HISTORY of ARCHITECTURE

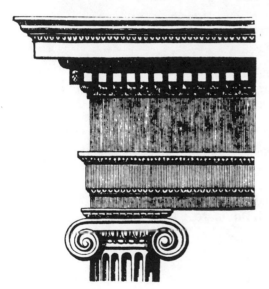

From The Earliest Times;
Its Present Condition in
Europe and the
United States

Mrs. L. C. Tuthill

Introduction by
Lamia Doumato

GARLAND PUBLISHING, INC.
NEW YORK & LONDON 1988

This volume was reproduced from a facsimile of
the1848 Philadelphia edition in the
Yale University Library

Introduction © 1988 by Lamia Doumato

Library of Congress Cataloging-in-Publication Data

Tuthill, Louisa C. (Louisa Caroline), 1798–1879.
     History of Architecture from the earliest times : its present
condition in Europe and the United States / Mrs. L. C. Tuthill ;
introduction by Lamia Doumato.
     p. cm.
     Reprint. Originally published: Philadelphia : Lindsay and
Blakiston, 1848. With new introduction.
     Bibliography: p.
     ISBN 0–8240–3717–0 (alk paper)
     1. Architecture—History. I. Doumato, Lamia. II. Title.
√ NA200. T8 1988
     720' .9—dc19   88-10283

Design by Renata Gomes

This volume is printed on acid-free,
250-year-life paper.

Printed in the United States of America

ACKNOWLEDGMENTS

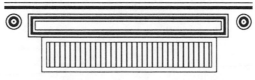

Initially, I must thank Professor Alan Gowans who introduced me to Tuthill's History and suggested that her work deserved further study. Professor Richard Longstreth of George Washington University guided my research and provided helpful insights. Thomas McGill, my colleague at the National Gallery of Art, was of great assistance in locating some of Tuthill's obscure publications and finally, thanks are due to Ralph Carlson of Garland Publishing for his support.

INTRODUCTION

In a letter of February 15, 1841, Louisa Tuthill offers the publishing firm of Cary and Hart her recently completed manuscript, a general work on American architecture. "It is a book on architecture designed for general circulation and not alone for artists. The title will be somewhat as follows; Architecture, Ancient and Modern: The past and present condition of the Art in the United States, with plans for its improvement. The Mss. is ready for the press and has been examined by several literary and scientific gentlemen and (I trust I shall be pardoned for adding) highly approved. The object of it is to improve the public taste by bringing the topic before readers of all classes, and furnishing correct models for imitation. No work of the kind has hitherto appeared in the United States, and you will find gentlemen, that it is much needed."[1]

This volume, the first history of architecture published in the United States, would not actually appear until 1848 and then under an expanded scope and format. A publication of this genre was a deviation from Mrs. Tuthill's existing work—sentimental and moralistic books for "young ladies" to prepare them for marriage and their domestic duties.[2] These publications played a crucial role in the development of family life and were as common in the nineteenth century as cookbooks are today. Louisa Tuthill also edited and wrote a series of children's books with the same blatant moral overtones; these volumes were quite successful, with some going into as many as forty editions.

Louisa did not begin her life with hopes of a career in writing. She was born in New Haven, Connecticut to an affluent family, descendents of Theophilus Eaton, one of the city's founders. Her father, Ebenezer Huggins, was a prosperous merchant while her mother, Mary Dickerman, was a typical middle class housewife. Louisa, the youngest of seven children, was nonetheless educated at Litchfield and New Haven in seminaries whose curricula were compared to that of Yale College. A contemporary relates that Louisa's middle-class lifestyle included, "to the fullest extent the opportunities of education which these seminaries afforded, as well as the more general, but not less important element of education, the constant intercourse with people of refined taste and cultivated minds."[3]

In 1817 Miss Huggins married Cornellus Tuthill, a recent Yale graduate who had studied law but opted instead to become a minister and soon after their marriage was licensed to preach. This career was somewhat short-lived due to an attack of typhus and a resulting weakening of his health. He turned instead to literary pursuits and edited (along with a number of male friends) the *Microscope* in 1820 and later in 1822–23 the *Christian Spectator*. His health continued to deteriorate and in 1825, Mrs. Tuthill found herself widowed with four children.

Louisa Tuthill's literary talents which she had earlier disdained (refusing to write except to please her husband who published at least one of her pieces anonymously in the *Microscope*) were now a source of both revenue and solace for her. A contemporary critic, Sarah Hale, discusses Louisa Tuthill's work in her 1870 publication entitled, *Woman's Record, or Sketches of All Distinguished Women from Creation to A.D. 1868*. After a brief biographical sketch and a selected list of titles, Mrs. Hale characterizes the author, stating that "Mrs. Tuthill is a pleasant writer; her cheerful spirit and hopeful philosophy give an attractive charm even to good advice; which like medicine requires often to be sugared before it is willingly taken. All her writings bear the stamp of an earnest purpose to promote the best interests of society; she has read much and uses her knowledge of books skillfully to illustrate her own views. There is also a pure current of pious feeling flowing, as it were, from her warm heart, that freshens old thoughts and keeps her literary field bright with the flowers that never die."

To the contemporary reader, Sarah Hale presents a most unappealing portrait of a do-gooder subjectively lecturing on morals and lifestyle through her writings; Mrs. Hale intimates that Louisa rehashes ideas and ideals which have been presented extensively by other authors.

However, one could use Mrs. Hale's apt description of Tuthill's writings in discussing any other woman writer of the period by simply substituting names. At this time in America there were a good number of women writers who produced etiquette books similar to Mrs. Tuthill's. The Beechers are a case in point; Catherine and Harriet coauthored *The American Woman's Home* which concerns itself more with the economics and day to day upkeep of a home than did the writings of the "genteel" Mrs. Tuthill. Nonetheless, the audience was basically the same and the issues brought home were just that—issues about the home brought to the home. Another important voice raised to the homemaker was that of Lydia Sigourney, who like Tuthill, had moved in an affluent circle which included the stylish literary and artistic personalities influential in society. (Ithiel Town was one of Signourney's acquaintances who would later prove useful to Tuthill). Sarah Hale, widowed early in life just as was Louisa Tuthill, was rescued by a number of her deceased husband's friends who supported her initial literary venture as editor of the popular journal, *Woman's Companion*.

More important to perceive in the similarities among these women are elements common to their background: all were well-educated women, exposed to the polite society of the day; all were descended from important families of a city; all were pious (the Beechers' father was, like Louisa Tuthill's husband, a preacher). But these factors would be insignificant if there was not a willing audience ready and waiting to consider their thesis. The period of 1815 to 1865 was a time of complex and numerous changes in many aspects of American life: mechanization of manufacturing and of agriculture; swifter and more widely available means of transportation; progressive and more efficient business techniques all combined to force the American into a swift transition from a traditional to a more modern way of life.

The middle class wished to preserve its traditional values while embracing selected new ones, and since the home was recognized as the most effective place for inculcating values, it was therefore the place for reconciling old and new. This was a major preoccupation of the era. Music and literature emphasized the vital role of house and home as in John Howard Payne's exceptionally popular 1823 song, "Home Sweet Home."[4] Music, art and all cultural events were embraced by American womanhood. "'High art' was enlisted in an effort to improve or reform the American character."[5] Art and taste were blended with religion and morals to create an ideal conception of truth and beauty, and these twin ideals appeared in the writings of many popular authors. Morality became inextricably tied to domestic architecture.

Besides being enterprising and dilligent, Louisa Tuthill was perceptive. She understood her society and seized this opportunity to provide the public with its wants. In publishing this first history of architecture she paved the way for two vital American phenomena. One: she established a precedent for a tradition of female authors writing architectural history and criticism; this was the first attempt by a woman writer to influence style (taste) in architecture. Two: she defended the validity of a truly American architecture (a belief propogated by earlier architectural writers, e.g., Thomas Jefferson and A.J. Davis) with indigenous regional building materials, with a relationship between art and the American landscape, with architects trained here in the United States— ultimately an architecture for America not dependent on Europe. Tuthill's influence becomes immediately apparent through the efforts of her long-time acquaintance, Sarah Hale, editor of the popular *Godey's Lady's Book*.[6] In 1849 *Godey's* boasted an unprecented 40,000 subscribers. It was also in 1849 that *Godey's* established a regular feature of each issue, the "Model Cottage" column that for the next thirty years would influence house styles as strongly as *Godey's* fashion articles would dominate American women's standard of dress. Tuthill's pleas for an American style did not go unheeded by *Godey's* (which published 450 model-house designs between the years 1846 and 1898); in 1854 the magazine announced that all future "Lady's Book Houses" would be by American designers.[7] Another female author following the pioneering tracks of Tuthill was Frederika Bremer who discussed American architecture in her prefaces to a number of Andrew Jackson Downing's books. Harriet Monroe and later Mariana Griswold van Rensselaer and a host of other writers would continue to keep the American public aware of the aesthetics of architecture. Included in this group was Helen Gaut, writer and illustrator for several magazines and newspapers in the United States, who wrote articles on domestic architecture in the *Ladies Home Journal* for more than two decades.[8]

Writing a history of architecture was a formidable task,

probably more so in the 1840s than it would be today; while the existing source publications were fewer, the book collections and libraries were not so accessible. Being a well-connected woman of New Haven society, Mrs. Tuthill was privy to the library of architect Ithiel Town. A contemporary source relates that Town's private library, amassed by the architect over a thirty year period, consisted of approximately ten thousand volumes, (many of which were rare or expensive) and a collection of more than twenty thousand individual engravings by ancient and modern masters. The library also housed Town's collection of objects d'art which included "one hundred and seventy oil paintings, besides mosaics, and other works of art and objects of curiosity."[9]

The complete name as it appears on the title page of Tuthill's volume is this: *History of Architecture from the Earliest Times; Its Present Condition in Europe and the United States with a Biography of Eminent Architects and a Glossary of Architectural Terms.* The history is composed of twenty-eight chapters in 426 pages; supplementing the text are forty-six engravings and over one-hundred wood cuts. The preface, dated 1847, is followed by lists of the plates, while two appendixes, a chronological table of the principal architects before and since the Christian era, and a glossary of architectural terms complete the book.

A glance at the table of contents immediately identifies the idiosyncracies of this volume: no chapter on Early Christian or Byzantine architecture; chronological arrangement interrupted by chapters on architectural principles, on building materials, and on qualifications for an architect; an entire chapter devoted to arrangements of a city, i.e., city planning. Future histories of architecture would consist of several volumes and provide more even and comprehensive coverage of periods, cultures, and styles. To these Tuthill's history could not compare in scope or in thoroughness. Her intention, however, was not to provide the definitive history of architecture. In her writing Tuthill combines verse, flowery sentiment, sociological insight, social history, explanation of terms, and personal ideology. Louisa Tuthill is highly subjective. On occasion, this need to include her own highly colored observations renders her account interesting and thought-provoking, as it would the writings of any historian. Chapter eight on Grecian architecture, the most substantial in the early part of the book, presents a discussion of origins of the orders in a narrative which verges on a chatty style. "It has been remarked that the doric column is in fact Egyptian modified to a new position and worship, and that the nobler specimens are but reduced and petty imitations of those ancient and indestructable supporters to the temples of Thebes, of Memphis and Tentyra" [sic].

At other times, the author grasps a somewhat sophisticated concept; this is best exemplified in her discussion of the inception of the Corinthian order by Callimachus who observed the acanthus naturally draping its leaves around a basket and was thus inspired to create the Corinthian capital. Tuthill finds fault with this tale and points once again to similarities in Egyptian prototypes; she does not, however, disregard the former argument, choosing instead a theory of accidental circumstances and making it seem plausible that Callimachus' genius may have reproduced what had long been invented.

Quite often this subjective stance is neither positive nor subtle as when evaluating the Greek Revival in a chapter entitled "The Grecian Orders in Domestic Architecture." After establishing some of the traits of the style, Mrs. Tuthill continues "happily a better taste is now prevailing. The Grecian mania has passed by, and some caution is necessary that the people become not so rabid with the Gothic and Elizabethan mania that has now seized them."

Even as she wrote, Louisa Tuthill was herself "rabid with the Gothic"; chapter twenty devoted to a study of this style is twenty pages long with four full page plates and several small illustrations inserted within the text. The glories of Gothic are praised to the skies and detailed accounts of individual buildings prevail (detailed not in modern terms but rather compared to Mrs. Tuthill's concise and often pithy writing style; in some early chapters she sees fit to dismiss Hindu and Arabian architecture with a three or four page survey). The thoroughness of coverage is also evident in the number of sources the author acknowledges in this chapter.

This history has no formal bibliography or list of sources, but useful references are provided in footnotes throughout the book. Here again, Tuthill is concise to a fault, often listing only the author's last name and the first few words of the title, i.e., Britton's *Architectural Antiquities*; Pugin's *Specimens of Gothic Architecture*; Loudon's *Architectural Encyclopedia*. One might argue that the rationale for such a brief citation was due to the popularity of these books and that her audience was well-acquainted with these resource tools.

This may prove true for the above mentioned reference

works; however, Mrs. Tuthill is not discriminating enough to adjust her policy for books that were not standard sources. Her procedure for citing remains constant even for those books which could not have been "household" items for her readers, i.e., Jahu's Biblical Archaeology, Callaud in his Journey to Meroe, Gau in his Nubia. The simple answer comes with the understanding that few, if any, readers would consult Mrs. Tuthill's references even if they had an opportunity to do so.

Important and recent publications such as *Views of Ancient Monuments in Central America, Chiapas, and Yucatan* by Frederick Catherwood, published in London in 1844, and Lord Kingsborough's seven volume folio series on the *Antiquities of Mexico* attest to the serious research commitment of the author and to the quality of Town's book collection.

If Louisa Tuthill's historical methodology is not all that it should be, her essays on current topics in the art realm and her awareness of American architecture are her strong points; this is where Louisa shines. As a roundabout method for introducing the concept of an art school in the United States (a cause espoused by Ithiel Town, Lydia Sigourney, and a number of the New Haven elite), Tuthill presents causes which have hindered the progress of art in America: she relates most problems to a lack of developed "taste" in the United States. The lack of cultivated taste functions in very practical terms like the law of supply and demand. Why should artist or artisan develop his art to a superlative point when no one is there to recognize the heights of his achievement? She sees this phase of American life coming to an end with more people traveling to Europe and returning to their homes with an appreciation of and a desire for the finer things experienced on their sojourn; it is unnecessary that art objects, architectural elements, or drawings be carted back to their home when Americans are an industrious and talented lot and perfectly capable of providing products as good if not better than their European counterparts.

"In order that the fine arts may be successfully cultivated, taste must be diffused among the higher classes of the community. Among the arts of design", she continues, "architecture must precede painting and sculpture: they are but the hand maidens who decorate her palaces, her capitols, her churches." There is nothing of the Democratic ideal in Tuthill's writings. She lives in a world of definite hierarchies, both in thought and in actuality.

Tuthill encourages the development of the architectural profession and the suitable reward for its practitioners in her comment, "to the young men of our country, Architecture offers a lucrative and honorable profession. Instead of devoting so large a proportion of talent and active energy to the three learned professions, and to commercial pursuits, it is high time to direct them into other channels. This Art opens a fair field for laudable ambition." (She would have been startled to know that only a generation later young women of the country were beginning to follow this advice.)

Later in the text, she introduces a chapter entitled, "Qualifications for an Architect" with the declarative statement that "in order to rise to eminence in art, *genius* is indispensable." Equating the architect with poet, painter, and musician, she continues to underline the significant role played by professional architects of earlier eras. The remainder of this essay enumerates the qualities essentials to the practicing architect—ingenuity, mathematical talent, invention, practicality; she goes on to define each at some length.

Louisa Tuthill advises young men who have shown a talent in this area to begin their studies at a young age and keep this "noble art" foremost in their mind; she urges them, once their formal studies are complete, to make the European tour with one definite objective: "study the chef d'oeuvres of art in the cities and galleries of Europe, and return home with correct taste and skill in the Fine Arts, and moreover, with enthusiasm. . . ." Exposure to the edifices themselves is of supreme importance in the author's judgement and a basic necessity for the success of a young architect. Tuthill respects professionalism and in this regard distinguishes herself from contemporary women authors who advocate self-help in the home; the Beechers went as far as including sketches for cupboards and closets to assist the house wife in a do-it-yourself fashion. Louisa Tuthill articulated the need to have each working person fulfill the task for which he was trained and was therefore more adept. Even in her earlier writing of home books, she illustrates this point effectively with a short story of a homemaker who, by attempting to carry out her cook's functions, foils an important dinner party. But the message is clear—people should be trained for their professional duties; this is a vital point to comprehend and differentiates Tuthill's philosophy from that of her contemporaries.

The need for professionally trained architects is not Tuthill's only issue. Equally important is the need for domestic architecture planned and built in America. Her unequivocal belief was that

Americans should utilize American architects to build their American houses. "In adopting the domestic architecture of foreign countries, we may be . . . ridiculous." Even the English architectural prototype, which she acknowledges as a part of America's heritage, is rejected because Louisa Tuthill believes that a truly American architecture must be indigenous; "an American architect must possess the power to adopt what is suitable to our soil, climate, manners, civil institutions and religion without servile imitation."

Perhaps her statement did not pass unheeded. Beginning with Richardson in the 1870s, we find prestigious American Architects reassessing seventeenth-century American house types, materials, and elements, and reinterpreting them into a new eclectic style. This trend continued in the works of Emerson, Price, and finally through the 1890s with McKim, Mead, and White. The practice of borrowing and integrating elements of early American architecture into new buildings of the 1870s through the 1890s was so marked as to reverse the usual patterns of influence, making American achievements in architecture highly desirable and emulated in Europe[10]

Although Louisa Tuthill refuses to identify the important professionals of her day, she does not shrug from the task of "merely mentioning" some of the principal public buildings in the United States. In a few instances, she provides location, a sentence or two on style, measurements, and a unique architectural element. In the course of this survey, she names a few specific architects, among them Thomas U. Walter, John Notman, Richard Upjohn, James Renwick, and, understandably, the firm of Town and Davis.

Tuthill's entreaties to working architects do not end with a publication of their work; she has a more serious matter to discuss—building materials—and she devotes an entire chapter to it. After defining the indigenous types of marble, stone, metals, and trees, she offers these words of caution against depleting natural resources. "Instead of cutting down and wasting trees. . . farm houses might be constructed of the stones that now encumber the soil. . .. There has hitherto been a great want of economy in this respect, and it is therefore the more earnestly urged upon the attention of the community." Since none of the author's writings show a significant regard for frugality, we may rightfully conclude that Tuthill was genuinely concerned with environmental issues, namely preservation and conservation of the country's natural resources.

Although much of the volume is seemingly directed at practicing architects, Mrs. Tuthill makes very clear her prime motivation for writing this book in her dedicatory statement: "To the Ladies of the United States of America, the acknowledged arbiters of taste, this work is respectfully inscribed." Very little in this statement is unusual for nineteenth-century publications. Educating the female of the northeast and midwest was a commonly shared goal as attested to by the number of publications directed at women. The uniqueness of Louisa Tuthill's concept is concern for visual rather than verbal education; her intention is to provide American women with sufficient knowledge of the art of architecture to enable them to make aesthetic decisions. She presents convincing arguments to persuade readers of the necessity of visual education. "Every person has an individual interest in Architecture as a useful art and all who cultivate a taste for the Fine Arts must give it a high place among them. The best way of effecting improvement in any art or science . . . is to multiply as far as possible those who can observe and judge."

She believes in the basic and enriching value of a knowledge of architecture. "It is a ubiquitous art, available to all for contemplation and appreciation. For women, a taste for architecture is as vital as a taste for flowers." She makes the perceptive statement that architecture provides a sense of history and a link to understanding elements of the past: religion, government, social institutions, science, and art.

Despite the fact that Mrs. Tuthill's history did not go through numerous editions nor attain the great popularity enjoyed by some of her less significant books, it emerges as a noteworthy contribution to nineteenth-century architectural history. She realized that she had made a unique contribution in publishing the first history of architecture in the United States. She was also undoubtedly aware that she raised many vital issues: the importance of an informed consumer; the need for a school for the proper training of American architects; the significance of function as the most important element of a building; and finally, the existence of architecture as an integral part of daily life.

Could she know that she was pioneering a tradition of women architectural writers and critics, stronger at some periods than at others, but nonetheless continuing into our own time? Could she realize that she was preparing women readers for the next generation of architectural thought? Prophetically, the ideals proposed in her history — the insistence on professionally trained architects (which would, of course, come with the founding of the AIA in 1857), the use of indigenous regional building materials, and the development of a uniquely American architecture—were the wave of the future. Seen in this light, Mrs. Tuthill's study for "the Ladies of the United States of America" documents the philosophy of American and European architecture and ably provides a transition from her time into the epochs to come.

NOTES

1.　Original letter from Mrs. Tuthill to publishers Cary and Hart in the collection of the Historical Society of Philadelphia. The original manuscript discussed in Tuthill's letter of 1841 has not survived but we know from the context of the letter that it was a history limited to American Architecture. In the seven intervening years, Mrs. Tuthill expanded her work to include architecture of all nations.

2.　In these etiquette books, Tuthill intended to present to the public what was socially and tastefully acceptable in America. In this sense, her history of architecture is not so different from her earlier writings. Tuthill's work included books for children as well as collections of essays by other authors.

3.　Johns S. Hart. *Female Prose Writers of America*. Philadelphia: E.H. Butler and Co., 1892. p. 100.

4.　David Handlin. *The American Home*. Boston: Little, Brown and Co., 1979. p. 4.

5.　Frank L. Mott. *A History of American Magazines*. Cambridge, Mass: Harvard University Press, 1966. p. 351.

6.　After publishing nine volumes, Mrs. Hale's magazine was bought by Godey in 1837 (Mrs. Hale was retained as editor) and merged with his *Lady's Book*. Ultimately, the title would be changed to *Godey's Lady Book*.

7.　Ruth E. Finley. *The Lady of Godey's: Sarah Josepha Hale*. Philadelphia: J.B. Lippincott, 1931. p. 138.

8. John William Leonard, editor. *Women's Whos Who of America, 1914–1915*. Detroit: Gale Publishers, 1976. p. 63.

9. Lydia Sigourney. "The Residence of Ithiel Town, Esquire." *Ladies Home Companion and Literary Expositor.* . 10 (1839–40) p. 123.

10. James D. Kornwolf. "American Architecture and the Aesthetic Movement," in *In Pursuit of Beauty: Americans and the Aesthetic Movement.* New York: Rizzolli, for the Metropolitan Museum of Art, 1986.

WORKS EDITED OR WRITTEN BY LOUISA C. TUTHILL

Louisa Tuthill's writings consist of moralistic tales for children (many of which were published as part of the Juvenile Library); etiquette manuals for young men and ladies; and several volumes dealing with aesthetics. Included in the latter category are several works of the popular British aesthete, John Ruskin. Tuthill selected essays by Ruskin and provided brief introductions to his collected work. Earlier in her writing career Tuthill's books were published with no author indicated while others listed only "a Lady" as the author.

Ancient Architecture. New Haven: Babcock, 1830.

Anything for Sport. Boston: Crosby & Nichols, 1846.

Beautiful Bertha. New York: Scribner, 1855.

The Belle, the Blue and the Bigot: Or Three Fields for Women's Influence. Providence: S.C. Blodget, 1844.

The Boarding School Girl. Boston: Crosby & Nichols, 1848.

The Boy of Spirit: A Story for the Young. Boston: Crosby & Nichols, 1848.

Braggadocio: A Book for Boys and Girls. New York: Scribner, 1851.

A Course of Calisthenics for Young Ladies. . . . Hartford: H.F.J. Huntington, 1831.

Edith: The Backwoods Girl. New York: Scribner, 1859.
Ellen Stanley and Other Stories. Boston: Crosby and Ainsworth, 1865.

Get Money. New York: Scribner, 1858.

History of Architecture, from the Earliest Times. . . . Philadelphia: Lindsay and Blakiston, 1848.

Home: A Book for Young Ladies. London: Nelson and Sons, 1853.

Hurrah for New England: Or the Virginia Boy's Vacation. Boston: Crosby & Nichols, 1847.

I Will Be a Gentleman. Boston: Crosby & Nichols, 1845.

I Will Be a Lady. Boston: Crosby & Nichols, 1844.

I Will Be a Sailor. Boston: Cosby & Nichols, 1864.

I Will Be a Soldier. Boston: Crosby & Nichols, 1862.

James Somers: The Pilgrim's Son. New Haven: A.H. Maltby, 1827.

Joy and Care: A Friendly Book for Young Mothers. New York: Scribner, 1855.

Larry Lockwell or I Will Be a Sailor. Philadelphia: Perkenpine & Higgins, 1864.

Love of Admiration or Mary's Visit to Boston. New Haven: A.H. Malty, 1828.

The Merchant. New York: G.P. Putnam, 1850.

The Mirror of Life. Philadelphia: Lindsay & Blakiston, 1847.

My Little Geography. Philadelphia: Lindsay & Blakiston, 1847. This volume is sometimes attributed to Tuthill's daughter, Cornelia Tuthill Pierson.

My Wife. Boston: Crosby & Nichols, 1846.
The Nursery Book. New York: G.P. Putnam, 1849.

Onward! Right Onward! Boston: Crosby & Nichols, 1844.

Queer Bonnets or Truthfulness and Generosity. New York: Scribners, 1853.

Reality Or The Millionaire's Daughter. New York: Scribners, 1856.

Romantic Belinda. Boston: Crosby & Ainsworth, 1864.

A Strike for Freedom Or Law and Order. Boston: Crosby, Nichols, and Co., 1850.

Success in Life: The Artist. Cincinnati: Derby, 1854.

Success in Life: The Lawyer. New York: G.P. Putnam, 1850.

Success in Life: The Mechanic. New York: G.P. Putnam, 1850.

Success in Life: The Merchant. New York: G.P. Putnam, 1850.

Tip-top. New York: Scribner, 1853.

True Manliness Or The Landscape Gardner. Boston: Crosby & Ainsworth, 1867.

When Are We Happiest Or The Little Camerons? Boston: Crosby & Nichols, 1846.

Young Lady at Home and in Society. New York: Allen Bros., 1869.

Young Lady's Home. New Haven: S. Babcock, 1839.

Young Lady's Reader. New Haven: S. Babcock, 1839.

JOHN RUSKINS'S WRITINGS, SELECTED AND EDITED BY LOUISA TUTHILL:

Beauty and Nature. New York: H.M. Caldwell, 1896.
Pearls for Young Ladies. New York: Wiley and Sons, 1878.

Precious Thoughts. New York: Wiley and Sons, 1866.

The True and the Beautiful in Nature, Art, Morals and Religion. New York: Wiley and Sons, 1858.

BIOGRAPHICAL SCOURCES ON LOUISA TUTHILL:

Adams, Oscar Fay. *A Dictionary of American Authors.* Boston: Longwood Press, 1897. 292.

Allibone, S. Austin. *A Critical Dictionary of English Literature and British and American Authors.* Vol. 3. Philadelphia: J.B. Lippincott & Co., 1871. 2485.

Davis, Dorothy R. ed. *The Carolyn Sherwin Bailey Historical Collection of Children's Books: A Catalogue.* New Haven: Southern Conn. State College, 1966.

Duyckinck, Evert A., and George L. Duyckinck *Cyclopaedia of American Literature.* Vol. 2. New York: Scribner, 1855.

James, Edward T. *Notable American Women, 1607-1950.* Vol. 3. Cambridge, Mass: Belknap Press, 1971. 487–488.

Shaw, John MacKay. *Childhood in Poetry.* Vol. 3. Detroit: Gale Research Co., 1980.

Wilson, James Grant and John Fiske *Appleton's Cyclopaedia of American Biography.* Vol. 6. New York: D. Appleton and Co., 1889. 189.

GENERAL SOURCES:

Abell, Mrs. L.G. *Woman in Her Various Relations.* New York: R.T. Young, 1853.

Beecher, Catherine, and Harriet B. Stowe. *American Woman's Home.* New York: J.B. Ford and Co., 1869; reprint: New York: Arno Press, 1971.

Beecher, Catherine. *Miss Beecher's Housekeeper and Healthkeeper.* New York: J.B. Ford and Co., 1874.

Beecher, Catherine. *The New Housekeeper's Manual.* New York: J.B. Ford and Co., 1874.

Carey, M. *Practical Rules for the Promotion of Domestic Happiness.* Philadelphia, 1838.

Chapman, Josephine Wright. "The Real New Woman: A Woman Who Builds Houses." *Ladies Home Journal.* (October, 1914) 3.

Cole, Doris. *From Tipi to Skyscraper: A History of Women in Architecture.* Boston: i Press, 1973.

Dye, Judith. *For the Instruction and Amusement of Women: The Growth, Development and Definition of American Magazines for Women, 1780–1840* Ph.D. Dissertation. University of Pennsylvania, 1977.

Fitch, James Marston. "When Housekeeping Became a Science." *American Heritage.* 12 (August, 1961) 34–37.

Garcia, Hazel. "Of Punctilios Among the Fair Sex: Colonial American Magazines, 1741—1776." Journalism History, 3 no. 2 (1976) 48–51, 63.

Geer, Emily Apt. "Haynes and the New Women of the 1880s. "*Hayes Historical Journal,* 3 no. 1/2 (1980) 18–26.

Gowans, Alan. *Images of American Living.* Philadelphia: Lippincott, 1964.

Hale, Sarah. *Woman's Record.* New York: Harper and Bros., 1870.

Hamlin, Talbot. *Greek Revival Architecture in America.* New York: Oxford University Press, 1944.

Hanaford, Phoebe. *Daughters of America*. Boston: Russell, 1883.

Handlin, David. *The American Home*. Boston: Little, Brown & Co., 1979.

Hart, John S. *Female Prose Writers of America*. Philadelphia: E.H. Butler and Co., 1852.

Hayden, Dolores, and Gwendolyn Wright. "Architecture and Urban Planning." *Signs*, 1 no. 4 (1976) 923–33.

Heisner, Beverly. "Harriet Morrison Irwin's Hexagonal House." *North Carolina Historical Review*, 58 no. 2 (1981) 105–23.

Lantz, Herman. "The Preindustrial Family in America: A Further Examination of Early Magazines." *American Journal of Sociology*, 79 no. 3 (1973) 566–88.

Mather, Linda Lee. *The Education of Women: Images from Popular Magazines*. Ph.D. Dissertation, University of Pennsylvania, 1977.

Matthews, C.T. "Influence of Women in Architecture." *American Architect and Building News*, 59 (January 1, 1898) 3–4.

Mott, Frank L. *A History of American Magazines*. Cambridge, Mass: Harvard University Press, 1966.

Signourney, Lydia H. *Letters to Young Ladies*. Hartford: William Watson, 1835.

Sigourney, Lydia H. "The Library of Ithiel Town, Esq." *Ladies Companion and Literary Expositor*, 10 (1839-40) 123–26.

Skylar, Kathryn Kish. "American Female Historians in Context, 1770–1930." *Feminist Studies*, 3 no. 1/2 (1975) 171–84.

Stuart, Robert. *A Dictionary of Architecture*. 3 vol. London: Jones and Co., 1830.

Torre, Susana. *Women in America: A Historic and Contemporary Perspective*. New York: Whitney Library of Design, 1977.

Trollope, Frances. *Domestic Manners of the Americans.* New York: Alfred A. Knopt, 1949.

Van Rensselaer, Mariana Griswold. "Client and Architect." *North American Review.* (September, 1890) 320.

von Holst, H.V. *Modern American Homes.* Chicago: American Technical Society, 1916.

Wharton, Edith, and Ogden Codman, Jr. *The Decoration of Houses.* New York: Scribner's Sons, 1897.

Wheeler, Gervase. *Rural Homes or Sketches of House Suited to American Country Life with Original Plans, Designs, etc.* Auburn: Alden Beardsly and Co., 1853.

Wright, Julia McNair. *The Complete Home.* Philadelphia: Bradley, Garretson and Co., 1879.

Wright, Gwendolyn. *Building the Dream.* New York: Pantheon, 1981.

Wright, Gwendolyn. *Moralism and the Modern Home.* Chicago: University of Chicago, 1980.

HISTORY

OF

ARCHITECTURE.

A. B. Wilson.

Waterbury,

Conn

HISTORY

OF

ARCHITECTURE,

FROM

THE EARLIEST TIMES;

ITS PRESENT CONDITION

IN EUROPE AND THE UNITED STATES;

WITH

A Biography of Eminent Architects,

AND A GLOSSARY OF ARCHITECTURAL TERMS.

BY MRS. L. C. TUTHILL.

WITH NUMEROUS ILLUSTRATIONS.

" Behold those broken arches, that oriel all unglaz'd,
That crippled line of columns bleaching in the sun,
The delicate shaft stricken midway, and the flying buttress
Idly stretching forth to hold up tufted ivy."
                                      M. F. TUPPER.

" Some pretend to judge of an individual by his handwriting; but I would
rather say, 'show me his house.' "—LONDON ARCHITECTURAL MAGAZINE.

PHILADELPHIA:

LINDSAY AND BLAKISTON.

1848.

C. SHERMAN, PRINTER,

19 St. James Street.

TO THE LADIES

OF

THE UNITED STATES OF AMERICA,

THE ACKNOWLEDGED ARBITERS OF TASTE,

This Work

IS RESPECTFULLY INSCRIBED.

PREFACE.

THE perception of the beautiful, is among the noblest of God's gifts to man. When improved by culture, it diffuses over the poor wants of human nature a glory, like sunlight upon the dark and frozen earth.

The peasant of the genial South, trains the jessamine over his rude porch, and beneath it, after the weary labour of the day, enjoys the " stilly eve."

The Swiss mountaineer hangs his picturesque chalêt amid the embowering trees of his native Alps, and its beauty delights the passing traveller.

With the same earnest longing for the beautiful, the man of wealth calls in the aid of Art, to decorate his more lofty dwelling-place.

But not alone the home of man must minister to his love of the beautiful ; the Temple, which he consecrates to the worship of his Creator, must rear its stately columns and spread its overarching vault, to form a fit sanctuary for holy thoughts and heavenward aspirations.

As society advances, all the edifices which the multiplied wants of civilized life demand, must be beautified ; hence arises Decorative Architecture.

Every person has an individual interest in Architecture as a useful art, and all who cultivate a taste for the Fine Arts must give it a high place among them. The best way of effecting improvement in any art or science, says Alison, " is to multiply as far as possible those who can observe and judge."

On this principle, an able writer in the Foreign Quarterly Review, strenuously recommends that *ladies* should cultivate a taste for Architecture. He says, " When we consider how wide is the province, how influential the authority which the sex are apt to claim in such matters, how much depends upon the refined taste of our *fairer halves*, it must be acknowledged, that to initiate them into this study would not be an act of perfect disinterestedness." This writer considers a taste for Architecture as adding to the innocent pleasures of life as much as a taste for flowers, or *furniture*, and as suitable for women as a knowledge of Chemistry or Astronomy.

To the *painter*, the *poet*, the *sculptor*, and the *novelist*, to the *traveller*, to the *reader* and the *writer* of books of *travels* and *history*, some acquaintance with Architecture is indispensable. This Art has the advantage over painting and sculpture in one respect,—its treasures are open to all—free as air; its *illustrations* stand upon the hill and in the vale ; in the crowded street and in the wooded glen.

The study of ancient Architecture, is the study of history. It reveals the religion, government, social institutions, science and art of the mighty past. Its monuments have perpetuated the names and deeds of the great, when the perishable materials to which they were committed in writing, have been swept away by the wings of Time. What sublime emotion fills the mind, when contemplating the structures which may have been revered as antiquities, by the Patriarch Abraham, as he gazed upon them and mourned over the idolatry of Egypt! What a quickened sense of the beautiful steals over the perceptions, while admiring the glory of Greece, in her Parthenon ! What intense interest is experienced while tracing the rise and progress of a new and beautiful mode, as the Art adapts itself to the pure and holy worship of Christianity !

Goethe says, " The influence which flows upon us from Architecture, is like that from music;" and Coleridge calls it, " frozen music."

To the *young men* of our country, Architecture offers a lucrative and honourable profession. Instead of devoting so large a proportion of talent and active energy to the three learned professions, and to commercial pursuits, it is high time to direct them into other channels. This Art opens a fair field for laudable ambition.

The history of the rise and progress of Architecture in other nations, should excite effective emulation.

> " Emulation and Endeavour :—
> To freemen, labour is renown."

The immense resources for building in the United States, will be profitably and tastefully appropriated, whenever the people themselves have sufficient knowledge of the Art, to employ and remunerate scientific architects.

The limits of this work will not allow a description, or even the mention, of many edifices in the United States, which are an honour to the architects and their employers ; the few specimens given, may be compared to those which a lecturer on science collects upon his table, merely for illustration.

A few of the introductory pages of this History of Architecture were published anonymously, some years since. No apology is offered for giving the entire book to the Public ; as nothing of the kind has hitherto appeared, it is hoped that it will be an acceptable addition to every family library. Much time and labour have been expended upon it, and the most humble apologies would be offered for its execution, could they but shield from that severity of criticism, which the author earnestly deprecates.

L. C. T.

Philadelphia, November, 1847.

NOTE.

THE BANK OF NORTH AMERICA, (Plate XXXIV.) The design for this engraving was not received in time for the description to appear in its proper place, among the public buildings of Philadelphia. The edifice is now being erected. It is of red sandstone, commonly called freestone; one of the best materials for architecture which this country affords. The windows and doorway are in remarkably fine style. The foundation and corner-stones in rustic, and the richly-ornamented cornice, add to the bold expression and effective character of this beautiful edifice. John Notman, architect.

LIST OF ENGRAVINGS.

LIST OF WOOD CUTS.

CONTENTS.

CHAPTER I.

ORIGIN AND PROGRESS OF ARCHITECTURE.

CHAPTER II.

EGYPTIAN ARCHITECTURE.

CHAPTER III.

HINDOO ARCHITECTURE.

CHAPTER IV.

PERSIAN ARCHITECTURE.

CHAPTER V.

JEWISH ARCHITECTURE.

CHAPTER VI.

CHINESE ARCHITECTURE.

CHAPTER VII.

ABORIGINAL OR AMERICAN ARCHITECTURE.

CHAPTER VIII.

CYCLOPEAN AND ETRUSCAN ARCHITECTURE.

CHAPTER IX.

GRECIAN ARCHITECTURE.

CHAPTER X.

ROMAN ARCHITECTURE.

CHAPTER XV.

REVIVAL OF GRECIAN AND ROMAN ARCHITECTURE IN THE FIFTEENTH CENTURY.

CHAPTER XVI.

PRESENT STATE OF ARCHITECTURE IN EUROPE.

CHAPTER XVII.

PRINCIPLES OF ARCHITECTURE.

CHAPTER XVIII.

QUALIFICATIONS FOR AN ARCHITECT.

CHAPTER XIX.

HISTORY OF ARCHITECTURE IN THE UNITED STATES.

CHAPTER XXV.

USE OF THE GRECIAN ORDERS, GOTHIC AND ELIZABETHAN STYLES,
IN DOMESTIC ARCHITECTURE.

CHAPTER XXVI.

CHAPTER XXVII.

ARRANGEMENTS OF A CITY, AND BEAUTIFYING OF TOWNS AND
VILLAGES.

CHAPTER XXVIII.

CEMETERIES.

HISTORY OF ARCHITECTURE.

CHAPTER I.

ORIGIN AND PROGRESS OF ARCHITECTURE.

ARCHITECTURE is both an essential, and an ornamental art. While society is in its infancy, and strength and convenience alone are regarded, it ranks with other mechanic arts necessary to the comfort of man; but, when it adds to these, beauty of design, or a regard for effect, it becomes an ornamental or fine art, taking its place beside the sister arts, poetry, painting, and sculpture.

The art of building, in its widest signification, includes naval, military, and civil architecture.

Civil architecture, comprehending all edifices constructed for the use of man in civil life, forms the topic of the present work.

In that advanced condition of society, to which moral and intellectual culture has given form and order, buildings are required for religion, education, legislation, public exercises, amusements, commerce, manufactures, for perpetuating heroic deeds and historical events, and for domestic life.

Respecting the origin and early practice of this art, historical testimony affords no aid; some shelter, however, has been necessary for the comfort and protection of man ever since his creation.

In the bland and healthful air of Paradise, Milton imagined "a blissful bower," as the dwelling-place of our first parents.

> "It was a place
> Chosen by the Sovran Planter, when he framed
> All things to man's delightful use; the roof
> Of thickest covert and interwoven shade,
> Laurel and myrtle, and what higher grew
> Of firm and fragrant leaf; on either side
> Acanthus and each odorous bushy shrub
> Fenced up the verdant wall; each beauteous flower,
> Iris all hues, roses and jessamine
> Reared high their flourished heads between, and wrought
> Mosaic; underfoot the violet,
> Crocus and hyacinth with rich inlay,
> Broidered the ground, more coloured than with stone
> Of costliest emblem; other creature here,
> Bird, beast, insect, or worm, durst enter none,
> Such was their awe of man."

Alas! how soon fallen Adam and Eve needed a more substantial shelter! Expelled from lovely Eden, the first man probably laboured "in the sweat of his brow," to build the first habitation.

Every invention has its origin in the wants of man.

As the human mind increases in power, the whole material world is brought under its dominion and made to minister to physical comfort and pleasure. Man advances by slow degrees to this proud elevation. It matters not, in this connexion, indeed it is out of our province, to discuss the vexed question of man's progress. Art is progressive.

Before man exercised the faculty of invention as an architect, he may have crept into hollow trees, or inhabited caves, as tenant in common with the beasts of the earth. Trees, with their wide-spreading branches, offered a natural shelter; by twining them together at the top, where they grew at a convenient distance apart, and filling in the sides with branches, something like a house would be formed. The wigwams of our North American Indians are only one step in advance of this kind of shelter. They cut down the trees, place them in a circular form, fasten them together at the top, interweave branches " to fence up the verdant wall," and fill the interstices with clay.

These miserable huts do not equal in their mechanical construction, the nest of the oriole. The primitive huts of the Caffres, advance one step farther. They are regular domes, covered with mud, which hardens in the sun. The doors, or holes for entrance, are only two or three feet high, and the king himself is obliged to enter his regal residence " on all fours." The mud structures of the beaver are superior to them; but, as Dr. Johnson says, " the beaver of the present

day can build no better than could the beaver, four
thousand years ago."

Tents were among the earliest habitations. They
were made at first of the skins of animals, afterwards
of felt and various kinds of cloth.

The Patriarchs of the Old Testament dwelt in tents,

> " While on from plain to plain they led their flocks,
>   In search of clearer spring and fresher field."

On each green and chosen spot, these portable habitations could be spread in a moment, and as readily
removed.

The Israelites, during their wanderings in the wilderness, dwelt in tents. Their Tabernacle for religious
worship was a spacious and magnificent tent, divided
into three parts. Coverings of skins, rendered it im-
pervious to rain and dampness. The first or inner
covering, was of "fine twined linen," wrought with
needlework in various colours; the second covering was
of goat's hair; the third, " of skins dyed red," and the
fourth, of " skins dyed blue."

Even at the present day,

> " The Arab band
>   Across the sand,
> Still bear their dwellings light,
>   And neath the skies
>   Their tents arise,
> Like spirits of the night;
>   While near at hand
>   The camels stand,
> And drink the waters bright."

It was a mighty step in the art of building when trees were smoothed into posts and placed in a rectangular form, with a covering or roof over them. Simple as this invention now appears, the inventor ought to have been " known to fame," for houses have continued nearly of the same form ever since. The most splendid Grecian temple is only an ornamented copy of the oblong house with its upright posts.

Log cabins were used, thousands of years before they were built by American backwoodsmen.

In the rude navigation of savages, the advance from paddles and oars to sails, was not greater than this stride from wigwams and mud huts, to a regular log house.

The employment of stones for buildings, was another important onward step in the art. The want of stones in some places, and the difficulty of shaping them into the forms desired, led to the manufacture of bricks, by reducing a mass of clay to a regular form, and hardening it in the sun, or burning it with fire. A convenient and enduring material was thus obtained, which has continued to be used ever since. From the only authentic record of this period—the Bible —we learn, that the city and tower of Babel were built of brick. The ambitious daring of some mighty leader projected this tower.

"Go to," said he, "let us make brick, and burn them throughly. And they had brick for stone, and slime had they for mortar. And they said, Go to, let us build us a city, and a tower, whose top may reach unto heaven; and let us make us a name, lest we be scattered abroad upon the face of the whole earth."

This presumptuous undertaking was arrested, after the walls had been raised to a great height, by one of the most striking miracles recorded in Holy Writ.

> "Among the builders, each to other calls,
>   Not understood, till hoarse and all in rage;
>   . . . . . Thus was the building left
>   Ridiculous, and the work *Confusion* named."

BABYLON.

It is supposed that the City of Babylon and the Temple of Belus afterwards occupied the same site as the Tower of Babel upon the plains of Shinar, between the rivers Euphrates and Tigris. It was founded B.C. 2000, by Nimrod, and was rebuilt by Semiramis, B.C. 1200. Strengthened and beautified by succeeding sovereigns, it became one of the wonders of the world. Walls, three hundred and sixty feet high, eighty-seven feet in thickness, and sixty miles in length, surrounded this city. We are apt to be somewhat incredulous about these measurements, yet, when so many stupendous monuments remain, to demonstrate the power and skill of ancient nations, we know not where to fix the bounds of our belief.

Eastern writers, in their usual hyperbolical manner, describe the Temple of Belus, as twelve miles high, while St. Jerome more moderately asserts that it was only four miles in height! The geographer Strabo, who may perhaps be relied on, says it was six hundred and sixty feet high.

The city was laid out in regular squares, the streets of fifteen miles in length crossing each other at right angles. Its hundred gates of brass opened at the end of these streets. The hanging gardens of "the golden city" gave it the beauty of Paradise. But prophecy had spoken its doom, and Babylon the Great fell never to rise again. Travellers, as they wander over the desolate ruins, startle "the mole and the bat" from the prostrate temples of idolatry. The site of this stupendous city has been identified, and confirmation thus added to the truth of prophecy. Sir Robert Ker Porter, who visited these ruins, gives the following account of the present condition of the Temple of Belus:—"It is an immense pile of ruins; at its base it measures 3082 feet in circuit; it presents two stages, the first about sixty feet high, cloven into a deep ravine by the rain, and intersected by the furrows of ages; the second ascent is about two hundred feet; from thence to the top thirty-five feet.   On the western side, the entire mass rises at once from the plain in one stupendous, though irregular pyramidal hill, broken in the slopes of its sweeping acclivities by time and violence.   On the north side there are large piles of ruins of fine and solid brickwork, projecting from among immense masses of rubbish at the base. The remains of the masonry are furnace-burnt bricks, united by a calcareous cement.   The base of the structure was not altered, but the piles of fine bricks thrown down were vitrified with the various colours. The consuming power appears to have acted from above, and the scattered ruins fell from a higher point than the summit of the present standing fragment. The heat of the fire which produced such amazing effects must have burned with the force of the strongest furnace.   I should be inclined to attribute the catastrophe to lightning from heaven."

NINEVEH.

Nineveh, the splendid capital of the Assyrian Empire, was sixty miles in circuit, and surrounded by high walls.

Recent discoveries have been made on the site of this ancient city, which promise to open a new volume of historical facts. A traveller thus writes to his friend in America:

"The principal mound (of these lately discovered ruins) is very large, being about sixteen hundred feet in length. My first excavation brought me on walls with inscriptions of the cuneiform character. I soon found that I had got into a palace that had been buried for many centuries. I have cleared out several rooms, the walls of which are covered with figures. They are religious and historical. The former, the lion with the head of a man and the wings of a bird; the bull with similar head and the wings of the eagle. The historical subjects are chiefly interesting for the insight they afford into the manners and customs of the ancient Assyrians, their mode of warfare, the state of the arts, &c. From an examination of them, there results a conviction that this people had risen to the greatest power; that they were highly civilized, and had attained a very remarkable proficiency in the fine arts."

The traveller who has made these interesting and invaluable discoveries, inclines to the opinion that the Greeks received their first knowledge of the arts from the Assyrians, instead of the Egyptians. There is, he thinks, more similarity between these remains of Ninehvite art and the Grecian, than between the Grecian and the Egyptian.

"Tyre and Sidon, cities of Phœnicia, probably excelled in the arts and sciences which were known in the more distant parts of Assyria. We know that the Tyrians and Sidonians were esteemed among the ancients for their skill in astronomy, arithmetic, commerce, and navigation, and that we are indebted to them for the invention of glass, linen, and even of letters. May we not conclude, then, that a people so enlightened had arrived at some excellence in the fine arts; and that they spread a knowledge of them in all their colonies, thus laying the foundation of that perfection which has been the glory of Grecian art?"

Sacred history is thus constantly being verified by the discoveries of modern travellers, and Prophecy is confirmed. We rejoice that Sculpture and Architecture were so skilfully practised in bygone ages, for we are thus put into communication with them, and enjoy a retrospective clairvoyance. As the discoveries of modern geology have brought to light extinct races of gigantic animals, preserved in solid rock, to tell us what wonders have been in the natural world, so the remains of art reveal to us the power, knowledge, religion, and character of races of men, and remain "solemn marks of the frailty of human greatness."

CHAPTER II.

EGYPTIAN ARCHITECTURE.

THE accounts of the few travellers who long ago visited Asia and Africa, were ridiculed, and treated as extravagant fictions. During the last century, and more especially since the commencement of the present, the investigations of learned and scientific men have more than verified those seemingly incredible narratives. Stupendous edifices remain, to demonstrate the truth of those wonderful stories. Structures of surpassing magnificence astonish the travellers in Egypt, Hindostan, and Persia. When, or by whom, these everlasting monuments of man's might were erected, the present inhabitants of these countries cannot inform the amazed traveller. Their antiquity dates back to a period shrouded in dark uncertainty, upon which authentic history throws no light, of which they are themselves the only, the mysterious, the indestructible records.

It is impossible to determine with certainty which of the three countries, just mentioned, first brought Architecture to that degree of excellence which these remains exhibit. Sir William Jones and some other oriental antiquaries contend for the superior antiquity

of Hindostan, and assert that the East was not only
the birthplace of art and science, but that they were
there nurtured till they grew to manhood.   This may
be true, but there is also strong testimony on the side
of Egypt.   From that land, it is supposed by some
learned antiquaries, that inventive genius in Architecture arose, and thence was spread throughout the
then civilized regions of the earth.   Others trace it
still farther down the Nile, and consider Ethiopia as
the land from which light emanated.*

Egypt is a country of small extent, but its geogra-
phical position, and geological formation, render it
capable of supporting an immense population.   The
river Nile, enriching its soil, opens a passage through
its whole extent.   The traveller is struck with wonder
and admiration, at the number, size, and magnificence
of the structures still standing upon the banks of that
mysterious river.

" Rent palaces, crushed columns, rifled moles,
    Fanes rolled on fanes, and tombs on buried tombs."

---

* *Les Savans* of France, Gau in his Nubia, and Callaud in his
Journey to Meroe, describe the monuments of Upper Nubia as massive, and many of them, magnificent.   It is supposed that Egyptian
Architecture was only an imitation or improvement upon the Ethio-
pian.   There is in Herodotus a passage to this effect : " Meroe, the
parent city of the Ethiopians, is a large city.   The people worship
only Zeus and Dionysius, (Ammon and Osiris,) and them they
honour greatly ; and they make their expeditions whenever the deity
by his oracular answers orders them."   From this it is inferred
that the Ethiopians settled colonies, and that Egypt was one of them.

Egypt contains ancient buildings of three distinct characters: pyramids, excavations, and temples or palaces with flat roofs, supported by rows of columns.

The famous pyramids of Egypt stand upon a plain which extends from Cairo about fifty miles along the Nile. Forty, or more, of different sizes, and of various materials, are irregularly scattered over this plain; the three largest, the pyramids of Cheops, of Cephrenes, and of Mycerines, are in the neighbourhood of Djiza.

The great pyramid of Cheops, is the largest structure in the world; or in other words, it is the greatest mass of materials which men have ever placed together, to form a single building; and one of our distinguished countrymen says, "the oldest pyramid is yet the most perfect work of art." It has stood through the moral and physical convulsions of more than thirty centuries, and may remain until

> "The cloud-capt towers, the gorgeous palaces,
> The solemn temples, the great globe itself,
> Yea, all which it inherit, shall dissolve,
> And like the baseless fabric of a vision,
> Leave not a rack behind."

This pyramid is five hundred feet in height, and seven hundred and twenty feet on each side of the base; thus covering 518,400 square feet. It is ascended by steps to the summit, which is a platform of nine large stones, each of which would weigh a ton.

Some of the stones in other parts of the pyramid are still larger. They are of hewn granite and limestone on the outside, cemented together with fine mortar; in the interior the stones are so nicely smoothed and fitted together, as not to need cement of any kind. Machinery of immense power, of which all knowledge is lost, must have been employed to raise these stones to such an amazing height. The pyramid is ascended by steps.*

---

* The following description of the manner of ascending the Pyramid, is from " Letters from the Old World, by a Lady of New York."

" When about to ascend the great Pyramid of Cheops, we were very glad to avail ourselves of the services of another tribe of Bedouins, who reside in a village near at hand. I had four of them assigned to me as conductors, with a promise of a good *backshee* in case they took me safely to the top, and returned me again where they found me. The gentlemen had each two to attend them. The effect produced upon the senses when standing beside a wall of stone *eight hundred feet* long by nearly five hundred feet high, unbroken by columns to lighten the heavy aspect of the mass, is indeed very imposing; but before I had time to reflect on the danger of ascending, the gentlemen hurried me onward, and I soon found myself lifted from shelf to shelf, without time to look behind me. After about half an hour's climbing, we came to a part of the edifice where it appears attempts have been made to penetrate the interior, and a large chamber, or rather notch, had been cut in one of the angles. Here a halt was called, and all gathered to this point. It is about two-thirds of the way to the top, and affords quite as fine a view as that from the summit. But when we looked down, and saw the precipice below us, some of our hearts, or rather nerves, failed. My husband persisted that I should proceed no further, and prevailed upon me to return. Early the

The second pyramid, that of Cephrenes, is about
four hundred feet high, and six hundred and sixty-five

---

next morning, however, he ascended to the top in a very few minutes,
and enjoyed the fine prospect exceedingly. The gentlemen cut their
names on the summit, but I was obliged to content myself with doing
it by proxy, as did Chateaubriand, who, when at Cairo, left Egypt
without going at all to the Pyramids! which in so sentimental a
traveller seems unpardonable. He requested a gentleman on the
first opportunity to inscribe his name on them, adding, ' in order to
fulfil all the duties of a pious traveller!'

" The north side of the largest pyramid is so steep as to be dangerous
of approach. A short time since, a young Englishman was precipitated
from the top to the bottom, and of course dashed to atoms. Near
the bottom the layers of stone are about four feet thick, and the mode
of my ascent was as follows: first, an Arab got down on his hands
and knees, thus forming a sort of extra step, while two others
mounted on the edge above, and giving me their hand, I was enabled,
by making two good long *Taglioni-isms*, to reach the place where
they stood; a fourth Arab remained always behind and below me, to
be ready in case I made a false step. This went on very well for a
short time, while each shelf or step was of sufficient width to permit
the placing of my four-footed stool, but frequently the steps were
not more than six inches wide, while yet they were four feet high,
thus rendering the footing very insecure, and the position sufficiently
alarming for weak nerves. In such cases another mode of proceeding
became necessary: an Arab would kneel with one knee and present
the other as a step, the one below holding him against the rock, that
he might not topple over. At about half-way from the ground, the
layers of stone are not over three feet thick, and from thence to the
top they diminish gradually. Difficult as the ascent is, it is as nothing
when compared with the descent. In the first operation, the face
being turned to the wall, neither the giddy height is observed, nor the

feet on each side at the base. The enterprising traveller, Belzoni, discovered the entrance to this pyramid, in 1818. When he forced his way to the interior,
he found inscriptions in Arabic, showing that the pyramid had been entered by a Saracen conqueror some
centuries before. Nothing of great value has been discovered in them in modern times. We are told that
under one of the Caliphs, an order went forth for the
destruction of these edifices, and that the work was
committed to one of the most skilful engineers of the
age. He wrought at it for a long time, expending
much labour and treasure, and finally gave it up. Of
course, he had no gunpowder. The engineer began at
the top; but how he got there, up the smooth plane
of five hundred feet, is beyond comprehension, unless
by cutting a flight of steps from the bottom. "Nothing
can be farther from the truth than the idea that there
was a regular series of steps for ascent in the original
plan of either of these pyramids." The attempts to

---

tapering point for which one is aiming; the whole attention being
taken up with the matter on hand, and the climber being hurried on
without time to turn around, so that a fearful height is reached before
he is aware of it. Curiosity satisfied, and the constant excitement
over, the descent becomes a regular matter of business. On looking
down, the first few tiers of steps are quite perceptible, and their lines
are distinctly marked, but all lines soon become confused, and nothing
but a smooth surface is visible from fifty feet in advance down to the
very ground. At first the stoutest hearts recoil at this optical delu-
sion, but gradually gaining assurance as they descend, they get
through with it tolerably well."

destroy them, or to effect an entrance, have uncovered these steps.

All the pyramids are finished in the interior with much labour. They contain many long and intricate passages, the walls of which are sculptured and painted, the colours remaining as fresh as if recently executed. For what purpose these stupendous edifices were erected, remains an enigma which the most learned antiquaries have in vain attempted to solve. Were they for tombs, or for temples for religious worship? Probably they united both purposes. The ancient Egyptians believed that the soul existed as long as the body could be kept from dissolution, and they therefore preserved the bodies of the dead by embalming and placing them in situations where they would not be disturbed. From this fact it has been inferred that the Pyramids were the sepulchres of kings.

> " And round a tyrant's tomb, who none deserved,
>   For one vile carcass, perished countless lives."

They were thus consecrated as the burial-place of a hero or king whom they idolized ; and in them were probably celebrated the most sacred mysteries of their strange religion. From some fancied derivation of the word *pyramid* from a Greek word signifying *corn,* some antiquary conjectured that the pyramids were the granaries which were built by Joseph to preserve the grain of Egypt ! But M. De Lacy has proved that the word *pyramus* belonged to the primitive language of Egypt.

The Pyramids of Saccara, at some distance from the Great Pyramids, are in a ruinous state. Some of them are rounded at the top; others are flat, and ascended by steps.

These are supposed to be of more recent origin than the larger pyramids. One, which has partly fallen down, was built of unburnt bricks, badly made with gravel, shells, and chopped straw. It has been suggested that these were the works upon which the Israelites toiled under their hard task-masters. " The immense pyramid of unburnt bricks on our right was, no doubt, the work of a portion of the oppressed Israelites, whose lives the task-masters of Pharaoh made 'bitter with hard bondage in mortar and in brick;' and when they murmured against their hard fate, the command of the tyrant was followed out to the letter, 'ye shall no more give the people straw to make brick, as heretofore; let them go and gather straw for themselves,' 'and the tale of the bricks which they did make heretofore, ye shall lay upon them; ye shall not diminish aught thereof.' In this dry climate, unburned bricks are mostly used; and in order to give the clay more tenacity, a large proportion of chopped straw is worked into it in the pit; without which, or something for a substitute, as coarse dry grass or 'stubble,' the bricks would crumble to pieces in handling, after being dried in the sun."

Caverns or *grottos*, excavated from the solid rock, were used as tombs by the Egyptians. These Hypogées, as they are termed by the French, were domestic tombs. At Thebes, they remain in great numbers, and afford habitations to the miserable Arabs of the present day. They are varied almost infinitely. The most magnificent have a vestibule carved into the face of the rock; thence there is a descent of a few steps into a passage which leads to halls, which in some instances are more than six hundred feet in length. Doors open from them at irregular intervals into chambers where are placed the mummies. The architecture of these tombs has nothing in common with the temples and pyramids, excepting the sculptured and painted decorations. For this reason it is not necessary here to describe them minutely. The sculptures and pictures exhibit the modes of domestic life; the employments of the people; the navigation of the Nile; funerals, combats, domestic animals, &c., &c.

TEMPLES.

These are so numerous and so interesting, that it is exceedingly difficult to know which to select for description. The splendid work* prepared by the *savans* who accompanied the expedition of Napoleon to Egypt, gives a perfect representation of these

---

* " Description de L'Egypte, ou, Recueil des observations et des recherches qui ont été faites en Egypte pendant l'expedition de l'armée Française; publie par les ordres de sa Majesté l'Empereur Napoleon le Grand."

wonderful remains of Egyptian architecture. They
are scattered in rich profusion all the way, on both
sides of the Nile, as far as the Cataracts. "The
hundred-gated" Thebes, spreads its solemn ruins on
both sides of the river.

Here, the oldest specimens of true Egyptian art
may be found.

Luxor, El Kusr, "the ruins," one of the oldest
edifices, stands on the eastern bank of the river. Professor Heeren attempts to prove that Luxor was a
palace, or a building for some civil purpose, though
the general plan resembles that of the temples. He
gives, among other circumstantial evidence to this
effect, the fact, that the occupations and scenes of daily
life are depicted upon the walls of some of the apartments.

It is mentioned first among these mighty ruins,
before the more minute description of temples, on
account of its beautiful obelisks or monoliths.

An obelisk,* is a tall, quadrilateral structure, hewn
out of a single block of granite or other stone, gradually
diminishing from the base to the top, where the four
sides meet at last, in a pyramidal form. They were
usually placed in pairs, at the entrance of temples.
The question, as to their use and origin, is still de-
batable ground. That they served for something
more than ornament, is certain. They are doubtless

---

* Sometimes termed *a monolith*, but this word is applicable to any
structure formed from a single stone.

Plate I

THE PYRAMID OF CHEOPS.

ENTRANCE TO LUXOR.

books of religion, and the sculptured history of mighty monarchs.

The entrance to Luxor (Plate I.) is distinguished by two beautiful obelisks, more than eighty feet high, and ten feet square at the base. A modern traveller thus describes them : " Before the grand entrance of this vast edifice, two lofty obelisks stand, proudly pointing to the sky, fair as the daring sculptor left them. The sacred figures and hieroglyphic characters are beautifully cut into the hard granite, and have the sharp finish of yesterday. The very stone looks not discoloured. You see them as Cambyses saw them, when he stayed his chariot-wheels to gaze up to them, and the Persian war-cry ceased before these acknowledged symbols of the sacred element of fire. Very noble are all these remains, but my eyes were continually attracted towards the aspiring obelisks, and again and again you turn to them with increasing wonder and admiration."

Alas ! for these beautiful obelisks ! They no longer stand like twin deities to guard the entrance to Luxor. A solitary one remains, " ready in anger to dart at the sun, for not having annihilated at a stroke, the barbarous Gaul who so lately robbed it of its mate. The French, by permission of the Pacha, have taken one of these beautiful obelisks to Paris."

This monolith has since been erected in La Place de la Concorde, where it has excited the wonder of the Parisians, and been gazed at with awe by travellers from all lands.   Much labour has been bestowed upon

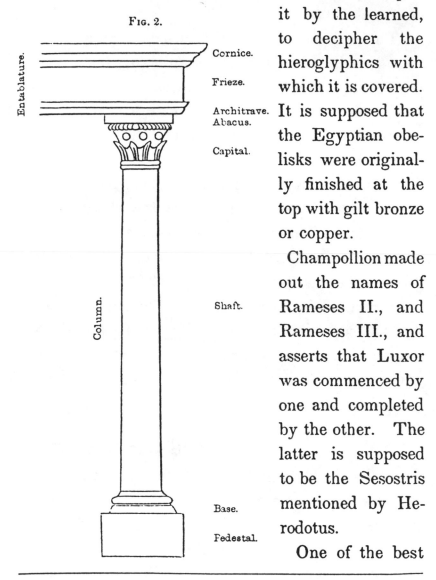

FIG. 2.

Entablature.

Cornice.

Frieze.

Architrave.
Abacus.

Capital.

Column.

Shaft.

Base.

Fedestal.

it by the learned, to decipher the hieroglyphics with which it is covered. It is supposed that the Egyptian obelisks were originally finished at the top with gilt bronze or copper.

Champollion made out the names of Rameses II., and Rameses III., and asserts that Luxor was commenced by one and completed by the other. The latter is supposed to be the Sesostris mentioned by Herodotus.

One of the best

NOTE.—The wood-cut in the margin is introduced merely to show the several parts of a column, and the entablature which it supports. The proportions and the design are not those of any established order.   A complete column is formed by the *base, shaft,* and *capital :* the entablature by the *architrave, frieze,* and *cornice.*

Plate II

PROPYLÆA OF THE TEMPLE OF EDFOU.

THE PRONAOS OF THE TEMPLE OF DENDERA.

descriptions of " the arrangement of the parts" of an
Egyptian Temple, is an ancient one, given by the
Greek geographer, Strabo. " In a line with the entrance into the sacred enclosure, is a paved road or
avenue, about a hundred feet in breadth, or sometimes
less, and in length from three to four hundred feet, or
even more. This is called the *dromos*, as Callimachus
has it. This is the sacred dromos of Anubis. Through
the whole length of the dromos, and on each side of it,
sphinxes are placed at the distance of thirty feet from
one another, or somewhat more, forming a double row,
one on each side. After the sphinxes, you come to a
large *propylon*, (Plate II.) and as you advance you
come to another, and to a third after that; for no definite number, either of propyla or sphinxes, is required
in the plan. After the propyla, we come to the temple
itself, which has always a large and handsome *pronaos*
or *portico*, and a *sekas* or *cella* of only moderate dimensions, with no image in it, or, at least, not one of
human shape, but some representation of a brute
animal."

The temples of the Egyptians, and all their edifices,
were painted with rich bright colours.

The portico or pronaos was more elevated and larger
than the sanctuary or temple; it was sustained by
columns, and closed laterally with walls.

The great temple at Esne, the ancient Latopolis,
had a splendid portico with twenty-four columns, six
in a row, (Plate II.) The architrave is sculptured with

figures of men and animals; the frieze is wide and ornamented with triglyphs; the cornice is narrow and filled
with hieroglyphics.   Over the door is the favourite
ornament of the winged globe.   The temple itself is
entirely in ruins.   It is conjectured that the people
were only admitted into the pronaos or portico; the
priests alone entered the precincts of the mysterious
cella, the inner sanctuary.   The base of the columns
is a small square block; the circumference of the
shaft where it rests upon it is small, enlarges suddenly, and then continues of nearly equal size to the
capital.   They are ornamented with sculpture in *bas-
relief*, near the base, and higher with reedings and
filletings.

This temple was dedicated to Jupiter Ammon.
Alexander the Great, when Egypt submitted to his
authority, marched with a part of his army to this
temple, and there caused himself to be proclaimed the
son of Jupiter Ammon.   The obedient priests paid
him divine honours, which he afterwards claimed as
his due.   The temple was twelve days' journey from
Memphis, through inhospitable deserts.   The soldiers,
when they found themselves surrounded by these
boundless seas of sand, where the eye for days could
not rest upon a sign of vegetation, were greatly
alarmed, and doubtless cursed in their hearts the mad
ambition of their leader.   The water which they had
brought with them in goatskins upon camels, entirely
failed; in this extremity they were relieved by the

timely falling of a shower, which was cunningly
ascribed to the peculiar favour of Jupiter Ammon.
At length, the splendid edifice burst upon their longing sight, filling them with delighted wonder.   It
stood upon a fertile plain, surrounded by groves of
beautiful trees, above which its towering columns rose
in majestic grandeur.

One of the artists who accompanied the expedition
of Napoleon says of the remains of this temple : " Its
architecture made upon each one of us the same impression; we were seized with a certain confused admiration,
which we hardly dared to avow, and casting our eyes
alternately upon the monument and upon our fellow-
travellers, each one sought to assure himself whether
he was deceived by his sight or by his mind ; if he
had lost suddenly the taste and the principles which
he had gained by the study of Grecian monuments of
art.   This struggle between the real beauty of the
architecture which we had before

Fig. 3.

our eyes, and our prejudices in
favour of Grecian forms and proportions, held us some time in sus-
pense, but at length we were carried away by a unanimous movement of admiration."

Some of the Egyptian vase-
shaped capitals, are ornamented
with leaves of the lotus, or lily of the Nile, others
with the palm, date, and papyrus. These show a
fine conception of the beautiful, and were, doubtless,

FIG. 4.

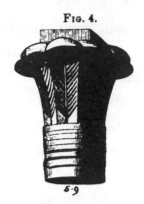

FIG. 5.

afterwards imitated in Grecian architecture. No. 6

FIG. 6.

is a column from the temple of Isis, at Dendera. It is composed of four heads of the Goddess Isis, with drapery about them; the profiles may be seen on the sides. Observe the abacus above this capital; it is not a square, flat stone, like the others; it is of a cubical form and richly ornamented with hieroglyphics. The temple from which it was taken, was one of the most perfectly executed of the numerous works upon the Nile. It was in one of the courts of this temple that the famous Zodiac was discovered, which has afforded so much speculation to the astronomers of Europe.

In all these columns the *abacus* is smaller than the shaft, and separates the capital from the entablature in a more distinct manner than was afterwards practised by the Greeks.

Of all the remains of Egyptian architectural greatness, the temple or palace of Karnac, or Carnak, is the most elaborate and extensive. It contains such an immense number of sphinxes, colossal statues, obelisks, propyla and porticoes, that the mind is bewildered, and lost amid the endless variety. All descriptions fail to convey a just idea of its size and magnificence. We can form no conception of a hall so large that the Cathedral of Notre Dame, at Paris, could be placed in it entire; or as a *Frenchman* remarked, "eight of our churches might dance a cotillon in it." This is the great hypostyle hall, supported by one hundred and thirty-four colossal columns, some of which are twenty-six feet in circumference, and others thirty-four. Six men with their hands united might clasp one of the shafts of these columns, but not the capitals; they are sixty-five feet in circumference, and ten feet high!

Champollion says : " The imagination, which in Europe rises far above our porticoes, sinks abashed at the foot of the one hundred and forty columns of the hypostyle hall of Carnak."

Yet this prodigious hall forms but a small part of the whole temple. There are twelve principal approaches to it, with their propyla, sphinxes, and colossal statues. As the devotee to this shrine walked through the long avenue, " between the majestic and tranquil sphinxes, and the mighty gates 'grated harsh thunder,' or turned on 'golden hinges,' " his soul must have been filled with religious awe ;—travellers who now wander among the prostrate ruins, are overpowered by their sublimity.

Alexandria, the splendid city built by Alexander, at the Delta of the Nile, was ornamented with obelisks, columns, and sphinxes, from the ruins of ancient Egypt. Thebes itself, was an immense quarry from which alone vast quantities of sculptured granite were transported to the new city. Cairo was built out of the ruins of Alexandria. Rome shared in the spoil. The superb obelisk still standing in the Piazza del Popolo, at Rome, was brought from Heliopolis by order of the Emperor Augustus. The solar obelisk of red granite in the square of Mount Citoria, at Rome, was also brought from Hieropolis by the same Emperor; it is ninety feet high, and covered with hieroglyphics, executed in fine style.

France, England, Germany, and other European countries, are rich in spoils, brought by travellers from that land of wonders.

The character of Egyptian Architecture is grave and sublime. " No people," says Champollion, " either ancient or modern, ever conceived the arts of architecture and sculpture on so sublime a scale as the ancient Egyptians. Their conceptions were those of men a hundred feet high." The straight lines and angles, unbroken by a single curve, give to the outline of all

their structures a heavy, massive appearance. There
is a general resemblance in the plan of the edifices, but
the architecture offers numberless varieties in detail.
The columns, for instance, have endless variety in
their proportions and ornaments; sometimes every
column in the same edifice is different in its decorations. The richness and profusion of sculpture with
which every part of the walls and columns are covered,
is one of the most remarkable characteristics of Egyptian Architecture. These sculptures are in *bas-relief*,
and often brilliantly coloured. The effect which this
richness of decoration produces, is overpowering and
bewildering; language seems to fail the various travellers, who attempt to express their emotions on behold-
ing these stupendous relics of ancient genius.

The Egyptians must have been a very numerous
people under a severe despotism. Whether the despotism which could command such immense power
was that of a cunning priesthood, or a long line of
ambitious monarchs, is uncertain; the probability is,
that it was the former, as most of the remains are
temples dedicated to the worship of their deities,
among whom the ibex and cat hold a conspicuous
pre-eminence. It is supposed by some that these
were symbolical, and that many of the other figures
were astronomical signs. The wily priests exacted
the hard earnings and ceaseless toil of millions to support an absurd, a monstrous system of idolatry. To
keep the people in awe and maintain their blind ado-

ration, the temples of their idols must be magnificent and imposing. Thus, what was at first a useful art, arising from stern necessity, became among the Egyptians the most expensive, and considering the objects to which it was devoted, the most useless of all arts. Yet to the historian, the architect, and the antiquary, these grand remains are not useless. They contain the *chiselled record* of the manners, customs, arts, sciences, literature, and religion of a portion of the human race who would otherwise have been buried in oblivion.

The dust of ages has been brushed away from these faithful records, and a gleam of light has been cast upon the Egyptian darkness that had shrouded this mysterious nation. We are indebted to Champollion, Dr. Young, and others, whose indefatigable labours have been devoted to this occult science.*

---

* The many who have heard the very interesting lectures of Mr. Gliddon, can testify to the patient persevering labour of the men who have endeavoured to decipher and explain Egyptian hieroglyphics.

CHAPTER III.

INDIAN OR HINDOO ARCHITECTURE.

ALTHOUGH nothing can be known with certainty as to the priority of the Egyptian or the Hindoo Architecture, some very scientific men claim that there is internal evidence that Hindostan led the way. We will not discuss the question.

The ancient edifices of Hindostan resemble those of Egypt in their form and general character, and yet are sufficiently marked to produce a peculiar style. " All countries in adopting a neighbouring style seem to have worked it with some peculiarities of their own, so that a person conversant with examples can tell, upon inspecting a building, to what nation it belongs."

The sacred edifices of the Hindoos were of five different kinds—pyramids, excavations, square or oblong temples, temples in the form of a cross, circular temples.

The pyramids are far inferior to those of Egypt, and are so much surpassed by other more perfect remains of Hindoo Architecture, that they are not worthy of particular notice.

EXCAVATIONS, OR TEMPLES CARVED FROM THE SOLID ROCK.

The most celebrated are at Elephanta, Salsette and Ellora.

The Island of Elephanta is near Bombay, and is so called from a colossal figure of an elephant carved upon the rocks on the southern shore of the island. A temple, one hundred and twenty feet square, is here cut out of the solid foundation of the earth. (Plate. III.)

Fig. 7. The large columns, of which there were four rows, stand upon high square pedestals; the bases have a peculiar ornament; the shafts are reeded, very short, and much smaller at the top than near the base. The capitals, though reeded like some of the Egyptian capitals, are larger, and flattened out as if the superincumbent weight had pressed them down. Along the sides of the cavern are about fifty statues, from twelve to fifteen feet high, having their heads ornamented with crowns, helmets, and other decorations. Like most of the Hindoo deities, they are each endowed with three or four pair of hands, and hideously unnatural countenances. The face of the great three-headed bust, is five feet long, and the breadth across the shoulders is twenty feet.

This subterranean temple is constantly exposed to

Plate III

INDRA SUBBA.

ELEPHANTA.

the sea breeze, and is yielding to the ruthless spoiler, Time,

> " Whom stone and brass obey,
> Who gives to every flying hour
> To work some new decay."

Canara, in the island of Salsette, is represented by travellers as very magnificent. There are four stories or galleries hewn out of a high perpendicular rock, into which open more than three hundred apartments. Before the entrance into this grand temple, stand two colossal statues, twenty-seven feet high. Thirty-five octagonal columns support the roof, which is not flat like Elephanta, but finely arched. The bases and capitals of these columns are formed of tigers, elephants, and other animals finely carved, and represented crouching down, as if to support the superincumbent weight. There are said to be not less than six hundred figures of idols within the excavations of Salsette.

But wonderful as are the excavations at Salsette and Elephanta, they are far surpassed by those of Ellora. A traveller says: " No monuments of antiquity in the known world are comparable to the caves of Ellora, whether we consider their unknown origin, their stupendous size, the beauty of their architectural ornaments, or the vast number of statues and emblems, all hewn out of the solid rock."* It would require volumes to give a description of these amazing works. It

---

* Seely, " Wonders of Ellora."

seems a land of enchantment, "the eye and imagination are bewildered with the variety of interesting objects, that present themselves on every side. The feelings are interested to a degree of awe, wonder and delight, that at first is painful, and it is a long time before they become sufficiently sobered and calm, to contemplate with any attention the surrounding wonders. Conceive the burst of surprise, at suddenly coming upon a stupendous temple, within a large, open court, with all its parts perfect and beautiful; standing proudly alone upon its native bed, detached from the neighbouring mountain, by a spacious area all around, nearly two hundred and fifty feet deep, and one hundred and fifty feet broad; the unrivalled fane in the midst, rearing its rocky head to a height of nearly one hundred feet, its length about one hundred feet, its breadth sixty-two; having well-formed doorways, windows, and staircases; containing fine large rooms of a smooth and polished surface, regularly divided by rows of pillars."—Thus stands "KEYLAS THE PROUD, wonderfully towering in hoary majesty, a mighty fabric of rock, surpassed by no relic of antiquity in the known world."

Far inferior to this vast building in size, is the exquisitely beautiful temple of Indra Subba, (Plate III.) It is a copy on a small scale of the mighty Keylas. Like that, Indra Subba is an insulated temple at Ellora, with a wide area or open space around it, which is terminated by a spacious gallery supported by columns, carved into the perpendicular rock. The little temple is left completely insulated as represented in the plate, the galleries being some hundred feet distant. It would seem to the observer, that these curious works must have been constructed downward; the workmen beginning at the top of the rock, chiselled first the roof, scooping out at the same time the area around it; thus working gradually down till the temple was finished to its base, where the foundations remain immovably fixed, a part of the primitive rock, which nothing can disturb, but the convulsions of the final catastrophe, when

" Rocks fall to dust, and mountains melt away."

The columns of the Temple of Indra have capitals consisting of two reeded cushions pressed down; the shafts diminish suddenly near the capital; the bases are moulded and rest upon a plinth.

The single column, standing alone, reminds one of the two pillars of brass, Jachin and Boaz, which stood in Solomon's Temple. For what purpose this isolated column was designed, it is difficult to determine; it has no base, but rests upon a pedestal, beautifully sculptured. The roof to this elegant little temple is finished with circular ornaments resembling cupolas, at each corner, and upon the top. The chiselling of the ornaments shows that the artists had arrived at a degree of skill, far surpassing that of the modern Hindoos.

Visvacarma, also at Ellora, is a vaulted temple,

eighty feet in length, and forty-four feet in breadth. From the sides of the roof project rafters of rock, meeting in the centre of the vault, and resting upon sculptured figures which stand upon a heavy entablature. Square massive columns without base or capital support this entablature. The great altar at the end of the temple is twenty-four feet high; in front of it is a canopy under which is the idol, Visvacarma.

> "The ancient pillars rear their rocky heads,
> To bear aloft its arched and ponderous roof,
> By its own weight made steadfast and immovable;
> Looking tranquillity, it strikes an awe
> And terror to my aching sight."

What and who were the men who designed and executed these mysterious temples?

They were not like the feeble and indolent Hindoos who now wander among them, incapable of appreciating the genius, which brought out these forms of beauty from their rocky beds. Conjecture is at fault; history gives no clue to the mystery. "The first view of the desolate religious city of Ellora," remarks Mr. Erskine, "is grand and striking, but melancholy. The number and magnificence of the subterraneous temples, the extent and loftiness of some, the endless diversity of sculpture in others, the variety of curious foliage, of minute tracery, highly wrought pillars, rich mythological designs, sacred shrines, and colossal statues, astonish but distract the mind. No trace re-

mains to tell us the hand by which they were designed, or the populous and powerful nation by which
they were completed.   The empire whose pride they
must have been, has passed away and left not a memo-
rial behind it.   The religion to which we owe one
part of them indeed, continues to exist; but that which
called into existence the other, (the Boodhist,) like the
beings by whose toil it was wrought, has been swept
from the land."

The rock of which these sculptured caverns are
formed, varies; black and gray basalt, granite, "a
hard vesicular rock, and a rock of gritty loose texture,"
are mentioned by travellers; from which we infer, that
there is in the geological formation occasional stratifica-
tion, and that the reason why some of the caves are in
a more ruinous condition than others, is the less enduring nature of parts of the material of which they are
formed.   It is impossible not to be forcibly struck
with the resemblance between Hindoo and Egyptian
Architecture.   The massive columns, the varied and
curious capitals, the solemn grandeur of the *tout en-
semble*, seem to point out a common origin; yet great
diversities occur, and in some instances, (Visvacarma
and several other vaulted temples for example,) of an
entire departure from the straight lines and angles of
the Egyptian style.

Of Hindoo temples, which are of more modern
origin, there are an endless variety.   Many of those,
composed of square or oblong courts, are of immense

extent. One of the most magnificent is that of Sering-ham, near Tritchinopoly. This pagoda is composed of seven square enclosures, the outermost being four miles square; the walls are twenty-five feet high, four feet thick, and three hundred and fifty feet from each other, leaving a space about a thousand feet square in the centre, upon which stands a high pagoda. To each of the enclosures are four gateways with lofty towers; these gateways are in direct lines leading to the centre.

Another kind of Indian Pagoda is in the form of a cross, with lofty cupolas at the centre and at the ex-tremities of the cross.

There are many pagodas of a circular form. The horrid Temple of Juggernaut is compared to an im-mense butt or wine-cask set on end. The sacred do-mains of this pagoda afford pasturage for twenty thou-sand sacred cows. In Tanjore is a pyramidal pagoda, which Lord Valentia says is the finest specimen of the kind in India, and is a very beautiful piece of archi-tecture. As there is a strongly marked resemblance between Egyptian and Hindoo Architecture, there is also a striking similarity in their idolatry. From these facts it is inferred that the communications between these two mighty nations were frequent and intimate, or, that one was founded by a colony from the other, after the arts and sciences had been for a long time cultivated in the fatherland.

CHAPTER IV.

PERSIAN ARCHITECTURE.

THE beautiful ruins of Persepolis afford a fine specimen of ancient Persian Architecture. Nothing however remains but a few splendid remnants of the palace
which Alexander partially destroyed in one of his mad
frolics.

Persepolis is situated in the province of Faristan,
latitude 30° 40′ N., longitude 84° E. Le Brun spent
three months in exploring and delineating these ruins,
and after much discussion, conjectures that Darius and
Xerxes built Persepolis.

These ruins were probably the summer palace of a
Persian monarch. From the name *Chilmenar*, which
signifies forty columns, it has been inferred that only
that number belonged to the edifice; but Le Brun
counted the traces of two hundred and five, although
only nineteen were then standing entire. The doorways
or entrances resemble those of Egyptian temples.
The columns are much more slender in proportion to

Fig. 8.

their height, than either Egyptian or Hindoo columns, being seventy-two feet high, and only seventeen inches in diameter at the base.

The capitals (Fig. 8) are very high, occupying nearly a fourth of the whole height of the column. The bases (Fig. 9) are a little more than four inches high, and twenty-five in circumference, very beautifully and delicately carved. It is supposed that these capitals were intended to represent bunches of feathers as they had formerly been tied around the tops of tall wooden pillars. No fragments of a roof have been discovered, and the columns are too slender to have borne any but a light one. These beautiful marble columns probably sustained temporary awnings of silk, which, as it was a summer palace, could be taken down at pleasure.

In Shushan, the palace of Ahasuerus, there were

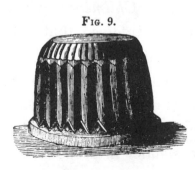

Fig. 9.

" white, green and blue hangings, fastened with cords of fine linen and purple, to silver rings, and *pillars of marble ;* the beds were of gold and silver upon a pavement of red, and blue, and white, and black marble."

Like Shushan, the mouldering solitary ruin of Persepolis was once the chosen seat of merriment and splendour. It is silent now, silent as the desert, save when some tall column which long has tottered upon its base, startles the amazed traveller by falling at his feet with thundering sound. There stood the gorgeous throne, there bowed the abject throng; soft, sweet music floated around these stately columns, fragrant incense filled the air. Desolation reigns sole monarch now; the mournful sighing of the wind the only music; damp vapours load the unwholesome air. The dust of the mighty is mingled with that of their meanest slaves, as it is scattered by every breeze over this mouldering monument of their brief glory.

The Tombs of the Kings at Persepolis are sculptured and elaborately ornamented. They are excavations, and carved from the rock. The tomb of Darius, as it is called, is the most magnificent. The perpendicular front, which presents itself, is seventy feet high, seventy feet in breadth at the base, and forty feet above. The lower columns support a heavy entablature; their capitals are composed of the heads of oxen. Above this first gallery are two rows of human figures supporting entablatures, and above them the sculptured figure of a king performing his devotions before an altar.

It is thought by some authors that Persepolis was built by Egyptian architects, carried thither by Cambyses, but that the Persians, abhorring the Egyptian mythology, obliged them to erect and to decorate their structures according to some rude models which had previously existed. The sculptures represent religious processions, and sacrifices to the sun and moon; some of the persons in these processions carry umbrellas, an invention, which has been generally attributed to a much later period.

It cannot be doubted that there was a communication of architectural knowledge between the three countries, which possess the most magnificent specimens of ancient art.

CHAPTER V.

JEWISH ARCHITECTURE.

SEVENTY years after the birth of our Saviour, in fulfilment of prophecy, the destruction of Jerusalem was accomplished by the Romans under Titus. Very little can now be known of the architecture of that once beautiful city.

Following the description with which we are furnished in the Old Testament, we cannot make out a very exact architectural delineation of Solomon's temple. Previously to its erection, the Israelites had made very few of the higher efforts in the art. The cities of the Canaanites were surrounded with walls, and their dwellings were such as to accommodate their conquerors; when they built for themselves, their most stately houses were of the cedar of Lebanon, and other kinds of wood, and were rendered magnificent by carving, gilding, and embroidery.

This gorgeous style of ornamenting is still practised in the East, where the want of beauty of design in the structure, and unskilfulness in the architect, must be concealed by everything costly and dazzling in decoration. The Israelites might have received some knowledge of Architecture from Egypt, yet when Solomon was about to build the Temple, the workmen of his own kingdom were not sufficient for the task. The Tyrians and Sidonians were more skilful, and Hiram, King of Tyre, received a large sum annually while the Temple was building, for the labour of his subjects who were employed upon it. He also supplied large quantities of materials for the structure.

The Temple was built upon the summit of Mount Moriah. It was enclosed by a gallery or portico, which was divided into two courts, the great or exterior court, and the interior, or " court before the temple." These courts were separated from each other either by a wall, or a slight partition of lattice-work. There were various apartments around the main building, for the vases and other utensils used in the Jewish service, for the provisions for the priests, and for their accommodation while employed about the sacred duties of the temple.

The great *altar* stood in the court of the temple, or the court of the priests, as it is sometimes called.

The large brazen laver, "the molten sea," which stood in one of the courts, could contain three thousand baths.* It was supported upon the backs of twelve oxen, three facing to each point of the compass, and

---

* Jahu's Biblical Archæology.

its brim was ornamented with lilies of brass, an appropriate ornament for the water's edge. Beside this immense laver there were ten smaller ones, resting upon highly ornamented bases, and wheels, "like chariot wheels," that they might be moved about the court.

The part of the Temple called the sanctuary, was sixty cubits (about ninety feet) long, twenty cubits broad, and thirty high, with the exception of the part called the *Sanctissimum*, or *Most Holy*, the height of which was only twenty cubits, so that there remained over it a room of ten cubits in height. In front of the sanctuary was the porch or pronaos, (similar, perhaps, to the Egyptian,) one hundred and twenty cubits high, having a lofty entrance without any door. The entrance to the sanctuary was closed by a folding door, ornamented with carved work covered with gold, and turning on golden hinges, and a similar door was at the entrance of the Holy of Holies ; both of them were covered with veils of embroidered linen. Near the entrance of the porch were two columns of brass, Jachin and Boaz, which seem to have been merely for ornament, as they supported no part of the edifice. These columns were twelve cubits, (about eighteen feet,) in circumference ; the *shafts* were eighteen cubits high, the *capitals* five, and the *bases*, thirteen ; making the whole altitude, thirty-six cubits, (about fifty-four feet.)

These proportions resemble those of the columns at Elephanta ; the capitals with their *leaves, pomegranates,* and *lilies*, remind us of the profusely ornamented Egyptian capitals. The shafts and bases were hollow, the brass of which they were made being a hand's breadth in thickness.

The sanctuary was built of large square stones, hewn and fitted at the quarry. This seems to have been the usual practice among the ancients; "the splendour and magnificence of a building seem to have been estimated by the size of the square stones of which it was constructed;" in Solomon's Temple, however, they were covered within and without with boards of cedar profusely carved, and overlaid with gold.

The sacred historians mention several other buildings with which Solomon adorned Jerusalem, but so concisely, that we can form no accurate conceptions of them.

The Temple, repaired and beautified by Herod, is the one so often mentioned in the New Testament, and was exceedingly magnificent. The gates and porches were lofty and richly ornamented with gold and Corinthian brass. The sanctuary was of white marble, and the roof of it was covered with sharp rods of iron covered with gold.

It was in the porch of this Temple that Judas threw down the price of his treachery, the thirty pieces of silver. The porch on the south side was the highest part of the Temple, and was probably "the pinnacle," from whence our blessed Saviour was shown the glories of the kingdoms of this world, by the arch-deceiver. From another porch in the court of the Gentiles, Jesus drove out " the money-changers, and those who sold doves," for the sacrifices of the temple worship.

In studying Egyptian, Hindoo, and Persian Architecture, we are aided by splendid remains: here we have no such certain guides ; our researches, therefore, cannot lead to anything very satisfactory.

CHAPTER VI.

CHINESE ARCHITECTURE.

THE earliest attempts at buildings in China, were close imitations of tents, and to this day they have not departed from the original design. Although remarkably ingenious, the Chinese are an imitative people, and it is impossible to say, how many centuries their works of all kinds may have continued precisely the same.

The Great Wall was constructed by Thsing-chi-hoang-ti about two hundred and fourteen years before our era. A French writer calls it a "monument le plus colossal, comme le plus insensé, peut-être, qu'ait jamais conçu la pensée humaine."

But Thsing-chi-hoang-ti knew what he was about; the Tartars might invade his dominions, but that was not his only or chief reason for this immense structure. Having brought under his sway a great number of petty kingdoms, into which the Celestial Empire had been previously divided, and widely extended his conquests over neighbouring countries, the illustrious

Hoang-ti issued a decree worthy of the immortal Jack Cade; namely, that all the books of morals and history in his wide dominions should be burned. Tyranny of course would be best secured by ignorance. But discontent, revolt, and vengeance threatened him, and the people must be employed; hence arose the great wall Wen-ti-tchang-tching, upon which millions of men were occupied for ten years. His neighbours, the Tartars, might invade his dominions, but his most dangerous foes were his own subjects. Wen-ti-tchang-tching means the wall of a thousand leagues. It is supposed to be about half that length, fifteen hundred miles. Its thickness is such, that six horsemen might ride abreast upon the top of it. It varies from twenty to forty feet in height. Throughout its prodigious length it is flanked with towers at the distance of two flights of an arrow apart. Thus it is carried over high mountains, and through deep valleys, and ravines, and rivers. The wall was built with much care and skill, with hewn stone on the exterior, filled in between with earth. "The materials which have served for the construction of this wall," says M. Barron, "would be more than sufficient to build a wall twice round the globe, six feet high and two feet thick."

Thsing-chi-hoang-ti embellished his capital with buildings of the greatest magnificence. He augmented the number of regal edifices by causing three hundred royal palaces to be erected within the walls of the city, and four hundred in the country. All these edifices, which he endeavoured to render as magnificent as possible, were to be placed, say the historians, so as to present upon the surface of the earth a *coup d'œil*, like that which *the milky-way* and the constellations near it present in the vault of the heavens. This was, indeed, making a Celestial Empire!

Another Emperor confessed as a sin, that he had made his palaces too superb, and otherwise expended superfluously in buildings. The Chinese have built large structures of their favourite porcelain. The famous pagoda at Peking is of this material.

Their pagodas all have nearly the same form. (Plate IV.) Chinese gates and garden-houses have lightness and grace, but there is comparatively little in their architecture worthy of imitation. Their dwelling-houses (Plate IV.) are lacquered, painted, and gilded, and it is doubtful whether the palaces mentioned by the ancient historians were anything more than wooden structures thus gaudily ornamented.

Sir William Chambers says, that " some consideration is due to a race of men who, separated from the polished nations of the world, have, without any model to assist them, been able of themselves to mature the sciences and invent the arts. What is really Chinese has at least the merit of being original."

Plate IV

CHINESE PAGODA & DWELLING HOUSE.

CHAPTER VII.

AMERICAN OR ABORIGINAL ARCHITECTURE.

THE discovery of architectural ruins in Central America of immense extent, and of a style perfectly anomalous, excited throughout Europe and in our own country the most extravagant expectations.

The antiquary looked for revelations concerning a race older than Assyria and Babylon; antediluvians, perhaps, who built with the skill and magnificence of the " giants of those days."

The man of science was on tiptoe; the poet was ready to place his ideal creations amid splendid edifices which would surpass all the wild imaginings of the Arabian Nights.

The architect anticipated new designs, superior to those of classic Greece.

These rash expectations were in a measure disappointed, when the thorough investigations of Stephens and Catherwood, restored those long-hidden remains. Restored, we may say, for the beautiful " Views" of Catherwood, bring them, in all their fantastic and grotesque forms, before our eyes as realities. The inde-

fatigable and amusing writer, to whom we are indebted
for the most valuable information that has been given
with regard to Central America, says, of the ancient
American cities, " There are not sufficient grounds for
belief in the great antiquity that has been ascribed to
these ruins." " We are not warranted in going back
to any ancient nation of the Old World for the builders
of these cities." " This opinion was not given lightly,
nor without due consideration. It was adverse to my
feelings, which would have fain thrown around the
ruins the interest of mystery and hoary age."

Although we acknowledge the force of the internal
and circumstantial evidence, by which travellers have
arrived at this conclusion, yet the antiquity of these
remains is not settled. As it is impossible to assign
American Aboriginal Architecture to the exact chronological period to which it belongs, it has been introduced
here, as the fitting place, although it breaks in upon
the regular course.

The colossal edifices of the Aborigines of Mexico,
Central America,* and Yucatan, are mostly pyramidal
in form (Plate V.); the pyramid rises by terraces,
which gradually decrease in size ; upon the top is left

---

* Central America lies between 8° and 18° N. latitude. It com-
prehends that part of the long isthmus between North and South
America which, lying between the Atlantic and Pacific Oceans, extends
from New Grenada to Mexico. Yucatan is a peninsula projecting
from its northern extremity into the Gulf of Mexico.

Plate V

CASA DEL GOBERNADOR.

A MEXICAN TEOCALLIS.

a level space of sufficient size for the building which crowns the summit.

In front of the pyramid was a hideous idol, and the stone of sacrifice upon which human victims were offered.

In Mexico these teocalli were very numerous. " They were solid masses of earth, brick, or stone. The bases of them were several hundred feet square, and they towered to a height of more than a hundred feet. There were said to be six hundred altars, or smaller buildings, within the great Temple of Mexico, which, with those on the sacred edifices, in other parts of the city, shed a brilliant illumination over its streets through the darkest night."

The great teocallis of Mexico was divided into five stories or bodies, each one receding so as to be of smaller dimensions than that immediately below it. The ascent was by a flight of steps on the outside, which reached to the narrow terrace or platform at the base of the second story, passing quite round the building, where a second stairway conducted to a similar landing at the base of the third. The breadth of this walk was just so much space as was left by the retreating story next above it. From this construction the visiter was obliged to pass round the whole edifice four times in order to reach the top. This had a most imposing effect in the religious ceremonials, when the pompous procession of priests, with their wild min-strelsy, came sweeping round the huge sides of the

pyramid, as they rose higher and higher, in the presence of gazing multitudes, towards the summit.

The dimensions of the temple cannot be given with
any certainty. It was, probably, not much less than
three hundred feet square at the base, and as the
Spaniards counted a hundred and fourteen steps, was
probably less than one hundred feet high.   On reach-
ing the summit, they found it a vast area, paved with
broad flat stones.   The first object that met their view
was a large block of jasper, the peculiar shape of which
showed that it was the stone on which the bodies of the
unhappy victims were stretched for sacrifice.*   Its con-

---

* Prescott's Conquest of Mexico. " Human sacrifices were adopted
by the Aztecs or Mexicans, two hundred years before the conquest.
One of the most important festivals was that in honour of the god
Tezcatlipoca, whose rank was inferior only to that of the Supreme
Being.   He was called ' the Soul of the World,' and supposed to have
been its creator.   He was depicted as a handsome man, endowed
with perpetual youth.   A year before the intended sacrifice, a captive, distinguished for his personal beauty, and without a blemish on
his body, was selected to represent this deity.   Certain tutors took
charge of him, and instructed him how to perform his new part with
becoming grace and dignity.   He was arrayed in a splendid dress,
regaled with incense, and with a profusion of sweet-scented flowers.
When he went abroad, he was attended by a train of the royal pages,
and, as he halted in the streets to play some favourite melody, the
crowd prostrated themselves before him, and did him homage as the
representative of their good deity.   In this way he led an easy, luxurious life till within a month of his sacrifice.

" At length the fatal day arrived. The term of his short-lived glories
was at an end. He was stripped of his gaudy apparel, and bade

vex surface, by raising the breast, enabled the priest to perform his diabolical task more easily, of removing the heart. At the other end of the area were two towers or sanctuaries, consisting of three stories, the lower one of stone and stucco, the two upper of wood elaborately carved. In the lower division stood the images of their gods. Before each sanctuary stood an altar with that undying fire upon it, the extinction of which boded as much evil to the empire, as that of the Vestal flame would have done in ancient Rome. Here also was the huge cylindrical drum made of ser-

---

adieu to the companions of his revelries. One of the royal barges transported him across the lake to a temple which rose on its margin, about a league from the city. Hither the inhabitants of the capital flocked to witness the consummation of the ceremony. As the sad procession wound up the sides of the pyramid, the unhappy victim threw away his gay chaplets of flowers, and broke in pieces the instruments of music with which he had solaced the hours of captivity. On the summit he was received by six priests, whose long and matted locks flowed disorderly over their sable robes, covered with hieroglyphic scrolls of mystic import. They led him to the sacrificial stone, a huge block of jasper, with its upper surface somewhat convex. On this the victim was stretched. Five priests secured his head and his limbs, while the sixth, clad in a scarlet mantle, emblematic of his bloody office, dexterously opened the breast of the wretched victim with a sharp razor of itzli, a volcanic substance hard as flint, and inserting his hand in the wound, tore out the palpitating heart. The minister of death, first holding this up towards the sun, cast it at the feet of the deity to whom the temple was devoted, and then expounded the tragedy as the type of human destiny, which, brilliant at its commencement, too often closes in sorrow and disaster."

pents' skins, and struck only on extraordinary occasions, when it sent forth a melancholy sound that might be heard for miles. " The temple rising high above all other edifices in the capital, afforded the most elevated as well as central point of view. From this position could be distinctly traced the symmetrical plan of the city, with its principal avenues issuing from the four gates and connecting themselves with the causeways which formed the grand entrances to the capital. This regular and beautiful arrangement was imitated in many of the inferior towns, where the great roads converged towards the chief teocallis as to a common focus."

The structures of Yucatan and Central America possess the same general characteristics as those of Mexico. The ruins of Uxmal, in Yucatan, are the most remarkable for their extent and variety of any which have been yet explored.

" They impressed my mind," says Catherwood,* " at the first glance, with the same feelings of wonder and admiration, with which I first caught sight of the ruins of Thebes."

The grand teocallis so nearly resemble the Mexican one already mentioned, that it is needless to give a particular description of it. It is called the " House of the Dwarf," and the " House of the Diviner."

Next in importance is the " Casa del Gobernador,"

---

* " Catherwood's Views, in Central America, Chiapas, and Yucatan."

or House of the Governor. (Plate V.) This immense
building is constructed entirely of hewn stone, and measures three hundred and twenty feet in front, by forty
feet in depth; the height is about twenty-six feet. It
has eleven doorways in front, and one at each end.
The apartments are narrow, seldom exceeding twelve
feet. The peculiar *arch* of the country has been employed in every room.

The Casa del Gobernador stands on three terraces;
the lowest is three feet high, fifteen feet wide, and
five hundred and seventy-five feet long; the second is
twenty feet high; the third, nineteen feet high, and
three hundred and sixty feet long; it is in a remarkably good state of preservation.

As this building is one of the finest that has been
explored, and gives a complete idea of the manner in
which those edifices were ornamented, we would com-
mend the reader to Mr. Stephens's full and accurate
description.*

It would *seem* as if this immense edifice had been first
built and the stones afterwards carved; for each stone
by itself is an unmeaning fractional portion, but by the
side of others it forms part of a whole, without which
it would be incomplete. All these ornaments may
have a symbolical meaning, and each stone be a part
of a history, allegory, or fable.

Up to the cornice, which runs round the whole
length and the four sides of the " Casa," the façade

---

* " Incidents of Travel in Yucatan."

presents a smooth surface; above, is one solid mass of rich, complicated, and elaborately sculptured ornaments, forming a sort of arabesque.

The finest ornament is over the centre doorway. It seems to have been a sitting figure with an enormous head-dress of bunches of feathers symmetrically arranged.

A peculiar ornament, called by Waldeck an elephant's trunk, appears all over the façade and at the

Fig. 10.

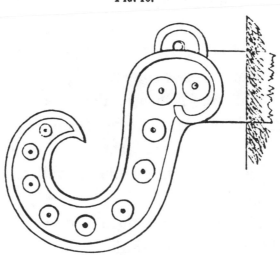

corners; and throughout all the buildings it is met with oftener than any other design in Uxmal. How astonishing, that all these carvings should have been executed without the use of iron!

The rear elevation of the " Casa" is a solid wall, nine feet thick. Like the front, it was ornamented with sculpture, but less gorgeous and elaborate. The roof is flat, and had been covered with cement, but is now overgrown with grass and bushes.

The long narrow apartments within, more resemble corridors or galleries, than rooms, some of them being twenty-three feet high, and only eleven or thirteen wide; some of them have but one door of entrance, and none of them windows.

The walls are constructed of square smooth blocks of stone. The floors are of cement.

The prints of a *red hand* were found upon all this, and all the ruined buildings of the country. They had been painted upon the stone by the living hand, with the thumb and fingers extended, moistened with red paint. The seams and creases of the palm were clear and distinct in the impression. What Champollion shall decipher the mysterious hieroglyphics which are everywhere sculptured upon these buildings?

Other buildings, that were once attached to the "Casa," still rear their solemn ruins in its vicinity.

Although these buildings afford no useful designs for the modern architect, and the sculptured ornaments are fantastic and grotesque, yet as specimens of art among a semi-barbarous people, they are exceedingly interesting. They have a picturesque appearance in the beautifully coloured "Views" of Catherwood, and the splendid engravings of the magnificent work of Lord Kingsborough. Some of the sculptures, as represented in the latter,* had a smooth, delicate finish, that would not disgrace the chisel of a modern artist.

Another feature in the Aboriginal Architecture, which must claim our attention, is the arch.

" A true arch is formed of a series of wedgelike stones, or of bricks, supporting each other, and all bound together by the pressure of the centre one upon them, which latter is therefore distinguished by the name of the keystone."

No such arch has been found among these ruins. Wilkinson, Gliddon, and others, give representations 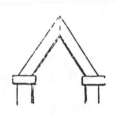 of the Egyptian arch, but may they not have been formed like these Aboriginal arches ? In many instances they were constructed of two large stones laid together and meeting at the top.

" The stones forming the side walls are made to overlap each other until the walls almost meet above, and then the narrow ceilings are covered with a layer of flat stones.   In every case the stones were laid in horizontal layers, the principle of constructing arches, as understood by us, being unknown to the original builders.   This accounts for the extreme narrowness of all their rooms.   In a few cases the covering stone

* " Antiquities of Mexico ;" a work in seven folio volumes, which owes its publication to the truly noble munificence of Lord Kingsbo·rough.

is wanting, and the two sides meet so as to form a sharp angle."*

In Yucatan, the inner surfaces of the stones were smoothed, and therefore must have presented the appearance of a regular arch, but not a semicircular one.

What are the nations of the Old Continent whose style of architecture bears most resemblance to that of the remarkable monuments of Chiapa and Yucatan? The points of resemblance will be found neither numerous nor decisive. There is indeed some analogy both to the Egyptian, and Asiatic style of architecture in the pyramidal terrace-formed bases, on which the buildings repose. A similar care also, was observed in the people of both hemispheres, to adjust the position of their buildings to the cardinal points. The walls in both are covered with figures and hieroglyphics, which on the American, as on the Egyptian, may be designed to record the laws and historical annals of the nation. These figures, as well as the buildings themselves, are found to have been stained with various dyes, principally vermilion, a favourite colour with the Egyptians also, who painted their colossal statues, and temples of granite.

" Notwithstanding these points of similarity, the Aboriginal Architecture has little to remind us of the Egyptian or the Oriental. It must be admitted to have a character of originality peculiar to itself."†

---

* Stephens.   † Prescott's Conquest of Mexico.

Their sculpture and their hieroglyphics give us no light to guide us to the discovery of their antiquity, and the origin of these singular buildings. Who inhabited these edifices, upon which the large trees now twine their roots among the loosened stones?

Le Noir, gives them an antiquity of "*trois mille ans*," and says, "Ceci n'est point mon opinion seule; c'est celle de tous les voyageurs qui ont vu les ruines."

Colonel Galindo, pronounces this country, "the true cradle of civilization."

Mr. Waldeck, from the old trees and the stalactites in some of the ruins, computes the age of the buildings at two or three thousand years.

Others have gone so far as to give them an antediluvian origin.

The old Spanish writer, Bernal Diaz, believed the Jews to have been the builders, and this is the opinion which Lord Kingsborough has laboured to establish. One thing is certain, that the Aztecs and the builders of Uxmal were a superior race to any that were found inhabiting this country, when it was conquered by the Spaniards.

CHAPTER VIII.

CYCLOPEAN AND ETRUSCAN ARCHITECTURE.

AGES before the Romans existed, the fair land of Italy was inhabited by nations who have left indestructible monuments as the only records of their history. Those wonderful cities of early Italy which have been termed Cyclopean, are thickly scattered throughout certain districts, and "are often perched like eagles' nests, on the very crests of mountains, at such an elevation as to strike amazement into the traveller who now visits them, and to bewilder him with speculations as to the state of society which could have driven men to such scarcely accessible spots for habitation, and to entrench themselves therein with such stupendous fortifications. The choice of such sites seems to indicate a state of society little removed from barbarism, in which there was no security nor confidence between the several communities, and the only law was,

> " The good old rule—the simple plan,
> That he should take who has the power,
> And he should keep—who can."

The walls of the Cyclopean cities are formed of huge blocks of limestone or other calcareous stone, roughly hewn, or, as in the walls of Tyrius, not shaped by the chisel, and in all cases laid together without cement. The Cyclopean gates are square; an enormous stone lying over two upright ones. There are, however, some rude attempts at an arch, the stones being arranged so as to meet at the top, in the same manner as they were formed, by the Aboriginal Architects of Central America. The true arch is never found in this style.

The cities of Etruria generally stood on low ground, although there are exceptions to this rule, and they were less ancient than the Cyclopean. The finest specimens of the Etruscan walls are built of large blocks of hewn stone laid in regular courses.

It is in the gateways and vaults of Etruscan Architecture, compared with those of the Cyclopean, that we find superior skill in the art. The perfect arch, formed of massive stones fitted together without cement, is the most striking feature in these architectural remains. There are many specimens in Etruria which the researches of modern travellers have brought to light.

Of Etruscan bridges with a single arch, several now stand as firmly as they did "twenty or twenty-five centuries ago." It is impossible to determine how long they have been built. The Etruscans were the people, doubtless, from whom the Romans in their early day derived the arts and sciences.

Their roads were cut through rocks to lessen the distance, like the tunnelling of modern times. "In their sepulchres there is a great variety of character ; in none is there any resemblance to the Roman; in most respects they differ from the Grecian, but they are very similar to the Egyptian ; some of them were excavated in the face of the rock, and others were below the surface of the ground."

The tombs of Etruria appear to have been an imitation of the dwelling-house of the living. They have sloping roofs, and in the interior the ceilings are finished with rafters in relief; the walls too, are panelled in relief; and a modern traveller exclaims, " Come, see, and believe, ye incredulous! *easy armchairs with footstools attached*, all carved out of the living rock. Then the articles of furniture bear out this view—the vases, the amphoræ, jugs, goblets, drinking-horns, the wine-coolers, glass bottles, the plates, cups, saucers, spoons, &c., &c., in bronze and earthenware—the mirrors, rings, and necklaces,—the armour and weapons. What mean all these as sepulchral furniture, if the belief were not entertained that departed spirits would in another state have similar necessities to what they had in this, and if the tomb were not intended to be, to a great extent, the counterpart of the abode of the living ?"

6

CHAPTER IX.

GRECIAN ARCHITECTURE.

GREECE—pride of the world!

> " Though broken is each consecrated shrine,
> Though crushed and ruined all,"

yet, every age shall own thee as the *alma mater* of poetry, eloquence, sculpture, and architecture.

Perfection, cannot be claimed for any of the works of man; it belongs only to the Divine Architect of the universe; His power and knowledge are but faintly reflected by human intellect.

The sages and philosophers of Greece, travelled into Egypt, Persia, and India, gaining a knowledge of the arts and sciences, and on their return, imparted it to their fellow-countrymen. The Grecian colonists who settled the peninsula and the beautiful islands of the blue Ægean, came from countries already far advanced in civilization.

Their architecture bears sufficient resemblance to the best specimens of the Egyptian, to prove that they had studied and improved upon it.

It was not till a short time before the Peloponnesian war, about B. C. 450, that the arts arrived at their highest excellence among the Greeks. The genius of this wonderful people was employed in the invention of mechanical and decorative architecture, until it was formed into three distinct orders, the Doric, Ionic, and Corinthian.

Every *order* is marked by the form, proportions, and ornaments, of the column and entablature. These are the governing members, with which every other part of a building must harmonize. It is not alone the costliness, magnificence, and antiquity of a Grecian edifice that render it beautiful; the beauty of proportion is independent of these. "The eye, even of an unpractised observer, when viewing a magnificent building, is never satisfied, unless the weights appear to be duly supported; and it receives a corresponding pleasure when that is the case." Hence, if the entablature, which is the only weight that appears, be heavy, the column which supports it must be large, to give it the appearance of strength; if the entablature be light, the column must also be light.

The proportions of the Grecian orders, connected as they are with the ideas of utility and fitness, have stood the test of time and experience, and are still the classic models for mankind.

> " First unadorned
> And nobly plain, the manly *Doric* rose;
> The *Ionic* then, with decent matron grace
> Her airy pillar heaved; luxuriant last,
> The rich *Corinthian* spread her wanton wreath."

DORIC ORDER.

The Doric, the most simple and ancient of these orders, was invented by the Dorians.

Their country abounded with forests, and the first habitations of the colonists, were probably constructed of wood. Upright posts were the pillars, supporting a roof with projecting eaves. Temples were, in time, built in the same oblong form, with columns of marble supporting an entablature. In the course of time, these simple structures were decorated to conceal the mechanical construction.

The column is without a base. (Plate VI.) The shaft is fluted, usually with twenty flat flutes or concavities. It has been suggested that the shaft was originally plain, and that the flutings were invented, to form a convenient place for the long spears of the soldiers who visited the temple. Although this appears fanciful, it may be true; many inventions have been designed for utility, and continued for ornament; the Egyptian columns, however, were reeded, and the change from convex ornamenting, to concave, seems very slight.

Among the many remains of the Doric order, the proportions vary. The most ancient columns are shorter in proportion to their diameter, than those of a later origin, being only five diameters in height.

Taking the diameter of the Doric column, Plate VI., at the bottom of the shaft, the height of the whole

Plate VI

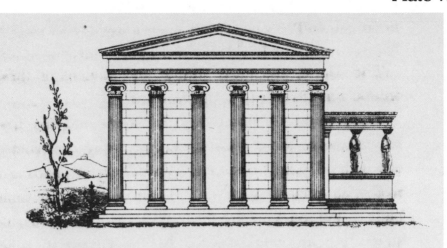

ERECTHEUM.

PARTHENON.

shaft is six diameters. From a careful comparison
of ancient Doric columns, the following proportions
have been established. The shaft, six diameters; the
capital, half a diameter; the abacus, quarter of a diameter. The shaft diminishes in thickness as it ascends;
where it joins the capital, it is nearly a quarter less in
diameter than at the bottom, where it rests upon the
platform. The *abacus* is considered the upper member
of the capital: it is here a flat square plinth; beneath
it, is the large, finely formed *ovolo ;* below this are three
annulets or rings, which complete the Doric capital.

The entablature is heavy. The *architrave* is ornamented with conical *drops*
or *guttæ*, as they are called.

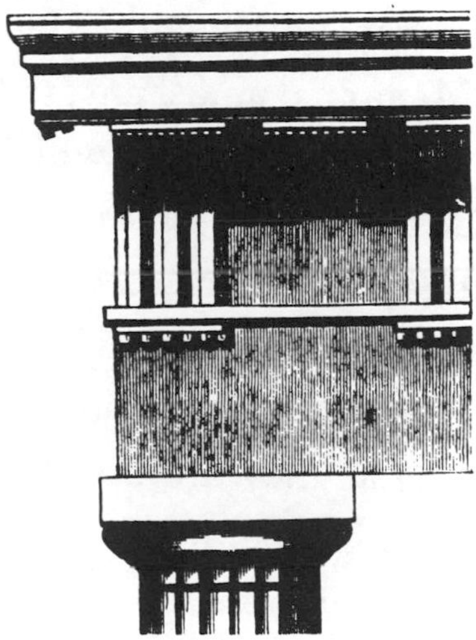

The *frieze* is sculptured
with *triglyphs*, an ornament
peculiar to this order. The
square places between these
triglyphs are called *metopes*,
and are often ornamented
with sculpture.

The *cornice*, has a large
projecting moulding, under
which are placed square

FIG. 12.

blocks, named *mutules*, ornamented with drops; these
mutules are placed directly over the triglyphs and
metopes.

The finest specimen of the Doric order is the temple
of Minerva Parthenon, at Athens. (Plate VI.) Peri-

cles resolved that Athens should be the admiration of the world, and that her architecture should keep pace with her military and intellectual renown. When the temple of Minerva Parthenon was to be built, many grand designs were offered to the Athenians for their choice. Ictinus was the successful architect, whose design met with their approbation. Callicrates was also employed upon it. A small temple, raised by Cimon, in honour of Theseus, was the model of the Parthenon. It has been remarked that "the Doric column is in fact Egyptian, modified to a new position and worship, and that the nobler specimens are but reduced and petty imitations of those ancient and indestructible supporters to the temples of Thebes, of Memphis, and Tentyra."

The sculptures which decorated this temple, were designed by Phidias, and executed by his scholars. Ictinus, the architect, wrote a work on the architecture of the Parthenon, which is quoted by Vitruvius. The Grecian temples are all oblong, and about twice as long as they are broad. The Parthenon was 225 feet in length, and 100 in breadth; the height of the entrance was thirty-six feet.

There were eight columns at each front, and seventeen on each side, counting those at the angle twice. Besides these, there was an inner row of columns at each end, which stood upon a platform two steps higher than the outer row. The diameter of the columns of the outer row, is six feet, two inches; their height, in-

cluding the capitals, thirty-four feet. The Parthenon
has an inclined roof, the ends of which are finished
with a cornice, similar to the one upon the entablature.
The triangular space formed by this cornice and the
entablature is called a *pediment.* On the eastern pediment of the Parthenon was an elaborate sculpture,
representing Jupiter and Minerva, with their atten-
dants; on the western pediment, Minerva and Neptune.
These sculptures, and others from the entablature,
were a part of the spoils now so famous as the Elgin
marbles, of the British Museum. Byron's indig-
nation was excited against Lord Elgin for these spoliations, and he has administered in several stanzas his
caustic reproof.

But who of all the plunderers of yon fane
   On high, where Pallas lingered, loth to flee
The latest relic of her ancient reign ;
   The last, the worst dull spoiler, who was he?
Blush, Caledonia ! such thy son could be !
   England ! I joy no child he was of thine :
Thy free-born men should spare what once was free ;
   Yet they could violate each saddening shrine,
And bear these altars o'er the long reluctant brine.

But most the modern Pict's ignoble boast
   To rive what Goth, and Turk, and time hath spared.
Cold as the crags upon his native coast,
   His mind as barren and his heart as hard ;
So he whose head conceived, whose hand prepared

Aught to displace Athena's poor remains,
Her sons too weak the sacred shrine to guard."*

Part of the beautiful Parthenon was destroyed by
the explosion of a magazine which the Turks had
placed within its walls, when Athens, in 1687, was
besieged by the Venetians. Enough of it remained
when Stuart visited Athens, about 1765, to enable
him to give a perfect representation of it, and Plate
VI. is from his view, as restored to its pristine glory.
When the columns or other parts fell, the Turks sometimes used them for their buildings, but it is said, that
they rarely destroyed or defaced these beautiful ruins.
The Parthenon stood upon the grand platform or area
of the Acropolis. On this elevation were accumulated
those edifices whose surpassing beauty will long remain the world's wonder. In sight of these splendid
structures, perhaps with his eyes fixed upon the sculptured Parthenon, St. Paul stood upon "Mars' Hill,"
the hill of Areopagus, and exclaimed, "Ye men of
Athens, I perceive that in all things ye are too superstitious. For as I passed by, and beheld your devotions, I found an altar with this inscription, 'To THE
UNKNOWN GOD.' Whom, therefore, ye ignorantly
worship, him declare I unto you. God, that made the
world and all things therein, seeing that he is Lord of

---

* Lord Elgin has given his apology for these spoliations in a small
work, entitled "Memorandum on the Subject of the Earl of Elgin's
Pursuits in Greece," London, 1811.

heaven and earth, dwelleth not in temples made with hands. Forasmuch, then, as we are the offspring of God, we ought not to think that the Godhead is like unto gold, or silver, or stone, graven by art and man's device."

The statue of the Goddess Minerva, executed by Phidias, occupied one apartment of the Parthenon. This statue was thirty-nine feet high, of ivory, covered with gold, and for richness and exquisite beauty of workmanship, was unsurpassed by any statue of antiquity. Another apartment was used for the public treasury.

There are splendid remains of temples of the Doric order in Italy and Sicily. The Greeks founded colonies in both these countries, and the monuments of their genius remain as a testimony to the power and opulence of those colonies. History contains no record of the architects who constructed these mighty temples; even the time when their majestic columns arose, or when they were prostrated in the dust, has been whelmed in oblivion.

There was a temple of Minerva at Syracuse; six temples at Selinus, one of which must have been so magnificent in size, as nearly to rival the massive monuments of Egypt. The porticoes of this temple were supported by Doric columns sixty feet high, and thirty in circumference; the length of the temple was three hundred and thirty-one feet; the immense piles of ruins attest the prodigious size of these temples.

At Agrigentum, are the remains of several temples, the largest of which was the Temple of Jupiter Olympus, one of the most imposing fabrics that was ever reared by man. The capitals of the Doric columns of this stupendous structure measure eight feet and two inches in height. The traveller wanders over these buried ruins with mournful solemnity, meditating upon the might and majesty of the genius of man, and the insufficiency of material structures to render his name immortal.

In Southern Italy are the ruins of Pæstum. Three temples may still be seen, two of which are very perfect. The columns are only a little more than four diameters in height; the entablature very heavy. The whole appearance of the temples, in consequence of these proportions, is less pleasing than that of the Parthenon.

No order can exceed the Doric in chaste simplicity and solemn grandeur. It is well adapted to public edifices, where strength and durability are sought, and where the expression intended is grave and majestic. The straight outlines and large square forms of Egyptian edifices are expressive of power, of strength, and durability, and fill the mind with wonder and awe; the perfect proportions of the Doric temples, with their simple ornaments, excite a different emotion. There is a harmonious distribution of the members, producing perfect unity in the whole building, and the emotion of beauty which fills the spectator, though less over-powering, is, perhaps, more pleasurable.

The details too, excite unqualified admiration. Every capital is perfect in its symmetry. The graceful ovolo, swells out into its beautiful form, as polished and smooth as the most delicate shell from "the dark unfathomed caves of ocean." Every stone in the majestic pile was so exquisitely prepared for its neighbour, that not the slightest crevice appears upon the exterior; the whole vast column seems hewn from a single block; the line is perfect to the lifted eye of the wondering artist, as again and again he follows the shaft from its firm rest upon the pavement, to the annulets of its capital.

This chaste and elegant style was the favourite order throughout Greece and its European colonies, until after the Macedonian conquest.

THE IONIC ORDER.

The colonies which were planted by the Greeks in Asia Minor, were called Ionia. Populous and rich, the sciences and arts were cultivated by the Ionians with great success. They have given their name to one of the three orders of Grecian Architecture, but whether they invented it, or only improved upon the Doric, is still a disputed point, not easy, and not important to decide.

The Ionic order is more light and delicate than the

Fig. 13.

Doric; the height of its column is greater in proportion to its diameter. The capital is ornamented with volutes. The origin of this peculiar ornament is conjectural. The curls in female head-dress; the beautiful spiral forms of seashells, particularly the cornu ammonis; the graceful unfolding fern; the horns of rams offered in sacrifice, and originally suspended about the temples: these all have been suggested as guiding the artist in designing the volutes of the Ionic capital. Encircling this capital is the eschinus, formed of the egg and dart; and the *astragal* having a beading formed of one large and two small beads, alternately. These are the mouldings usually found upon the Ionic capital.

Fig. 14.

The shaft is cut into about twenty-four deep flutes, which are sometimes filled in with reeding, for some distance from the base. The edges of the flutings do not meet like the Doric, but are separated by a flat surface or fillet. In some instances, Ionic shafts were plain, without fluting or reeding. The shafts were usually eight diameters in height.

The Ionic column has a base, and the entablature is

differently ornamented from the Doric. The cornice has dentils or teeth, and the egg and dart moulding; the frieze is generally plain: in some remains of this order it is wanting, the entablature consisting only of cornice and architrave. The triglyphs and sculptured metopes destroyed the unity of the Doric frieze; in the Ionic entablature the horizontal line was unbroken.

The Temple of Erectheus at Athens (Plate VI.) is a beautiful relic of the Ionic order. Its light and graceful proportions, and its beautiful capitals, Fig. 15, have been studied with pleasure and advantage by modern architects.

FIG. 15.

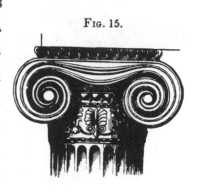

The celebrated Temple of Diana, at Ephesus, was of the Ionic order. It was four hundred and twenty-five feet in length, two hundred and twenty in breadth, and seventy feet in height. This splendid edifice, to which all the Grecian colonies contributed, was wantonly burnt, the same night on which Alexander the Great was born. The object of the villain, who perpetrated the deed, was to render himself famous throughout all time; the Ephesians forbade by a law, with severe penalties, that his name should be uttered. Nevertheless, Erostratus is a name too infamous to be forgotten. It was rebuilt by the artist Dinocrates, and had been standing for about four hundred years, when St. Paul preached to the Ephesians, and "filled the whole city with confusion." The pure gospel, which the Apostle declared unto them, would lead to the entire destruction of the worship of "the great Goddess Diana;" instead, therefore, of answering St. Paul with arguments, "they all with one voice, about the space of two hours, cried out, Great is Diana of the Ephesians!"

CORINTHIAN ORDER.

A fanciful origin has been given to this order. A young Corinthian lady died and was sincerely mourned by her faithful nurse; as a tribute of affection, this humble friend placed upon the grave of her young mistress a basket, covered with a tile, containing her jewels. As if to beautify this act of love, a graceful

Fig. 16.

acanthus spread its leaves around the basket, and thus was suggested to Callimachus, the sculptor, the Corinthian capital.

It does not accord with our feelings to prove so sweet a record in the annals of art to be apocryphal, but the Egyptian capitals were so frequently formed of rows of delicate leaves, that Callimachus cannot lay claim to the invention; we may still believe that in this case genius may have seized upon an accidental circumstance, and reproduced, in a more perfect and beautiful form, what had long been invented.

The body of the capital is a vase or basket; upon it rests an *abacus*, not square, but four-cornered, with concave sides, moulded and ornamented in the middle of each side with a honeysuckle or other flower. The lower part of the capital is decorated with two rows of leaves, eight

Fig. 17.

in each row. A space between the abacus and leaves is occupied by stalks formed into delicate volutes; larger volutes meet the four corners of the abacus.

The shaft of the Corinthian column originally had the same proportions as the Ionic, nine diameters in height; the moderns have made it still more slender, sometimes more than ten diameters. Anciently it was frequently found plain, but the finest specimens were fluted and filleted as it is when used at the present day.

The entablature and base were similar to the Ionic order, yet varied in different edifices, in the details.

One of the most perfect specimens of the Corinthian order (Plate VII.), is a beautiful little temple or monument at Athens. Why, or wherefore this has been called the Lantern of Demosthenes, would be difficult to discover. It is octagonal, with eight elegant columns.

The most magnificent temple at Athens, dedicated to Jupiter Olympus, was of this order. (Plate VII.) It was built of the purest white marble, and Art, in the zenith of her glory, could present no prouder shrine. Vitruvius says, this "structure is not spoken of with common praise; the excellence and sagacious contrivance have been approved of in the assembly of the gods."

The magnificent Corinthian columns of the exterior were sixty feet in height and six feet six inches in diameter. The area of the temple was half a mile in circumference. It had two ranges of columns on each side, twenty-one in each row, and ten columns at each end.

The Olympeium was founded by Pisistratus, five hundred and forty years before Christ, and completed more than two hundred years after, by the architect Cossutius, a Roman citizen employed by Antiochus Epiphanes. The ideal restoration given in Plate VII., may serve to convey a faint idea of its beauty. The Corinthian order was not much employed by the Greeks till after the conquest of Alexander. Subsequently, it was very generally chosen for all edifices

Plate VII

THE LANTERN OF DEMOSTHENES.

THE TEMPLE OF JUPITER.

where " elegance, gaiety, and magnificence were required."

The stern and massive simplicity of the Doric accorded much better with the taste of Greece in her palmy days, when her poetry and eloquence possessed the same characteristics.

Beside the three Grecian orders, human figures were sometimes employed by the Greeks as supports for entablatures. When these figures represented men, they were called Persians, from contempt, and a wish to degrade their enemies. When they were women, they were called Cariatides, from the people of Caria, who had been the allies of the Persians in some of their wars against Greece. (See Plate VI.) This was a great departure from correct taste.

In the Grecian orders there is an union of strength and lightness, of simplicity and ornament, of grandeur and beauty, which can never be surpassed. Modern architects, in endeavouring to improve upon Grecian designs, have been completely foiled; the closest investigation leads to the conclusion that the principles of Grecian Architecture were fixed by men of consummate science and skill, and have their foundation in immutable truth.

It is evident that the Greeks preferred the fine to the useful arts. Their temples were the only property which they possessed in common, and their munificence in affording the means for their erection, attests

the pride that they felt in making these monuments
the wonder of the world, when their private dwellings
were still humble.

The Greeks knew little of the comforts of domestic
life. The temple, the theatre, the forum, the schools
of the philosophers, were the places of resort for men;
wives were not intellectual companions, and the graceful embellishments of home, which depend upon them,
were not appreciated by their lordly masters.

" The houses of the Athenians in general, consist of
two sets of apartments; the upper story for the women,
and the lower for the men. The roofs have terraces,
with a large projection at each extremity. In the front
is a small court, or rather a sort of portico, at the end
of which is the house door, where we find sometimes a
figure of Mercury, to drive away thieves, or a dog,
who is a much more effectual guard."*

Such were the dwellings of Aristides and Themis-
tocles; but the men of wealth, in the later luxurious
days of Greece, erected more commodious mansions,
which they embellished with sculpture and painting.

The plan of a Grecian house, as given by the architect Vitruvius, exhibits a great number of apartments,
courts, and colonnades. In addition to the apartments
for the men and the women of the household, there were
suites of apartments for strangers, who came to attend
the great festivals, separated by passages and entered

---

* Anacharsis.

by gates apart from the main entrance. These apartments were furnished even with stores of edibles, that the guests might feel themselves quite at home.

Well might the comedian Lysippus say: " Whoever does not desire to see Athens, is stupid ; whoever sees it without being delighted, is still more stupid ; but the height of stupidity is, to see it, to admire it, and to leave it."

CHAPTER X.

ROMAN ARCHITECTURE.

FROM a state of extreme rudeness and barbarism, Rome gradually became the imperial mistress of the world. For a long time the gentle arts of peace could find no place among her rough warriors. Their dwelling-houses ungraced by the presence of woman, were at first, undoubtedly, less commodious than an American log-cabin.

Their first efforts of architectural skill were employed upon walls for defence. With the Tarquins, was brought the knowledge of the art as practised in Etruria. To the Romans, the invention of the *arch* has been attributed; but since arches have been discovered amid Etruscan ruins, older than Rome itself, it may rationally be inferred that they acquired the principles of its construction from Etruria. The unadorned works which they constructed during the early ages, were remarkable for solidity, being built of large blocks of stone, in the most substantial manner, proving the "early ambition which projected from its very infancy, 'the eternal city,' the capital of the world."

As Rome extended her conquests, wealth flowed in, and with it a taste for the luxuries of life. Greece and her beautiful colonies in Sicily and Italy, were among these conquests. The rude Romans must have gazed with savage wonder upon the chaste simplicity of the Parthenon, and the surpassing magnificence of the Temple of Jupiter Olympus at Athens; but their religion led them to reverence, and to spare the temples of deities whom they worshipped in common with the Greeks. The genius of the Greeks for Architecture, was gradually and perfectly developed by the rivalry of aspiring states and their ambitious, gifted artists; but as we now look through the vista of ages, it seems to have sprung up spontaneously, or rather to have come forth perfect in all its proportions and ornaments, like their own Minerva from the head of Jupiter. At Rome it was transplanted.

When Marcellus conquered Syracuse, a Grecian colony in Sicily, he carried the spoils, consisting of rich statuary, vases, and pictures, to Rome, to grace his triumph and astonish the Roman citizens. Plutarch tells us that on the occasion of the triumph decreed to Paulus Emilius, for his conquest of Macedonia, a whole day was scarcely sufficient to exhibit the specimens of classic art brought forth for that occasion. Two hundred and fifty chariots were employed to carry them in the triumphal procession. The acquisition of these models of art did not elicit genius; for a long time after, they imported their artists from Greece, or constructed their edifices from ancient ruins.   When the spoils of all nations were laid at the feet of the mistress of the world, she made a luxurious, a lavish use of them.   Augustus *boasted* hyperbolically, that he had found Rome "wood and brick, and had made it marble."

Instead of inventing any new orders, the Romans combined the arch and vault with the Grecian column and entablature.   In time, the art gained in richness and luxuriancy of decoration, but lost the pure and lovely simplicity of its native land.

The *Doric*, was very seldom employed by the Romans; when it was imitated, the proportions and ornaments were different from the Grecian.

Fig. 18.   Fig. 19.

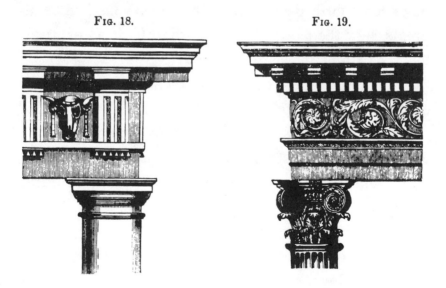

The *Tuscan* (Fig. 18) is sometimes called an order, although it cannot be so considered.   Neither does what has been termed the *Composite* (Fig. 19) deserve to be distinguished as an *order ;* it was only an inharmonious union between the Ionic and Corinthian.

The Romans varied the Ionic, making it more elaborate, without adding to its beauty. (Fig. 20.) Of the three orders, their favourite was the Corinthian. The decorative part of this order they varied, to suit the character of the building in which it was employed, or the taste of the builder. Thus, in place of the acanthus, they ornamented the

Fig. 20.

capitals with laurel, olive, thistle, and other foliage, differently disposed; in place of *volutes*, eagles, cornucopiæ, griffins, and other emblems; and upon the entablature they had an endless variety of mouldings; wreaths of flowers, heads of animals, &c. &c.

Although so little can be granted to the Romans as inventors, the splendid remains of their edifices testify how successfully they could employ the principles which they had acquired. These remains are public roads, aqueducts, temples, theatres, tombs, triumphal arches, historical monuments, thermæ or baths, basilicæ or courts of justice, and Forums or Forii.

The public roads were constructed with immense labour and expense ; they extended to the utmost limits of the vast empire.   Sometimes they were paved with flint and covered with gravel; often they were of large basaltic stones, neatly smoothed. These roads were raised, so as to command a view of the adjacent country, and had sidewalks for foot-passengers.

The aqueducts conveyed water to Rome, sometimes for a distance of fifty or sixty miles. They were carried through rocks, over hills, and through valleys on arches; where the valleys were deep, one row of arches was placed over another, and still another, to the height of more than a hundred feet. These aqueducts were constructed with as much regard to beauty as utility; they were ornamented with columns of finely sculptured stone and marble.

The temples of the Romans were not like those of the Greeks, uniformly oblong; they were circular, hexagonal, octagonal, and even triangular, and combined of all these and many other forms.

The most celebrated temple of a circular form is the Pantheon at Rome. (Plate VIII.) It is generally attributed to Agrippa; but careful researches have led to the conjecture that it was of earlier origin, and that Agrippa new-modelled and embellished the interior, and added the superb portico, upon which is an inscription which says is was *built* by Agrippa, 27 years before Christ. It was afterwards repaired and beautified by the Emperor Adrian. "The Catholics let the temple stand, and gloried in its conversion to Christianity."

Plate VIII

THE ARCH OF TITUS.

THE PANTHEON.

It was consecrated A. D. 607, by Pope Boniface IV., to the Virgin Mary and All Saints.

This immense temple has a wall nineteen feet in thickness, in which are six chapels, and between them eight small altars, which were niches for statues. The semicircle, in the same manner hollowed into the wall, now forms the choir of the great altar, and is opposite the main entrance. These walls surround an area of 132 feet in diameter; their height from the pavement to the springing of the dome, is sixty feet, and the whole height of the interior 132 feet! Over this spacious area, hangs that marble firmament, that self-balanced dome, the glory of Roman Architecture. The light is admitted through a circle in the dome, open to the bright Italian sky, twenty-seven feet in diameter. The magnificent portico in front is supported by sixteen Corinthian columns, the shafts of which are each formed from a single piece of Egyptian granite; the bases and capitals are of white marble. The eight columns of red granite, in front of the portico, sustain an entablature of beautiful proportions, upon which is the inscription of Agrippa, son-in-law of Octavius Augustus, by whom it was dedicated to Mars and Jupiter Avenger, in memory of the victory obtained over Mark Antony and Cleopatra, by Augustus. The temple was named *Pantheon*, from a Greek word, signifying an assemblage of all the gods, because it contained statues, in gold, bronze, silver and precious stones, of all the principal Roman divinities.

Opposite to the columns are six fluted pilasters,*
(the columns are plain,) between which the walls of
the portico are covered with beautifully sculptured
marbles; formerly the statues of Agrippa and Augustus
were placed in the niches on the right and left of the
grand entrance.   The threshold is of African marble;
the splendid door is covered with bronze; the door-
posts and architrave are of white marble.

In the interior of the Pantheon, the six chapels are
decorated each with two Corinthian columns, and two
pilasters, twenty-seven feet high, supporting an entablature which runs around the whole interior of the temple.   These columns are eight of violet marble, mixed
with yellow, and four of antique yellow marble; the
bases and capitals of white marble; the frieze is of
porphyry.

Over this order is an *attic*, a kind of half order, that
the Romans often added to their buildings.   In this
attic are fourteen small windows, which are now closed;
upon the entablature to this attic rests the great dome.

A very nice critic has said of the Pantheon : "Perhaps the interior elevation is beautiful, when it should
be grand; its Corinthian, though exquisite, appears too
low for the walls, and made the attic here a necessary
evil.   Had Adrian caught the full majesty of the naked
dome, and embellished its walls with one grand *order*,

---

* *Pilasters* are rectangular projections advancing from the wall,
with capitals and bases of the same order as the columns to which
they stand opposite.

that rose to the origin of the vault, the whole temple would have been 'more simply, more severely great.'"

So thought not one who viewed it with a poet's, rather than "a critic's eye."

> "Simple, erect, severe, austere, sublime;
> Shrine of all saints, and temple of all gods.
> . . . . Glorious dome!
> Shalt thou not last? Time's scythe and tyrant's rod
> Shiver upon thee—sanctuary and home
> Of art and piety, Pantheon! pride of Rome!
>
> "Relic of nobler days and nobler arts;
> Despoiled, yet perfect, with thy circle spreads
> A holiness appealing to all hearts;
> To art a model, and to him who treads
> Rome for the sake of ages, glory sheds
> Her light through thy sole aperture."

The aforesaid critic pronounces the portico, "more than faultless. It is *positively* the most sublime result that ever was produced, by so little architecture. Every moulding here becomes a model for the art."

The Pantheon has been thus particularly described, because, in many respects, it has served for ages as a model.

The temples of Vesta, at Rome and at Tivoli, were circular, and of the Corinthian order. This order prevailed over every other for centuries, throughout the Roman dominions. It was injured by a luxuriance and superfluity of ornament, which, however, accorded well with " the high and palmy state of Rome."

The largest temple at Rome, the Temple of Peace, was begun by Claudius, and completed by Vespasian. It was oblong ; " the ceiling, or roof of the nave was an immense groined vault, which rested upon eight Corinthian columns. The aisles had also vaults lengthwise, which were intersected by others, that covered the recesses or chapels, which projected outward from their side walls." Here seems to have been the origin of the naves and aisles of churches. There were recesses, in which were arched windows. Excepting the entrance, which had an ornamented portico, the exterior of this temple was quite plain.

The splendid ruins at Palmyra and Balbec are of extraordinary extent, and furnish many examples of the highly ornamented Corinthian. The Temple of the Sun, at Palmyra, with its magnificent porticos and long colonnades, has excited the admiration and wonder of travellers, who describe it as superior to any other Roman temple.

The theatre, amphitheatre, and circus, were among the most stupendous works of Rome. Of these, there are gigantic remains ; but as they were all constructed on a similar plan, a full description of one will suffice. The only difference between a theatre and amphitheatre was, that the former was a semicircular, the latter a circular edifice.

The Flavian Amphitheatre, called the Coliseum, was erected by the Emperor Flavius Vespasian, after his return from the Jewish war, A.D. 72. Many thousand Jews, who were made captives in this war, were employed upon the Coliseum. Titus completely finished it, and dedicated it to his father, Vespasian. On the day of its dedication, five thousand animals of different species were cruelly made to destroy each other for the amusement of the populace! But not animals alone were slaughtered in this amphitheatre. Here sat the conquerors of the world, coolly to enjoy the tortures and death of men who had never offended them. Two aqueducts were scarcely sufficient to wash off the human blood which a few hours' sport shed in these imperial shambles. Twice in one day came the senators and matrons of Rome to the butchery; a virgin always gave the signal for slaughter, and, when glutted with bloodshed, those ladies sat down in the wet and streaming arena to a luxurious supper. Such reflections check our regret for its ruin. As it now stands, the Coliseum is a striking image of Rome itself; decayed, vacant, serious, yet grand:—half gray and half green—erect on one side and fallen on the other, with consecrated ground in its bosom.

> " A ruin—yet what ruin ! from its mass
> Walls, palaces, half cities have been reared ;
> Yet oft the enormous skeleton ye pass,
> And marvel where the spoil could have appeared."

The shape necessary to an amphitheatre, has preserved it from destruction. Such was its stability that
it resisted earthquakes and sieges. Barbarian hands
commenced the work of dilapidation, and Popes, in
their turn, used it as a quarry for modern churches.
This colossal structure was oval in form, its length
being five hundred and eighty feet, and its breadth
four hundred and seventy. It was externally surrounded by three rows of arches, raised one above another to the height of one hundred and fifty-seven feet;
each row was composed of eighty arches, with as many
columns. The order of the lower part of the Coliseum is Doric; the next order is Ionic; the next, Corinthian; above this is a row of Composite pilasters,
and the whole is crowned with a heavy attic.

The first row of arches is marked with Roman
numbers; these arches were so many entrances which,
by means of twenty staircases, led to the upper piazzas
and to the seats; so that even a child could find his
way directly to his seat, and the numerous spectators
could quit the amphitheatre in a very short time, without confusion.

The arena, where the games were celebrated, is two
hundred and eighty-five feet long, and one hundred
and eighty-two wide; it was surrounded by a wall of
moderate height, to prevent the animals from escaping.
The seats for spectators were arranged around the
arena. Those destined for the emperor, his family,
and the *magnates* of Rome, were the nearest to the

arena; above these, were the seats for the people, gradually ascending, so that every spectator could have an uninterrupted view of the whole amphitheatre. Thus, eighty thousand spectators could be accommodated; and twenty thousand more could sit in the piazzas above.

There was no roof to this stupendous structure. The spectators were protected from the sun and rain by an awning, which was drawn over as occasion required.

During the reigns of Nero, Trajan, and other persecuting emperors, numbers of Christian martyrs bore testimony to the truth, by yielding up their lives in this amphitheatre:

"Butchered to make a Roman holiday."

Remains of amphitheatres, theatres, and circuses, are found wherever there were largo Roman cities.

Triumphal arches are numerous at Rome. These were solid structures erected to commemorate victories, and were lofty enough for the passage of giants.

The Arch of Titus (Plate VIII.) was erected after the destruction of Jerusalem by the army under his command; it is ornamented with sculptures in bas-relief representing the triumphal procession on the return of the conqueror. The Jews are bearing the consecrated vessels and emblems of their worship—the ark, the table of shew-bread, the seven-branched candlestick, &c., &c.

A scientific author says of the Arch of Titus, " It is so rich that I can hardly think it elegant.   The entablature, the imposts, the keystones, are all crowned with sculpture, yet meagre in profile ; but it is hard to judge the general effect of a mutilated thing."

In the Arch of Septimius Severus, the Composite starts so often and so furiously out, and the entablature meets you in so many points, as to leave no repose to the eye.

Constantine's Arch is larger, nobler, and even more correct in its architecture, the only object now in review ; but is that architecture its own ? We know that its columns, statues, and relievos are not ; and we may fairly suspect that its whole composition was stolen, as Constantine's reign was notorious for architectural robbery.   The Arch of Gallienus is a mere gateway, and that of Drusus seems part of an aqueduct ; yet, coarse as they are, each has its Corinthian columns and pediments stuck upon a fraction of the fronts.

" What business or what meaning have columns on any arch ? The statues of captive kings are but a poor apology for so idle a support.   The platform above the arch was well adapted to the curule statue. Here the triumphal car formed an historical record ; on a modern arch it is only a metaphor."

The *historical columns*, are true to no order of Architecture.* Trajan's column has a Doric shaft, a Tuscan

---

* Forsyth.

base and capital, and a pedestal with Corinthian mouldings. The shaft is eleven feet two inches in diameter at the base, and ten feet at the capital; the whole height of the column including the statue, is one hundred and thirty-two feet. Upon the summit formerly stood the statue of Trajan, in bronze; but Sixtus V. displaced the Emperor and elevated St. Peter, in bronze, notwithstanding the ashes of Trajan were buried beneath the pedestal, and the whole column is covered with sculptures in *bas-relief*, representing his victories. This splendid column is of marble, fastened together with bronze. A spiral cordon is represented as entwining it from the top to the bottom, in twenty-three windings, thus separating the figures that ornament it, and giving continuity to the subject or story. An interior winding staircase, chiselled out of the marble, conducts to the top, which commands a fine view of Rome. The pedestal is beautifully adorned with eagles, garlands, and trophies.

The column of Marcus Aurelius is similar to that of Trajan. It was erected by the Roman Senate, in honour of that Emperor, but he afterwards dedicated it to his father-in-law, Antoninus Pius. The pedestals to these columns are mentioned as unique in ancient Roman Architecture, though often employed in more modern days. The same critic,* who has been before quoted, remarks, that "The insulated pedestal, which in architecture acts as a stilt to the shaft, is beautiful,

---

* Forsyth.

8

because necessary only under insulated columns like these." The column of M. Aurelius having been injured by lightning, Sixtus V. repaired it, and placed upon the top a gilt-bronze statue of St. Paul.

The magnificent Corinthian column standing on a large pedestal in the square of St. Mary Maggiore at Rome, was the only entire column remaining of the Temple of Peace. It was not, therefore, an historical column, but as it now stands, in an insulated position, with a statue of the Madonna at the top, it has the appearance of such a monument.

The Romans were as magnificent in their *tombs* as in all their other architectural works.

The finest ancient sepulchral monument, and one of the best preserved at Rome, is that of Cecelia Metella. It is of a circular form, about ninety feet in diameter, the walls being *twenty-four feet* in thickness! The immense blocks of travertine of which it is constructed have sustained the attacks both of elemental strife and Roman war. A Corinthian entablature surrounds the edifice, ornamented with festoons and heads of oxen. This decoration has given it the name of Capo di Bove: (Ox's-head.)

> " There is a stern round tower of other days,
> Firm as a fortress, with its fence of stone,
> Such as an army's baffled strength delays,
> Standing with half its battlements alone,
> And with two thousand years of ivy grown,

The garland of eternity, where wave
The green leaves over all by time o'erthrown.
What was this tower of strength? Within its cave
What treasure lay so locked, so hid?—A woman's grave.

—" Thus much alone we know—Metella died,
The wealthiest Roman's wife; behold his love or pride."

" At what period the tomb of Metella was converted into the citadel of a fort, can be guessed only by the period at which the monuments in the city were occupied by the nobles. Certain it is, that the tomb was put at once to this purpose without any previous spoliation, and that the garrison unconcernedly dwelt over, not only the mausoleum, but the very ashes of Metella; for the coffin remained in the interior of the sepulchre until the time of Paul III., who removed it to the court of the Farnese Palace. The Savelli family were in possession of the fortress in 1312, and the German army of Henry VII., marched from Rome, attacked, took, and burnt it, but were unable to make themselves by force, masters of the citadel, that is, of the tomb, which must give us a high notion of its strength or their weakness."*

The tomb of Caius Cestius, stands near the ancient gate, now called St. Paul's Gate. This magnificent monument is a pyramid one hundred and thirteen feet high, and eighty-nine feet on each side at the base.

---

* Hobhouse.

It is covered with large slabs of marble on the exterior, and in the interior the sepulchral chamber is eighteen feet long, twelve wide, and thirteen high. The ceiling and walls are covered with stucco, ornamented with paintings. " It must seem singular that so little should be known of the two persons whose tombs were to survive those of so many illustrious names. Cestius is as little famous as Metella, and his pyramid is no less conspicuous than her tower."

The tomb of the Plautius family is in the form of a round tower, with an entablature similar to that of Cecelia Metella's monument. Like that, it was used as a fortress during the civil wars of the "dark ages."

The tomb of the Scipios was only discovered in 1780, after having been closed up perhaps, for more than eighteen centuries. The upper story is entirely gone; the lower is of a square form hollowed into the ground. The relics found in this tomb of "the most worthy family of the Roman republic," have been placed in the Vatican Museum.

These ancient monuments have been used as quarries, from whence more modern buildings have been erected. Other magnificent edifices have shared the same fate, their beautiful columns and finely wrought stones, serving to ornament buildings otherwise mean and inelegant. The mausoleum of Augustus, was used in the middle ages as a fortress; then it was hollowed out for a vineyard, and having at last become a circus, now serves for a place of amusement.

The magnificent *baths* of Rome shared largely in these spoliations. These baths were called Thermæ, or hot places. They were designed for bathing, gymnastic exercises, various kinds of amusements, and even had temples connected with them.

The Baths of Dioclesian covered several acres of ground. The general plan was a square, with a circular edifice at each angle. Two of these circular buildings remain; one is used for a granary, and the other for the church of St. Bernardo. The interior of the square, was filled with gardens, groves, porticoes, and an amphitheatre. One very magnificent apartment, called *Pinacotheca*, has been converted into the Church of St. Mary of the Angels. Pope Pius IV., wishing to consecrate this edifice, employed Michael Angelo to restore and ornament it for a Christian church. The entrance to this church is by a round vestibule, formerly one of the rooms belonging to the baths, of the same size as St. Bernardo's Church. Passing from this vestibule, you enter the nave of the church, which was the ancient *Pinacotheca*. This is a beautiful classical remnant of Roman Architecture. Eight granite columns, each of a single piece, support the roof. They are sixteen feet in circumference, and forty-three high.

The Baths of Caracalla are smaller than those of Dioclesian, yet they could accommodate three thousand people. The architecture and the ornaments were both beautiful. The Hall called the Cella

Solearis, one hundred and eighty-eight feet long and one hundred and thirty-four wide, has been much admired for its fine proportions and rich ornaments, and may give some idea of the general magnificence of these baths. The halls were filled with statues, the pavements were of the finest mosaic, and the porticoes were supported by columns of the richest marbles.

" The Baths of Titus were the first gallery of ancient painting that was restored to the world." These subterranean saloons, which were the lower story of the baths, are very numerous. They were opened in the time of Raphael d'Urbino, who studied the arabesque paintings upon the walls and imitated them in the Vatican. " Some of the ruins above ground rise up to the vaulting of their alcoves; but none show their specific relation to a bath, except the *Sette Salle*, the construction of which proves that it was a reservoir, and proves too, how well the ancients understood hydrostatics. The stucco with which it is covered is hard enough for the turning of iron, which could only arise from the tartareous penetration of water."

" To combine the scattered remains of those baths, to distribute their interior, to give light to every apartment, and find out offices for them all, would puzzle any regular surveyor; but what can daunt antiquaries ?" Their assiduous labours have brought to light what had remained for ages in obscurity, and proved beyond a doubt the extent, variety, and magnificence of the buildings which constituted the Roman Thermæ.

The old Roman *Basilica* seems at first to have been a part of a palace, but afterwards included those buildings devoted to law and trade. According to Vitruvius, a basilica had double porticoes, open on the four sides, an upper gallery, and an immense hall with vaulted ceiling. After the Christian religion was established, the basilicæ were converted into churches, and gave their form and name to those which were afterwards erected, as will be more specially mentioned hereafter.

The assemblies of the Roman people were held in the Forum, and public business was there transacted.

Of these, the most celebrated was the Forum Romanum, which has served in modern days as a *cow-market*, and from that circumstance is called *Campo Vaccino*. It was an oblong square, the exact dimensions of which cannot be ascertained. It is supposed to have extended from the Arch of Septimius Severus to the Temple of Antoninus and Faustina, and from thence in length to the Temple of Romulus.

The Capitol, which stood upon the Capitoline Hill, was raised above this Forum, and at its foot are supposed to have stood the Temples of Jupiter Tonans and of Concord; the latter is supposed formerly to have been called the Temple of Cicero. Nothing now remains but its portico, consisting of eight magnificent columns of oriental granite, of the Ionic order, twelve feet in circumference and forty in height.

" The barbarians, the fires, and the modern Romans have left but little of the temple where Cicero assembled the Senate, supposing these to be the ruins of that temple ; but it is something to hope that we tread the site, and may touch a fragment of the porch which was guarded by the equestrian patriots, who escorted the consul, and menaced Cæsar and the friends of the conspirators with swords."

Of the Trajan Forum, of which the celebrated Apollodorus was the architect, nothing now remains entire but the superb pillar which has been described. " The Forum of Trajan served, among other purposes, to perpetuate the memory of the good and great. Young men of great promise, who had died in the flower of their age, were honoured with a statue. The same place was devoted to the labours and the rewards of literary heroes ; here the poets and others recited their compositions, and here their images were allowed a place amongst conquerors and monarchs."

The Forum of Trajan is mentioned by ancient historians as the wonder and glory of Roman Architecture ; a perfect " miracle" in its gigantic splendour. Late excavations in this Forum, enable us at last to tread the floor of ancient Rome. The replacing the fragments of the columns on their bases, and the judicious arrangements of the other marbles, has created an effect little inferior to the wonders of Pompeii.

The admiring traveller is amazed at the dimensions
of the fragments, when compared with the space in
which so many buildings were raised. Here we
have a Forum with its porticoes, and statues, and
tribunals; a basilica, with a double internal portico
on every side; a quadrangular court, or atrium, also
adorned with enormous columns; two libraries; a
triumphal arch; the great column and the portion
of a temple, crowded into a space not so considerable as one of the smallest London squares. Whatever the earth covered of these magnificent structures
is now exposed to view, and the remnants are sufficient to show what must have been the subterranean
riches of Rome. The flooring and some of the many
fragments are so perfect as to make the *sudden burial*
of these parts of the city more probable than the gra-
dual decay."

Pompeii has revealed to us the *dwelling-houses* of
the Romans. A traveller says, that there " You forget
yourself, and the age you live in. Where am I? It
is Pompeii—the old city which has been dug out of its
grave—and the inhabitants! I stand, I move, among
the men of old times."

" The mode in which the largest dwellings are built,
was, on many accounts, the best fitted for the climate
and situation. All, except a very few, are of one story,
probably to guard against the effects of earthquakes;
and the rooms are very small. According to their
size, houses and villas contain one or more square

courts (Plate IX.), open above, and surrounded with
piazzas, which partially protect from the weather the
entrances to the sleeping rooms, usually ranged around
them by fours.   Other apartments of the house are situated according to the taste of the builder."—" The roof
is gone, nothing is seen above but the sky; this house
has been untenanted for ages; its last inhabitant was
a Roman citizen, and he lived under the reign of
Titus; a man who heard of the desolation of Judah
from captives taken fighting on the walls of Jerusalem;
and the first glad news of Christianity, perchance, from
the mouth of Paul himself.   Departed Pompeii!
Here time has left his glass unturned, for seventeen
hundred years."

The palaces of modern princes would suffer by a
comparison with the villas of Roman citizens.

Pliny, the consul, has left a minute description of
his winter residence at Laurentium, fourteen miles
from Rome.   It is probably a fair specimen of the
villas of Roman noblemen, but by no means equal in
magnificence to many of them.

" My villa," says Pliny, " is large enough to afford all
desirable accommodation, without being extensive.
The porch before it is plain, but not mean, through
which you enter a portico in the form of the letter D,
which includes a small, but agreeable area.   This affords
a very commodious retreat in bad weather, not only
as it is enclosed with windows, but particularly as it
is sheltered by an extraordinary projection of roof.

Plate IX

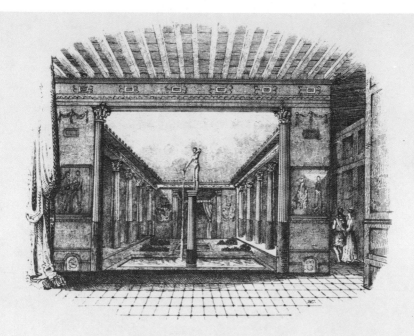

ATRIUM OF A ROMAN HOUSE.

PORTICO AT LORSCH

From the middle of this portico you pass into an in-
ward court, extremely pleasant, and from thence into a
handsome hall, which runs out towards the sea, so
that when there is a southwest wind, it is gently
washed with the waves, which spend themselves at
the foot of it. On every side of this hall, there are
either folding doors, or windows equally large, by
which means you have a view of the front and two
sides, as it were, of three different seas : from the back
part you see the middle of the court, the portico,
and the area, and by another view you look through
the portico, from whence the prospect is terminated
by woods and mountains, which are seen at a distance. On the left hand side of this hall, somewhat farther from the sea, lies a large drawing-
room, and beyond that, a second of smaller size,
which has one window to the rising, and another to
the setting sun. The angle which the projection
forms with this drawing-room, retains and increases
the warmth of the sun ; and hither my family retreat
in winter to perform their exercises. It is sheltered
from all winds, except those which are generally attended with clouds, so that nothing can render this
place useless, but what at the same time destroys fair
weather. Contiguous to this, is a room, forming the
segment of a circle, the windows of which are so
placed as to receive the sun the whole day; in the
walls are a set of cases, which contain a collection of authors, whose works can never be read too
often. From thence, you pass into a bed-chamber.

The remainder of this side of the house is appropriated
to my slaves and freedmen; but most of the apartments,
however, are neat enough to receive any of my friends.
In the opposite wing is a room ornamented in a very
elegant taste; next to which lies another room, which
though large for a parlour, makes but a moderate dining-
room.   Beyond is a bed-chamber, together with its
antechamber.   To this apartment another of the same
sort is joined by a common wall.   From thence you
enter into the grand and spacious cooling-room belonging to the bath; from the opposite walls of which
two large basins project, large enough to swim in.
Contiguous to this is the perfuming-room, then the
sweating-room, and next to that the furnace, which
conveys the heat to the baths.   Adjoining, are the two
little bathing-rooms, fitted up in an elegant rather than
a costly manner.   Annexed to this is a warm bath of
extraordinary workmanship, wherein one may swim
and have a prospect at the same time of the sea,
together with the beautiful villas that stand interspersed upon the coast.   At the other end is a second
turret, in which is a room that receives the rising and
setting sun.   Behind this is a large repository, near
to which is a gallery of curiosities, and underneath is
a spacious dining-room.   In the garden is a banquet-
ing-room; two apartments run round the back part of
it, the windows whereof look upon the entrance of the
villa.   From hence an inclosed portico extends, which,
by its great length, you might suppose erected for the

use of the public. Before this portico lies a terrace, perfumed with violets, and warmed by the reflection of the sun from the portico. On the upper end of the terrace and portico stands a detached building in the garden, which I call my favourite; and indeed it is particularly so, having erected it myself. It contains a very warm winter room, one side of which looks upon the terrace, the other has a view of the sea. Through the folding-doors you see the opposite chamber, and from the windows is a prospect of the enclosed portico. On that side next the sea, and opposite to the middle wall, stands a little elegant recess, which, by means of the glass doors and a curtain, is either laid open to the adjoining room, or separated from it. Adjoining to this is a bed-chamber, which neither the voice of the servants, the murmuring of the sea, nor even the roaring of a tempest can reach. This profound tranquillity is occasioned by a passage which separates the wall of the chamber from that of the garden; and thus, by that intervening space, every noise is precluded. Annexed to this is a small stove-room, which, by opening a little window, warms the bed-chamber to the degree of heat required. Beyond this lies a chamber and antechamber. When I retire to this apartment, I fancy myself a hundred miles from my own house; when my villa resounds with the mirth of my domestics, here I neither interrupt their diversions, nor they my studies."

If such was the villa of a subject, what might we

not imagine the magnificence of an imperial villa! The villa of the Emperor Adrian is said by some authors to have covered a space *ten* miles in circumference, by others *seven* miles. After having travelled through the Roman Empire, and seen the architectural wonders of Egypt, Greece, and Asia, Adrian wished to concentrate in his own villa everything that was most splendid in the fine arts. He was himself an architect, and it is said, that he was so conceited and vain, that the great Apollodorus fell a victim to his vengeance, the latter having criticised with some severity the Emperor's plan of the Temple of Rome and Virtue. In his own villa, Adrian showed a want of correct taste, by introducing every order and style then known. After the spoliations of the Goths, and the more slow but sure ravages of time, Adrian's villa has furnished to the museum and galleries of modern Rome an extraordinary number of statues and other relics, which fully attest its surpassing magnificence.

" This superb villa contained three theatres, one of which is better preserved than any other ancient theatre, for there are still seen some vestiges of the seats, of the scenery, the orchestra, and the actors' rooms; a riding-school; the Temple of the Stoics with seven niches for statues; a maritime theatre, (or naumachia,) surrounded by piazzas; a library, of which some rooms with paintings on the ceilings are still seen; the Temple of Diana and Venus; the imperial palace, two stories high; the Temple of Apollo, where are the niches for the nine Muses; the quarters of the Pretorian Guards; the baths for the men and for the women, of which four saloons are remaining; the temple made to imitate that of Serapis in Egypt; the Elysian Fields; and several other edifices, of which scarcely any other traces remain."

It was not alone in the imperial city and its vicinity that an architectural mania prevailed, it extended throughout the whole empire. The wall in Britain from Carlisle to Newcastle was only one among the many monuments that the Romans left in that island.

Palmyra and Balbec spread their sublime ruins over deserted plains, solemn mementos of the wreck of the mightiest of earth's kingdoms. They are in the most elaborate Romanized Corinthian order.

Roman Architecture, which was never so classically pure as the Grecian, in time degenerated into barbarous magnificence, overloaded with ornaments. The extent and splendour of Nero's Golden House, seem rather to belong to one of the palaces raised by Aladdin's Lamp than to anything real. After the people became vitiated by luxury, and lost their Roman dignity, and their emperors were the most monstrous examples of vice, every work that they undertook showed a want of taste and order, a departure from all simplicity and true beauty. Splendid and gigantic, but wanting in the beautiful and true proportions of the Grecian Temples, these works can never be safe models for imitation.

CHAPTER XI.

ARCHITECTURE OF THE MIDDLE AGES.

ARABIAN ARCHITECTURE,

KNOWN UNDER THE NAMES OF SARACENIC, MOORISH, AND BYZANTINE.

WHATEVER knowledge of the arts the Arabians acquired in the ages subsequent to Mahomet, they owed to the people whom they subdued, from the Indus to the Nile, and to their commercial relations with surrounding nations.

The first *Mosque*, which is known to have been erected out of the precincts of Arabia, was founded by Omar, immediately after the surrender of Jerusalem, on the site of the ancient Temple. This mosque was enlarged and embellished by succeeding caliphs until it was reckoned by the Arabians second only to the magnificent Mezquito of Cordova.

The ancient Arabians were a simple, frugal people, but as their conquests over more luxurious nations extended, their princes assumed the magnificence of Asiatic monarchs. As they acquired a greater relish for the arts, sumptuous edifices adorned their cities.

Plate X

MOSQUE OF ST. SOPHIA.

The great mosque founded by Alwalid I., at Damascus, is particularly celebrated; on this edifice first appeared the *lofty minaret.* This appendage was an innovation in the style, of which it has since become characteristic. Nothing can be more light and graceful than the general effect of minarets (Plate X.); the *pointed arches* with which these towers are decorated give great importance to this edifice in the eyes of architects, as they so nearly resemble those afterward employed in the Gothic, or pointed architecture of Europe.

When the seat of empire was removed from Damascus to Bagdad, neither labour nor expense was spared that the new capital might eclipse the splendour of the former. The gorgeous magnificence of Bagdad would seem only one of the inventions of the author of the Arabian Night's Entertainment, were it not authenticated by contemporary and ocular testimony.

Cairo arose to rival Bagdad, and its mosque is surpassingly rich and beautiful. In arts and sciences the Arabs of the West were not inferior to those of the East; the buildings erected by the Ommiad caliphs of Spain, are some of them equal to anything remaining of the most splendid cities of antiquity. Among these, the mosque at Cordova and the Alhambra or Alhamra in Spain are the most celebrated.

The Alhambra is a fortress and palace built by the Moorish Kings of Granada. The following description is extracted from "The Alhambra," by Washington Irving.

"Ascending a steep and shady avenue, we arrived at the foot of a huge, square, Moorish tower, forming a kind of barbacan, through which passed the main entrance to the fortress. This portal is called the Gate of Justice; the vestibule or porch is formed by an immense Arabian arch of the horseshoe form, which springs to half the height of the tower. On the keystone of this arch is engraven a gigantic hand, (a symbol of the omnipotent hand of God.) Within the vestibule on the keystone of the portal is engraven in like manner, a gigantic key, (a favourite symbol of the followers of Mahomet.) After passing through the barbacan, we ascended a narrow lane, winding between walls, and came on an open esplanade within the fortress. In front of this esplanade is the splendid pile commenced by Charles V., intended, it is said, to eclipse the residence of the Moslem kings. With all its grandeur and architectural merit, it appeared to us like an arrogant intrusion, and passing by it we entered a simple unostentatious portal, opening into the interior of the Moorish palace.

" The transition was almost magical; it seemed as if we were at once transported into other times and another realm, and were treading the scenes of Arabian story. We found ourselves in a great court paved with white marble, and decorated at each end with light Moorish peristyles. In the centre was an immense basin a hundred and thirty feet in length and thirty in breadth stocked with gold-fish, and bordered by hedges of roses. At the upper end of this court rose the great Tower of Comares. From the lower end we passed through a Moorish archway into the renowned Court of Lions. There is no part of the edifice that gives us a more complete idea of its original beauty and magnificence than this; for none have suffered so little from the ravages of time. In the centre stands the fountain famous in song and story. The alabaster basins still shed their diamond drops, and the twelve lions that support them, cast forth their streams as in the days of Boabdil. The court is laid out in flower-beds, and surrounded by light Arabian arcades of open filigree-work, supported by slender pillars of white marble. The architecture, like that of all the other parts of the palace, is characterized by elegance, rather than grandeur, bespeaking a delicate and grace-ful taste. When we look upon the fairy tracery of the peristyles, and the apparently fragile fretwork of the walls, it is difficult to believe that so much has sur-vived the wear and tear of centuries, the shocks of earthquakes, the violence of war, and the quiet, though no less baneful, pilferings of the tasteful traveller. On one side of the court a portal, richly adorned, opens into a lofty hall paved with white marble, and called the Hall of the Two Sisters. The latticed balconies still remain, from whence the dark-eyed beauties of the harem might gaze unseen upon the entertainments of

the hall below.   It is impossible to contemplate this
once favourite abode of Oriental manners, without
feeling the early associations of Arabian romance, and
almost expecting to see the white arm of some mysterious princess beckoning from the balcony, or some
dark eye sparkling from the lattice.

" A Moorish archway admitted us into a vast and
lofty hall, which occupies the interior of the Tower of
Comares, and was the grand audience-chamber of the
Moslem monarchs, thence called the Hall of the Am-
bassadors.   It still bears the traces of past magnificence.
The walls are richly stuccoed and decorated with ara-
besques, the vaulted ceiling of cedar wood, almost lost
in obscurity from its height, still gleams with rich
gilding and the brilliant tints of the Arabian pencil.

" An abundant supply of water, brought from the
mountains by old Moorish aqueducts, circulates
throughout the palace, supplying its baths and fish-
pools, sparkling in jets within its walls, or murmuring
in channels along the marble pavement.   When it has
paid its tribute to the royal pile, and visited its gardens and pastures, it flows down the long avenue leading to the city, tinkling in rills, gushing in fountains,
and maintaining a perpetual verdure in those groves
that embower and beautify the whole hill of the Alhambra."

M. Laborde in his " Voyage Pittoresque de L'Es-
pagne," assigns three distinct periods to the rise, progress, and decay of Moorish Architecture: the first

Plate XI

HALL OF JUSTICE, ALHAMBRA.

includes the space from the commencement of Islamism
to the ninth century; the second, from the ninth to
the thirteenth century; and the third, from that time,
to the annihilation of the Mahometan dominion in
Spain. The Alhambra belongs to the second period,
and presents the most perfect model of pure Spanish
Arabian Architecture.

CHAPTER XII.

THE great characteristic of the Architecture of the Romans, was the combination of the arch and vault, with the Grecian column. A prevalent form of their later buildings was the high vaulted hall, long and comparatively narrow, on each side of which were cells or chambers, communicating with the great hall and with each other, by arched openings or doorways. Upon this general plan are arranged the great halls of the Baths of Caracalla, and Dioclesian, and the Basilicæ or Halls of Justice. When Christianity was established by Constantine throughout the Roman Empire, these spacious halls were used as places of worship; many ancient buildings were repaired and adapted to this purpose, and subsequently, when new churches were built, the same general plan was followed. The principal entrance was at the west end, and the east end was of a circular form; the breadth was divided into three or four aisles, and upon the co-

lumns, arches were erected, to receive an upper wall, which supports a roof. An addition was
subsequently made of the transept, which completed the ground-
plan of a Christian church, in the
form of the Latin cross.

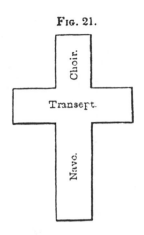

FIG. 21.

The great church of St. Sophia,
at Constantinople, was erected
under the Emperor Justinian,
about A. D. 637. Here was a mixture of the Grecian
and Roman Architecture, with new inventions, to
which the unskilfulness of the architects gave rise.
The dome fell twice in a few months after it was built,
and when it was rebuilt, huge buttresses were constructed to sustain the weight. Many columns which
had ornamented ancient edifices, were placed in the
new church of St. Sophia, and an immense number of
arches were raised in rows, one above another, to support various parts of the ill-constructed building. As
Christianity spread to the remotest regions of the Empire, ecclesiastical edifices were everywhere erected;
the rage for building churches in a short time became
general and excessive. Rome being at the head of the
Church of the West, very naturally prescribed the
mode of building, as well as the form of worship.

All countries, in adopting a neighbouring style of
building, have been obliged to accommodate it to some
peculiarities of their local situation, such as climate,

soil, and building materials.   Thus, while adopting the
Roman style, the architecture of every European
country was distinguished by peculiar and characteristic features of its own.   To the style which was
formed in this way, and was an intermediate or transition state between the old Roman and pointed or
Gothic style, the name "Romanesque" in English, and
"Romane" in French, has been given by some writers
of authority, though it may not yet have been generally adopted.   The foregoing remarks will sufficiently
show the propriety of the term, but the style is also
known as the Lombard or Lombardic.

One of its most characteristic features, is the compound semicircular arch.

THE ROMANESQUE IN ENGLAND,

COMMONLY CALLED THE SAXON AND THE NORMAN.

The Christian religion was early introduced into
England; it has indeed been claimed, on strong circumstantial evidence, that the foundation of the Church
was there laid by St. Paul himself.   Be that as it may,
when Christianity was first introduced into that island,
she came in the train of Roman art, and Roman power,
and when, her first footsteps being nearly effaced, she
once more appeared, it was again from Rome that she
came.

The *Saxons* landed on the island of Great Britain in
a state of barbarism.   Having subdued the ancient in-

Plate XII

CHURCH OF ST ETIENNE.

ANCIENT CHURCH OF RECULVER.

habitants, a general devastation took place; the Roman structures which had been left, when some time before the Romans evacuated the island, were now wholly destroyed, and scarcely a vestige of their improvements was suffered to remain.

In the course of one hundred years from the departure of the Romans, when King Ethelbert was converted to Christianity by St. Augustine, the zeal for erecting ecclesiastical edifices commenced. Various passages from old English writers might be adduced, to show that the Saxons had only two kinds of church buildings: the Roman style, and the unadorned manner in which they were built with "timber" by home-bred artisans. The ecclesiastics were the principal architects.

The venerable Bede has left us on record his admiration of the Coliseum. He mentions various buildings of stone in England, among which are two churches at Canterbury, in one of which Queen Bertha performed her devotions, and St. Augustine preached. Ina, King of the West Saxons, founded an English school in Rome, and Alfred the Great was presented at the early age of five years before the papal throne. From these facts we learn the predominating influence that Rome must have then exercised over the external forms, as well as the internal character of the Church of England.

One of the oldest churches in England is at Reculver on the Thames (Plate XII.); its spires were once held in such reverence that ships, entering the Thames, were wont to lower their topsails as they passed. This old church now hangs upon the cliff, which century after century the waves have been washing away, "and as successive portions have fallen, the bare sides have presented human bones, and coins, and fragments of pottery, and tessellated pavements, which told that man had been here, with his comforts and luxuries around him, long before Ethelbert was laid beneath the floor of the Saxon church, upon whose ruins the sister spires of the Norman rose, themselves to be a ruin, now preserved only as a sea-mark."

The Saxon style was doubtless but a barbarous imitation of the architecture of Rome. Although many parts of Saxon buildings still exist in churches which were afterwards repaired and remodelled by the Normans, it is doubtful whether a single church remains entire. Doorways (Fig. 22) and columns are occasionally found in castles and other buildings, which show decisive marks of Saxon origin. Towers were erected over the west front of Saxon churches and over the cross. In the interior, the sides were occupied by the arcade, the gallery, and the windows, forming three stories. The pillars were short, massive, and round. In arcades, doors, and windows, the arches were all *semicircular*,

Fig. 22.

and frequently compound. The principal door-cases were decorated with pillars and sculptured capitals. Round the arches were mouldings of great variety; and bas-relief ornaments of skulls, crossbones, and other hideous designs, were rudely carved in confused groups about the buildings. Among the Saxon mouldings the chevron or zigzag, and the embattled frette are conspicuous. The capitals of pillars were of strange and uncouth patterns.

Fig. 23.

The west door of the church of Cliff, near Dover, is undoubtedly Saxon. The triangular pediment is ornamented with the double-billet moulding. The keystone of the outer arch is a rude representation of the Deity in the act of benediction, and on each side is an angel. The head moulding and the crossed-circle moulding adorn this outer semicircle. Within is a narrow border of interlacing arches, upon which are the bead, corbel table, embattled frette, and flower mouldings. The small square door was probably added at a later period.

NORMAN ARCHITECTURE.

When the *Normans* conquered England, in 1066, they were far more cultivated than the Saxons. Many fine cathedrals had before that period been erected in Normandy. The Norman monks, it is said, were so partial to Architecture, that they studied both the theory and the practice; in their own structures they worked as artificers, while the abbots and superiors were the architects. Their connexion with Rome was still closer than that of the Saxons. After their establishment in England, pilgrimage was with them a practice in which the national fervour systematically vented itself. Italy was visited as well on account of its own scenes of legendary holiness, as because it was the way to the still more sacred regions of the East.

The Normans were much disposed to pomp and magnificence in their apparel and in their public and private buildings. They secured their conquests in England by building an immense number of fortresses and castles, and signalized their zeal in religion, by the number and splendour of their ecclesiastical edifices. Their style, although similar to that of the Saxons, demonstrating its Roman origin, shows progressive improvement in the art; the vaultings are more lofty and the pillars of greater diameter. Piers are frequently introduced. The mouldings are the zigzag, and other Saxon mouldings. The capitals are

Plate XIII

PETERBOROUGH CATHEDRAL.

elaborate, and often all different in the same building; the sculptures numerous, and exceedingly grotesque. The doorways and windows were deep, on account of the excessive thickness of the walls, and were always surmounted with a semicircular compound arch. The roofs were generally vaulted with stone; the groining, strong and plain, without tracery, but sometimes laced on one or both sides with a moulding.

The two finest structures of William the Conqueror's reign, are the Cathedrals of Canterbury and Battle Abbey. In the space of about one hundred years, a number of cathedrals were completed in England which still remain for the wonder and admiration of the present age. In those days, among the Normans, the highest dignitaries of the church were frequently architects. Gundolph, Bishop of Rochester, was the architect of Canterbury, Peterborough (Plate XIII.), and Rochester Cathedrals. The latter was completed by Ernulf, Bishop of Salisbury. Five other bishops during this period are known to have been skilful architects. The richness and splendour of these edifices can be accounted for in no other way, than by the supposition, that aid was furnished by the Roman Pontiffs, who were then in the plenitude of their power. They are so large and magnificent, that their execution would have required the whole revenue of the nation, poor as it then was, and even that would perhaps have been insufficient for the purpose.

THE ROMANESQUE IN IRELAND.

Christianity was introduced in Ireland very little later than in England. St. Jerome incontestably proves that there was a Christian church in Ireland as early as the fourth or beginning of the fifth century. The Hibernian legendary lore is so extravagantly marvellous, that it is difficult to gather a grain of wheat from the bushels of chaff. Many of the Irish ruins are in the Romanesque style. The Culdean Abbey at Monaincha has an arched portal, which the author of " The Antiquities of Ireland," (published in Dublin, 1790,) thus describes : " The arch is semicircular. Sculpture seems here to have exhausted her treasures. A nebule moulding adorns the outward semicircle of the portal, a double nebule with beads the second, a chevron the third, interspersed with triangular frette, roses, and other ornaments. It is also decorated with chalices artfully made at every stone so as to conceal the joint."

Cormac's Chapel is described as " one of the most curious fabrics in these kingdoms ; it is a regular church, divided into *nave* and *choir*, the latter narrowing in breadth, and separated from the former by a wide arch."

The remains of the cathedral or stone church at Glendaloch, in the Barony of Ballynacor, is a fine specimen of the Romanesque. " A semicircular arch forms the chancel," says the Irish author, "the eastern window is a round arch, ornamented with a chevron moulding." The sculptures of the inmost mouldings are *legendary*. One part is a dog devouring a serpent. Tradition tells us that a great serpent inhabited the lake, and being destructive of men and cattle was killed by St. Kevin. In another part the saint appears embracing his favourite willow,* and among the foliage may be discovered the medicinal apple.

---

* An Icelandic MS. gives the following account of this wonderful Hibernian Saint : "There was in Ireland one, among the body of Saints, named Kevinus, a kind of hermit inhabiting the tower of Glumelhagem, (Glendaloch) who, when that happened which we are about to relate, had in his house a young man, his relation, greatly beloved by him. This young man being attacked by a disease which seemed mortal, at that time of the year when diseases are most dangerous, namely in the month of March, and taking it into his head that an apple would prove a remedy for his disorder, earnestly besought his relation Kevinus to give him one. At that time no apples were to be had, the trees having then just begun to put forth their leaves. But Kevinus, grieving much at his relation's sickness, besought the Lord to grant him some relief for his kinsman. After his prayer he went out of the house and saw a large tree, a salix or willow, whose branches he examined, and as if for the expected remedy, when he observed the tree to be full of a kind of apples, just ripe. Three of these he gathered and carried to the young man. When the youth had eaten part of these apples, he felt his disorder gradually abate, and was at length restored to his former health. The tree bears every year a fruit like an apple, which from that time have been called St. Kevin's apples, and it is notorious that they are the most wholesome *medicine against all disorders to which*

The round towers of Ireland (Plate XIV.) are among the hobbies of antiquaries. They are scattered all over Ireland. Peter Walsh in 1684 observes: "That it is most certain those *high, round, narrow towers, built cylinderwise,* were never known or built in Ireland before the year of Christ 838, when the heathen Danes, possessing a great part of the country, built them in several places to serve themselves as watch-towers against the natives. Though ere long the Danes being expulsed, the Christian Irish turned them to another and much better use, that is, to steeple-houses or belfries." This is the most probable conjecture, yet another old writer asserts that they were the residences of anchorites, where "an incarnate angel upon earth led a celestial life."

A Mr. Smith who wrote upon the subject a learned dissertation, says of a tower at Ardmore, " That there were three pieces of oak still remaining on which the bell was hung; there were also two channels cut in the tile of the door where the rope came out, the ringer standing below on the outside." Upon which the

---

mankind are liable." The patience of St. Kevin was wonderful. On a certain time, putting his hand out of the window, and lifting it up to heaven, according to custom, a blackbird perched upon it, and using it for a nest, dropped her eggs therein. The Saint pitied the bird, and neither closed his hand, nor drew it in, but indefatigably kept it stretched out until she brought forth her young. In memory of this, all the images of St. Kevin have the hand extended and a bird sitting on it.

Plate XIV

ROUND TOWER.

ROCHESTER CASTLE.

author of "the Antiquities" remarks, "How quickly does the finest spun hypothesis disappear before this decisive evidence: this writer was not refined enough in antiquarian speculations to be whimsical." However, this same Mr. Smith changed his opinion, for in a subsequent work he says, an Irish MS. informed him, "they were penitential towers, the penitent descending from one floor to another, as his penance became lighter, until he came to the door, which always faced the east, where he received absolution."

These towers, of which nearly a hundred have been found in Ireland, are of various heights, from 50 to 140 feet. The walls are three or four feet in thickness. There are platforms dividing them into four, five, and even seven stories. Some of them are fifty feet in circumference at the base; in general, they are not more than nine feet in diameter at the base, and four feet at the summit. The doorways are at some distance from the ground, often as high as twenty, or twenty-four feet, without any steps on the exterior to ascend to them. These doorways are Romanesque; the arches are semicircular and compound, ornamented with the zigzag moulding. These peculiarities point out their architectural date and origin; their use must still remain an antiquarian enigma.

THE ROMANESQUE IN SCOTLAND.

Round towers have been found in Scotland, and
their use and antiquity have puzzled the Scotch antiquaries, and occasioned as many conjectures, as those
in Ireland. The footsteps of Rome may be traced in
the architecture, less distinctly than in England and
Ireland ; yet there were churches, rude indeed, before the eighth century, which doubtless had a Roman
origin.

THE ROMANESQUE IN GERMANY.

" The style of architecture in Germany, termed by
some writers Byzantine and Romanesque, corresponds
with the style in England which we term Norman,
though in some respects they vary considerably.
Thus we never find in German churches, the ponderous cylindrical piers which occur in English
buildings."*

At Lorsch, near the Rhine, a building still exists,
which was part of a church consecrated in 774 in the
presence of Charlemagne. In it are found, on the lower
floor, regular Corinthian semi-columns (Plate IX.), and
on the upper, Ionic pilasters ; the zigzag mouldings
and other ornaments show the commencement of the

* Stuart.

Plate XV

LOMBARDIE CHURCH AT COLOGNE.

Romanesque. The three colossal cathedrals of the
Upper Rhine, Worms, Mentz, and Spires, are Romanesque on a scale unrivalled in England.

There was no unity in this style, as in the Gothic
that succeeded it: the Ionic volute, and Corinthian
acanthus, are frequently traceable above the perpendicular Romanesque shaft (the same diameter at the
top as at the base).

While this *transition* was going on, from the classic
orders to a new and more perfect style, architecture
was of course mixed, and in some respects barbarous;
yet there were many striking and beautiful inventions,
which gave a distinctive character to the details (especially to the ornaments) of that period. The Church
at Cologne (Plate XV.) is a good example of the Lombardic style.

THE ROMANESQUE IN ITALY.

In Italy may be found every variety in this style.
The departures from classic models were not so striking as those of Northern Europe, yet there are splendid
specimens of the mixed or transition style. The west
door of the Church of St. Giacomo, at Venice, has a
canopy that shows one of these singular combinations.
Here the shafts of the columns rest upon lions. Four
retreating arches rest upon columns, with mixed capitals. Above rises the acute Romanesque pediment,
surmounted by the cross.

THE ROMANESQUE IN FRANCE.

Of all the Romanesque varieties, that of the south of France appears to possess the most simplicity and plainness of decoration, and yet the greatest complication of plan. Pilasters are used in the interior of churches of so classical an appearance, that if they were not almost universal, one would be tempted to believe them interpolations from more ancient structures. The celebrated Abbey of Clugny was built about 910, by Bermo, Abbot of Balme. Many other splendid edifices in the Romanesque style adorned other parts of France, and remain lasting monuments of the architecture of that period. The Church of St. Etienne (Plate XII.), at Caen, was founded by William the Conqueror, and "there the dead body of the sovereign before whom all men had trembled, was hurried to the grave."

There is not only great beauty, but there are many other excellencies, worthy of imitation in the Romanesque or Lombard style; the best specimens evince great architectural skill, and consummate knowledge in the freemasons who are supposed to have been the builders. "Some historians fancy they find symptons of freemasonry as early as the seventh century, and that a peculiar masonic language may be traced as far back as the reigns of Charlemagne and Alfred."

CHAPTER XIII.

GOTHIC OR POINTED ARCHITECTURE.

DURING the twelfth century, symptoms of a great architectural revolution began to show themselves in northwestern Europe. After the lapse of ages, an originative period in the constructive art once more approached. Various changes were introduced during the period of the Romanesque, which, though at the time may have seemed mere matters of detail, now that we can look back upon them, in one connected view, are clearly seen to have been the various partial developments of one grand and self-consistent whole. An internal principle of harmony was apparent in the newer works, clear and single, like that which had pervaded the buildings of antiquity.

It does not seem surprising that a new style of architecture should arise, adapted to a new and pure religion. The mighty, massive structures of the Egyptians excited awe bordering on terror; they were intended to conceal the mysteries which priestcraft imposed upon ignorance. The purer Grecian style was the embodying of a love of the beautiful, for

which the Greeks were remarkable ; they deified
nature, amid her most beautiful scenes, and made
their splendid temples to harmonize with the sunny
sky of clearest cerulean, her waving groves and sparkling streams, fanned by the bland breezes of the blue
Ægean.   This light and graceful beauty was united
with the lofty character, stamped upon all the works
of ancient Greece by the stern dignity of republican
simplicity.

The Romans, in their religion and architecture,
were imitators of the Greeks.   When, as mistress of
the world, Rome reared her gorgeous fabrics and hung
her lofty vaults in air, they were symbols of her
aspiring ambition.   Rich in decoration, and gigantic
in size, her finest structures were wanting in grace
and elegant simplicity.

The characteristic forms of Classic Architecture,
were " horizontal, reposing, definite ;" of the Christian
Architecture, " vertical, aspiring, indefinite."   " It
would hardly be too fanciful," says a reverend author,
" to consider the newer religious architecture as bearing the impress of its Christian birth, and exhibiting in
the leading lines of its members, and the aspiring
summits of its edifices, forms whose ' silent finger
points to Heaven.' "*

---

* " The principle of the Gothic Architecture is Infinity made
imaginable.   It is no doubt a sublimer effort of genius than the Greek
style."—Coleridge.

The term *Gothic*, "La maniera Gotica," was first given in contempt by the Italian writers to the *pointed* architecture of the middle ages. Sir Christopher Wren was the first English writer who applied it to English Architecture; he objected to the term, and proposed *Saracenic* instead, believing that to have been its origin. Britton has suggested the propriety of calling it the *Christian* Architecture; to this many objections might be urged. Though the Goths have no more claim to the invention of the style, than the Hindoos or the Mexicans, the name Gothic has so long been employed, and is so generally understood to designate the *pointed* architecture, that it would be unwise to attempt a change, even could a better be substituted.

As the pointed arch is the most striking and familiar feature of the Gothic style, it has been supposed the turning *point* of the revolution, which we have seen was progressively accomplished. Flying buttresses, tracery, clustered columns, and lofty spires are also distinctive features.

The Gothic style is said to have been suggested in various ways. From the lofty groves of heathen worship. The perfect form of the Gothic arch appears in avenues of trees, particularly the elm;* from huts made with the entwined twigs of trees; from the

---

* In Temple Street, New Haven, the high branches of weeping elms form a succession of beautiful arches, like the nave of a cathedral, ornamented with light and graceful tracery by the pendant branches.

FIG. 24.

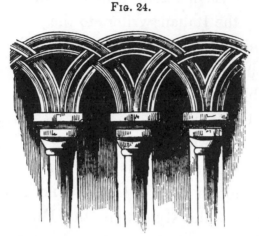

structure of framework in wooden buildings ; from the Pyramids of Egypt ; from the form of the keel of an ancient boat reversed ; from the intersection of semicircular arches. (Fig. 24.) These suppositions are, all but the last, fanciful and unsatisfactory.

All countries in adopting a neighbouring style, have been obliged to accommodate it to some peculiarities in their own condition, so that a person familiar with examples from all countries and ages, can tell upon inspecting a building, or even an important member of a building, to what age and country it belonged. The liability to heavy falls of snow, which would encumber and endanger flat roofs, could hardly fail to teach northern architects the necessity of raising and rendering acute the angle of the roof. The gable, wherever it appeared, would become proportionably acute, giving a new tone to the façade with which it was connected, and requiring, for the sake of uniformity, the adoption of pointed lines parallel to its own, in the portals, windows, and other parts of the building. For it may be here remarked, that the members and ornaments of a building must be governed by the form and character of the building itself.

"The parts of Gothic buildings are adapted to each other, as well as to the general design. The arched doors and mullioned windows are essential parts; and the spires, pinnacles, and buttresses serve by their weight to bind together the whole edifice. The history of the style accounts for its propriety, its chiefest merit. The Gothic Architecture, whatever its primitive elements may have been, was created in the *northern parts* of Europe; it was there adapted to the wants of a more inclement sky."

But if the hypotheses on the origin of the Gothic style are various, no less so are the opinions as to the nation to which the invention belongs. It has been ascribed to the Hindoos, Egyptians, Hebrews, Romans, Greeks, Saracens, French, English, Germans, Italians, Spaniards, Goths, Lombards, and Scotch.*

In the beginning of the twelfth century, the Crusades had drawn the flower of European chivalry to the East; vast numbers of ecclesiastics accompanied them, and as they were the repositories of art and science during that age, it is more than probable that they brought home to Europe many novel inventions in Architecture. There was also about this period a

---

* Authorities consulted : Dr. Stukely, Lord Aberdeen, Dr. Ledwich, Gunn, Whitaker, Knight, Barry, Lascelles, Wren, Warburton, Strutt, Wotton, Smirke, Whittington, Milner, Hall, Turner, Wilson, &c., &c.

corporation of builders or freemasons, consisting of Greeks, Italians, French, Germans, and Flemish, who kept secret the principles of their art. Protected by papal bulls, they travelled from place to place for the purpose of building ecclesiastical edifices. They had undoubtedly seen the finest specimens of art in the East, and would introduce from Saracenic Architecture whatever was suitable for northern buildings, especially in parts that were ornamental.

It must be confessed that the *origin* of pointed or Gothic Architecture is hid in the obscurity of " the dark ages;" the *principles* have been discovered only after long and careful examination of the buildings themselves.

Three modes in Gothic Architecture are mentioned under different names, by different architects. In England, these modes have been characterized by the terms " Early English," " Decorated," and " Perpendicular,"* the first being in fact the incipient, the second the perfect, and the third the degenerating Gothic of England.

The most prominent features of the " Early English" are exhibited in Salisbury Cathedral. These features are the high pointed roof and gable; the single or the triple lancet windows (Fig. 25); the

---

* Mr. Rickman was the originator of these terms, to which Britton and some others object; but as they designate more accurately the several modes, than any other terms hitherto employed, we adopt them, not as established, but quoted from the author.

Plate XVI

INTERIOR OF YORK MINSTER.

simple, bold doorway, frequently divided by a central
column, or cluster columns,
and headed by the same
pointed arches as the windows; the massive buttress,
with its deep water-tables,
between each stage.

FIG. 25.

The Early English, ac-
cording to Rickman, pre-
vailed from 1189 to about
1307. Its architecture had
throughout the lancet arch;
the piers of the interior
arches maintained the cir-
cular character common to the Romanesque style, but
were set around with four or
more slender shafts, attached like
reeds around a greater cylinder,
and in some instances bound together by mouldings at intervals.
The Rose or Catharine window,
is frequently found worked with
great care.

FIG. 26.

The general character of the Early English, was
that of severe and simple majesty; the ornaments were
bold and striking. In this style the best entire specimen in England is Salisbury Cathedral. Parts
of Westminster Abbey Church, the nave and aisles
of Peterborough, and parts of Ely, Worcester, and

York Cathedrals, furnish other examples of the Early English Gothic. This period includes the reigns of Richard I., John, Henry III., and Edward I.

The Decorated English* prevailed from about 1307 to 1377, or as some say, till 1460; or from the decease of Edward the First, till that of Richard II., thus including the long reign of Edward III.

Fig. 27.

Fig. 28.

During this period, the Gothic in England was distinguished for grace and elegance of proportion, for richness of decoration without exuberance, and for scientific skilfulness of execution. The windows of this period differ from those of the preceding, by being

---

* This second style in England, has also been called "the pure Gothic." An eminent architect has suggested that this division should be called "the *Triangular-arched* order;" as the form of the arch which was then principally in vogue admitted of an equilateral triangle being precisely inscribed between the crowning point of the arch, and its points of springing at the impost.

Plate XVII

YORK MINSTER.

larger and divided by slender upright *mullions*. Some were still adorned with *geometrical* tracery (Fig. 27); others were enriched with *flowing* tracery (Fig. 28), called in France, Flamboyant, from its resemblance to flames. This kind of tracery is beautifully described by Sir Walter Scott.

> " The moon on the vast oriel shone,
> Through slender shafts of shapely stone,
> By foliaged tracery combined.
> Thou wouldst have thought some fairy's hand,
> 'Twixt poplars straight, the ozier wand
> In many a freakish knot had twined;
> Then framed a spell, when the work was done,
> And changed the willow-wreaths to stone."

The arch is generally the equila-

Fɪɢ. 29.

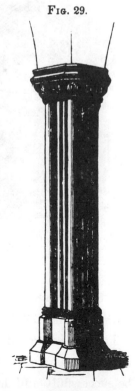

teral triangle, or more obtuse. Buttresses are richer and usually finished by pinnacles (Plate XVII.), ornamented with crockets. A common form of finish for doors was the pyramidal label (Plate XVII.), which was enriched with crockets at the top and sides like the pinnacles. In small works, the ogee arch is frequently found in the same manner decorated with crockets. In the interior, the clustered shafts are incorporated into quadrangular piers (Fig. 29), the roofs are elaborately groined (Plate XVI.), and the mouldings rich and varied.   Tapering spires now pointed "heavenward," breaking up the monotony of horizontal lines, and giving a pleasing, impressive effect to distant scenery.

Among some of the most beautiful examples of this style, from 1307 to 1377, are York Minster, the Chapter House of York Cathedral, and several parts of Exeter Cathedral.   Under Edward III., parts of Ely, Carlisle, and Gloucester Cathedrals.   Under Richard II., Henry IV., and V., parts of Winchester and Canterbury Cathedrals.

The "*Perpendicular*"* style is marked by its windows (Fig. 30), the mullions of which are carried

Fig. 30.

perpendicularly to the head, instead of finishing in flowing lines.   Arches are generally quite obtuse; arches still more depressed than Fig. 30 were frequently employed.   This style is distinguished by its superfluity of decoration and minuteness in the details.   If we include under this third period, (according to Rickman,) from 1377 to the decline of the Gothic style in the 15th cen-

---

* Several other appellations have been bestowed upon this third variety of the Gothic, viz.: " Florid Gothic ;" " The Tudor Style ;" " The Obtuse-arched Style."   Britton says, " Probably there is not any single phrase in the range of our vocabulary, by which it could be successfully and distinctively denominated."

Plate XVIII

KING'S COLLEGE CHAPEL.

tury, then King's College Chapel (Plate XVIII.) may be mentioned as its finest example. It is universally acknowledged to be "one of the most magnificent triumphs of architectural science in the kingdom." It was commenced by Henry VI., about 1443. The great interest of this building, architecturally considered, is in the stability and beauty of the stone vaulting, which, for the elegance of the fanlike tracery with which it is overspread in rich profusion, is perhaps unparalleled.

St. George's at Windsor was in progress during several reigns, and was not completed till after the tenth year of Henry VIII. The letters-patent of Richard II., are still extant (1390,) appointing the celebrated Geoffrey Chaucer, Clerk of the Works to this Chapel. Chaucer was empowered to "impress carpenters, and other workmen, for the necessary operations of the said chapel, and allowed *two shillings per day*, with the privilege of having a deputy." This chapel was repaired, at a great expense, by George the Third.

One of the finest specimens of the Perpendicular or Florid style, is the Chapel of Henry VII., at Westminster. This has been called by an English divine, "the miracle of the world." "It would seem, indeed, as though the architect had intended to give to the stone the character of embroidery, and enclose his walls in meshes of lace-work." The geometrical skill exhibited in the design, and the aspiring lightness, have justly called forth universal admiration. From the vault hang those stone *pendants* that are so rich and beautiful. Henry VII., it is said, was impelled to erect this chapel by the "compunctious visitings" of a guilty conscience; in order to make his peace with Heaven, he judged it necessary to expend a portion of his ill-gotten treasures in works of charity and devotion. The weal of his soul was to be secured by chaunting of psalms and requiems, and other superstitious ceremonies, as well as by costly sacrifices. Was there none to say to the alarmed monarch, "The sacrifices of God are a broken and a contrite spirit, which are in His sight of great price?"

Under the tyrannic and capricious sway of Henry VIII., spoliation and devastation superseded invention and design. The Chapel of Henry VII. is therefore left as the last gorgeous specimen of the Perpendicular or Florid Gothic in England.

> " Doomed to hide her banished head
> Forever, Gothic Architecture fled ;
> Forewarned, she left in one most beauteous place,
> (That much might of her ancient fame be said,)
> Her *pendant* roof, her windows' *branchy* grace,
> *Pillars* of *clustered reeds* and *tracery* of *lace*."

These succeeding epochs of the Gothic in England are not distinctly divided from each other; they may be said to overlap, so that buildings erected during the latter part of what is termed the "Early English," contain many examples of the " Decorated" style ; and the same may be said of the " Decorated" and "the Perpendicular."

In other countries beside England, the Gothic appears to have had three principal stages, *the early*, *the perfect*, and *the degenerating*. Starting from the same mode, the Romanesque, the various nations of Northwestern Europe seem to have proceeded, each in its own way, to the discovery of the principles of the *pointed* style, and the fact is striking, that in the second stage they all reached nearly the same goal. The perfect or Decorated Gothic is to be seen, varied only in unimportant points of detail, at York and Exeter, in England, at Cologne and Oppenheim, in Germany, in the beautiful church of St. Ouen, at Rouen, in France, and in " Fair Melrose," in Scotland. This point of union had not long been reached in each country before the style began to decline, each adopting various specimens of an after style peculiar to themselves until the great changes of the sixteenth century.

The Gothic cathedrals of Germany far surpass in size and magnificence any that England can boast.

Strasburg, on the Rhine, which formerly belonged to Germany, has a splendid cathedral, built in the thirteenth century. The façade of Strasburg measures about one hundred and eighty feet in breadth, and in height about two hundred and thirty feet, (far above the towers of York,) then rises the tower and the lofty spire two hundred and twenty-eight feet, making the whole height nearly four hundred and sixty feet.

Exclusively of the noble spire, the majestic west front of Strasburg exceeds the whole height of the loftiest fronts in England, including the towers. The extreme height of Westminster is two hundred and twenty-five feet to the top of the spire; it would therefore look like a dwarf, if placed before this gigantic structure of Strasburg. This immense cathedral is embellished with a richness of decoration almost unparalleled. " The building," says Mr. Whewell, " looks as if it were placed behind a rich open screen, or in a cage of woven stone."

The Cologne Cathedral is admired by many, as the finest specimen of the Gothic style in Europe; the richness of its decoration can scarcely be imagined. The Germans unquestionably preceded the English in perfecting the Gothic. The spire of England is generally a vast obelisk placed upon a tower, to which it seems to have been appended by an after thought, while the spire of Germany seems an integral part of the building itself, rising with the gracefulness and airy lightness of frostwork.

France has contested with England the honour of having first brought the Gothic style to perfection. She certainly can exhibit splendid testimony to support this claim. The cathedrals of Rheims, Amiens, Chartres, Beauvais, and St. Ouen, what can rival them in England ?

Rheims boasts the most celebrated cathedral in France, on account of its historical associations,* its immense size, and its antiquity. It was originally founded more than a thousand years ago, but was destroyed by fire in 1210; in the same year the new edifice was begun, and it was finished, excepting some of its ornaments, in thirty years. This cathedral has no mixture of designs; it is rich and light, massive below, but being in the pyramidal form, springs airy and graceful as it ascends. The western portal is magnificent, and the minute beauties are singularly fine.

Amiens Cathedral has, however, been considered by some learned critics, as the perfection of Gothic Architecture. It was begun in the same year with Salisbury, and is built on a similar plan; they have often been compared, but it is difficult to decide between their respective merits. It has been said, that Salisbury has the advantage of lightness, but Amiens surpasses it in loftiness and richness of decoration. The west front of the latter is crowded with armies of prophets, martyrs, and angels, which line the doorways, crowd the walls, and absolutely swarm around the pinnacles.

Spain, though some of its cathedrals, are surpassingly rich, seems to have been indebted for its principal honours to northern architects. Its general style of

* The kings of France were formerly crowned at Rheims. It was there that the unfortunate heroine, Joan of Arc, placed the crown upon the head of the ungrateful Charles.

Gothic Architecture is strong and massive, with ornaments of great delicacy, borrowed from the Moors.

There is no genuine Gothic building in Italy. Her artists never entirely lost sight of the classical structures around them, and mingled in their designs Gothic features with the classical; yet there are many splendid cathedrals which have called forth admiration. Milan Cathedral is a mountain of sculpture.

Batalha, the glory of Portugal, was founded by John I. in 1385. It bears incontestable proof that the general architecture is the offspring of a northern clime, incongruously modified by its southern situation. Its flat stone roof is adapted to the sunny skies of Portugal, yet its splendid west window is acute, as is also the portal, and the pinnacles are tapering. Notwithstanding these incongruities, it is one of the most highly finished specimens of the Gothic style in Europe, adorned with a profusion of ornaments, executed in a masterly manner, some of which are hieroglyphical and inexplicable to the learned. It was built by an Irish architect of the name of Hacket.

Fig. 31.

In Scotland, the ancient ecclesiastical edifices, although inferior in size to those in England, are generally in the best style of Gothic Architecture. During the reign of David I., many fine structures were built. History and poetry have united to throw a charm around Scotia's time-worn monuments, by

Plate XIX

giving them interesting, though melancholy, associations.

Melrose Abbey, although founded many years before, was increased and beautified in the reign of David I. It was in the "Decorated Gothic;" a part of the choir remains, in which is an immense window, with the mullions entire, and tracery broken.

" If thou wouldst view fair Melrose aright,
Go visit it by the pale moonlight ;
For the gay beams of lightsome day
Gild, but to flout the ruins gray :
When the broken arches are black in night,
And each shafted oriel glimmers white ;
When the cold light's uncertain shower,
Streams on the ruined central tower ;
When buttress and buttress, alternately,
Seem framed of ebon and ivory ;
When silver edges the imagery,
And the scrolls that teach thee to live and die ;
When distant Tweed is heard to rave,
And the owlet to hoot o'er the dead man's grave,
Then go, but go alone the while,
Then view St. David's ruined pile ;
And home returning soothly swear,
Was never scene so sad and fair."

" The darkened *roof* rose high aloof
On *pillars*, lofty, and light, and small ;
The *keystone*, that locked each *ribbed aisle*,
Was a *fleur-de-lys*, or a *quatre feuille ;**

---

* The French word, which was doubtless the original of *quatrefoil*, (Fig. 31.)

> The *corbells** were carved grotesque and grim,
> And the *pillars*, with *clustered shafts* so trim,
> With *base* and *capital* flourished around,
> Seemed bundles of lances which garlands had bound."

How perfect is this description by Sir Walter Scott! Washington Irving, in his visit to Abbotsford, mentions the delight with which Sir Walter spoke of old Melrose. "The Abbey was evidently a pile that called up all Scott's poetic and romantic feeling. He spoke of it, I may say, with affection. The heart of Robert Bruce, the hero of Scotland, *had been* buried in it. He dwelt on the beautiful story of Bruce's pious and chivalrous request in his dying hour, that his heart might be carried to the Holy Land and placed in the Holy Sepulchre, in fulfilment of a vow of pilgrimage; and of the loyal expedition of Sir James Douglas, to convey thither the glorious relic. Before dismissing the theme of the relics from the Abbey," says Irving, "I will mention another, illustrative of Scott's varied humours. This was a human skull, which had probably belonged of yore to one of those jovial friars, so honourably mentioned in the old border ballad:

> ' O the monks of Melrose made gude kale,
> 　On Fridays when they fasted;
> They wanted neither beef nor ale,
> 　As long as their neighbours' lasted.'

---

* "Corbells, the projections from which the arches spring, usually cut in a fantastic face or mark."—SCOTT.

"It was a matter of great wonder and speculation, among the superstitious housemaids, that the laird should have such 'an awsome fancy for an auld girning skull.'"

With the sixteenth century, that convulsive period which shattered the whole fabric and new moulded the whole moral constitution of society, the last vestiges of Gothic originative art disappeared.

We have confined our remarks on the architecture of the middle ages, to ecclesiastical edifices. We shall have occasion again to refer to the Gothic style under Domestic Architecture.

Although citizens of the United States feel comparatively little interest in the noble cathedrals of England, yet it would be strange if they had no sympathy with their ancestors of the father-land, of the same speech and blood, and faith, who worshipped with reverence beneath those venerable piles. These edifices have stood during the whole period most familiar to our historic recollections. We admire their magical lightness, their majestic loftiness, their grave solemnity, but even as we do so, a sentiment of wonder arises in our minds, and we ask involuntarily, "Why all this magnificence?" Was it, that the churchmen of old, wished to display their power, to increase their hold over the imagination of the people, or to give employment to a population of serfs? Was it because the people universally thought that they could buy Heaven with the positive merits of their good works?

Let us believe better things of them, although we know, that "thick darkness covered the people."

One thing is certain, that as the Romish church became more and more corrupt, cathedral building declined, and no subsequent edifices eclipsed those of the twelfth, thirteenth, and fourteenth centuries.

By the mechanism of our moral constitution, reverence, when rightly directed, increases happiness. This emotion is called forth in the highest degree by the worship of the Creator. " Thou shalt love the Lord thy God with all thy soul, mind, and strength." "Honour thy father and mother, is the first commandment with promise." The sentiment of reverence, it is to be feared, is too little cultivated in our own country. Perhaps our civil institutions are detrimental, nay, almost destructive to high and honourable reverential feelings towards our parents, guides, and superiors.

Can we not obviate this tendency by a careful culture of religious reverence? Should we not be anxious to honour our Maker, with the best gifts of the hands, the highest efforts of genius, and the strongest affections of the heart?

Even should we reverence the church edifice which is consecrated to the worship of God, it does not follow that we must of necessity be ignorant and superstitious.

Who shall say how often the traveller may have been taught to direct his thoughts heavenward by the sight of the distant tower or tapering spire; how often the inhabitants of a busy town may have been elevated in soul above its din and traffic, by the solemn witness borne by the massive repose of its noble church, to the solemn realities of a world unseen? While we avoid the errors and superstitions of a dark age, let us not be blinded by the false glare of the present, to our highest interests.

Authorities for Gothic Architecture: Britton's Architectural Antiquities, Pugin's Specimens of Gothic Architecture, Denkmäler der Deutschen Bankhunst, Dr. Georg Moller, Willis on the Architecture of the Middle Ages, Loudon's Architectural Encyclopedia, Rickman's Gothic Architecture, Rev. W. Whewell's Architectural Notes on German Churches, Plans, Elevations, &c., of the Church of Batalha, by James Murphy, Rich's Engraved and Coloured Cathedrals, Edinburgh Encyclopedia, British Critic, &c., &c.

CHAPTER XIV.

DOMESTIC ARCHITECTURE OF THE MIDDLE AGES.

THE feudal system, which for ages prevailed in Europe, had an influence upon the domestic architecture of that period. The barons dwelt in castles, often strongly fortified, their immediate retainers living within the castle walls, protected by their lord, and defending him in case of attack.

The serfs erected their miserable habitations around or near the baronial mansion. Nearly every town was originally thus formed, around the castle of the king, or of the powerful barons. In Knight's " Progress of Civil Society," towns such as these, are thus described:

" Hence by degrees the embryo town began,
As wants or habits formed its artless plan;
The increasing numbers part the chosen spot,
And each with rival toil adorns his lot,
Extends his little hut, and clears around,
The obtruding thorns and brambles from the ground;

Brings from the shattered tree the ponderous beam,
With thatch of reeds, and rushes from the stream ;
Constructs with rude design the simple shed,
From rains and tempest to protect his head ;
The walls with bark and pliant wattle weaves,
And spreads his easy couch of withered leaves."

Such temporary huts were the only shelter for the poor degraded serfs, who cultivated the soil for their liege lord, reaping for themselves only the bare necessaries that prolong a wretched existence.

The formidable strongholds of the chieftains, who in the feudal days were engaged in almost perpetual warfare, served the treble purpose of dwelling-house, fort, and prison. Every reader of history or of romance, will be reminded of the donjons (dungeons) dark, of these moated castles. In the erection of these edifices, strength was the first object of consideration. A rocky eminence was usually chosen for the site; if possible, surrounded by the sea on all sides but one, sometimes entirely insulated. There, perched proudly like a falcon's nest on the summit of an inaccessible rock, the frowning towers and battlements of stone bade defiance to the attacks of foes, and the storms of centuries.

When such a strong natural position could not be obtained, a deep ditch was formed around the whole outer wall, which was called the moat, and was generally filled with water; over this was thrown a drawbridge. A large area was sometimes thus walled in,

and entered only at one opening, which was a great
gateway with a portcullis, between two lofty towers.
In this area, stood the castle itself, varying in size and
form to suit the wealth and convenience of its lord.
Such was the general style of building throughout
Europe during the prevalence of the feudal system.

THE DOMESTIC ARCHITECTURE OF ENGLAND.

FROM THE FIFTH CENTURY TO THE SIXTEENTH CENTURY.

When the Saxons first landed in Britain, they must
have found many Roman edifices, which they partially
or entirely destroyed.   An ancient author, who wrote
as early as A. D. 560, says, "The walls of all the colonies were beat down to the ground with battering-
rams, and their inhabitants slain with the point of the
sword.   Nothing was to be seen in the streets, O,
horrible to relate! but fragments of ruined towers,
temples, and walls, fallen from their lofty seats, be-
sprinkled with blood, and mixed with mangled car-
casses."   It was thus that the Anglo-Saxons, coming
professedly as friends, at length became the deadly
enemies of the Ancient Britons, and finally subjugated
them.

For a long period after their establishment in England, their houses were rude structures of timber and
mortar, without chimneys, and with windows called

in Saxon *ehthyrl*, literally an eye-hole, destitute of glass, and covered with pitched cloth.

As the intercourse of the Anglo-Saxons with Rome increased, Christian bishops brought home artificers, and endeavoured to improve the condition of the people. Under the wise government of the great and good Alfred, the people began to emerge from a state of semi-barbarism, and gradually became more intelligent, ingenious, and civilized.

A Roman origin has been ascribed to some ancient ruins of castles, which more probably were Saxon, as they possess the leading features of the ecclesiastical remains of that period; namely, the semicircular, compound arch over the doors and windows, with the zigzag and fret mouldings. Among these ancient castles was that of Peveril of the Peak, which has been made familiar to every English reader by the genius of Sir Walter Scott. This castle, at Castleton, in Derbyshire, though held by Edmund de Peveril in the time of William the Conqueror, and from him descended to the hero of Scott's romance, is supposed to be of Saxon origin. "This feudal Baron," says the novelist, "chose his nest upon the principle the eagle selects his eyry, and built it in such a fashion as if he had intended it for the sole purpose of puzzling posterity."

There were but few strong castles in England, however, before the Norman conquest. William, and his chieftains, built strongly fortified castles in various parts of the kingdom.   The ecclesiastics too, lived in great state, and were themselves the principal architects of the age.

Roger, Bishop of Salisbury, and Alexander, Bishop of Lincoln, lived in their strong castles of Old Sarum and Newark, with large retinues of vassals and tenants, exciting the envy and fear of the monarch.

Within the space of one hundred years after the conquest, it is stated on the authority of Camden, that there were 1115 castles in England.   The buildings of England at this time were of five classes, namely : the castles of the monarchs ; baronial castles ; monasteries, including churches, chapels, hospitals, and the dwelling-houses of all orders of ecclesiastics, monks and nuns ; the town-houses of merchants, and their warehouses ; the mean hovels of artisans ; the houses or huts of the peasantry.

Among the most distinguished architects of this period, was Gundulph, Bishop of Rochester.   He was employed by William the Conqueror, to direct the building of the Tower of London, about the year 1078. His mode of building was greatly admired, and he was immediately employed in planning other castles.

Of the several castles built by Gundulph, that at Rochester, (Plate XIV.) erected about 1088, is one of the finest remains of antiquity in England.   A full description of this castle will be sufficient to give the reader a correct idea of a kind of building, which holds so conspicuous a place in poetry and romance.

Rochester Castle is built near the brow of a hill, on the banks of the River Medway, and its principal tower, which is 75 feet by 72, is so situated as to command both the river and the adjacent country. It was fortified by strong outworks and deep ditches, and had an area around it, enclosed for the use of the garrison.

In the construction of the castle, the circumstances most manifestly endeavoured to be provided for by the architect, were,

1. The security of the entrance, and the rendering it magnificent.

2. The protection of the whole garrison in case of a siege.

3. Contrivances to mislead besiegers with regard to the strength of the castle.

4. The security of stores, and of prisoners.

5. Easy conveyances for engines of war, into the various apartments and to the top of the tower.

6. The means of giving a quick alarm to all the garrison.

7. The supplying the garrison with water.

8. The carrying away the smoke from the apartments.

9. The providing a habitation for the lord of the castle, both stately and airy, and free from the annoyance of the enemy's instruments of war.

Many of these objects belong more properly to military than to civil architecture; but as the residence of most of the nobility, both of England and the continent, were, during the days of chivalry, thus constructed, we cannot with propriety omit that part which belongs to fortification.

First, as to the entrance. Nothing can be conceived more completely adapted to answer the double purpose of stateliness and security. In Rochester Castle, the entrance was by means of a grand staircase, which went partly around two of the fronts of the castle on the outside, and terminated in a grand portal, at a considerable height from the ground. Before this portal could be entered, there was a drawbridge to be passed, the pulling up of which cut off all communication with the flight of steps; and there was also a strong gate about the middle of the staircase, between the foot of it and the drawbridge. Nor was this the only security; for even the grand portal, beyond the bridge, was not the real entrance of the fortress, but merely the entrance of a small adjoining tower, the whole of which might be demolished without any material injury to the body of the castle. Within this little tower was a sort of vestibule, and from thence was a second entrance, (the real entrance of the great tower itself,) through a second portal, placed in the thickness of the wall, which was here about twelve feet thick; and the second entrance, as well as the first portal, was defended by a portcullis or herse, and also by a strong pair of gates; so that there were *three strong gates* to be forced, and *two portcullises* to be destroyed, before this entrance could be gained; and one pair of gates was to be broken down, and the drawbridge at a great height is to be retraced, before even the first portcullis could be approached.

The herse or portcullis, was a strong grating of timber, fenced with iron, made to slide up and down in a groove of solid stone-work, within the arch of the portal, just as a sash-window does in its frame, and its bottom was furnished with sharp iron spikes, designed both to strike into the ground or floor, for the sake of greater firmness or solidity, and to break and destroy whatever should be under it at the time of its being let fall. Its groove was contrived so deep in the stone-work, that it could not be injured or removed without pulling down the whole wall. For state, there were in the thickness of the wall, at the second entrance, two stone seats in large niches, for the warders, or for those who by military tenure kept castle guard.

Beside this grand entrance there was no other of any consequence, and indeed there was no possibility of getting in or out of the castle otherwise than by it, except by a small sally-port, or narrow doorway, situated directly under the drawbridge, and therefore in a place where any assailants might be easily annoyed. This little sally-port was at such a height from the ground that it could only be approached by a scaling-ladder, as it had neither stone nor other fixed steps; for further security, there was no communication with the grand apartments above, except by a winding staircase, so

narrow that it could easily be defended by a single
sentinel; it was also well secured by strong doors.

On the ground floor there were no windows, and but
few loop-holes, and even these were exceedingly small,
not being much above six inches square, their structure and situation being such that no weapon could
possibly enter far enough to fall into the apartments;
nor were there any but loop-holes above, where the
grand portals are situated.

The third story of Rochester Castle, contained the
rooms of state; and although there were in these
rooms magnificent windows, they were placed so high
in the apartments, (which were on that account more
than thirty feet high,) that it was almost impossible
for any weapon to be shot into the rooms, to do any
mischief.

As to the fourth or uppermost story, the rooms of
which were about sixteen feet high, there was no need
of precaution in the structure of the windows; it had
therefore, very large ones, not far from the floor.

Curious devices of false arches and solid round
towers, apparently weak, were constructed in various
parts of the castle, to draw the attacks of an enemy
upon the strongest places. The dungeon for the reception of prisoners was invariably attached to the old
English castle; in Rochester Castle it was beneath
the small square tower adjoining the keep itself. It
was entered by a narrow and steep flight of steps in

the wall. Air was admitted only by an aperture in the roof, which was secured by a trap-door.

Windsor Castle, in Berkshire, the principal seat and occasional residence of her present Majesty, Queen Victoria, belongs to the crown, and has generally been occupied by the English monarchs from the time the first building belonging to it was erected. It has been increased by successive monarchs, until it now occupies a space of about a mile in circumference. An irregular but connected series of buildings, completely encompass two large courts, having a grand keep-tower on a lofty mount between them. Around the upper court are numerous buildings appropriated to the royal family and their retinue. The lower court, is occupied by St. George's Chapel, the deanery and canons' buildings, poor knights' houses, seven towers of different sizes and shapes, with other subordinate buildings. On the northwest side of the upper court, are some apartments which were built by Henry VII. In them we recognise the same Florid Gothic with its fantastic decorations, that prevails in the ecclesiastical edifices of that age.

There are other apartments, built in the time of Elizabeth. A chimney-piece, in Queen Elizabeth's Gallery (as it is called), has an inscription which proves the time of its erection to have been A. D. 1583. The ceiling of this room is nearly covered with ornamental tracery, very different from the Gothic, with the emblematic figures of the harp, rose, crown, &c. Affec-

tation of elegance, and an ostentatious display of ornament, characterized the style of the domestic architecture, as well as the style of dress, of the haughty and
vain Queen.   As the peculiar manners and taste of a
popular monarch always produce a powerful effect in
regulating those of the higher classes of society, we
shall find that novelties in domestic architecture have
commonly their origin at court, and are thence progressively disseminated through the country ; hence,
we shall find that a profusion of puerile ornaments will
be found in nearly all the mansion-houses of the Elizabethan age.*   The shell-arched niche, grotesque
pilasters, caryatides, columns having the lower parts
covered with carved foliage, and upper parts fluted;
with a jumbled mixture of cherubim, birds, and lions'
heads, armorial bearings and mythological hieroglyphics, composed the heterogeneous designs for chim-
ney-pieces, fronts of houses, tombs, &c., during the
long reign of Elizabeth.

To return from this digression, suggested by Windsor Castle.   After the accession of Henry II., it was
deemed expedient to destroy many of the baronial
castles, and to prohibit the erection of others, as their
owners, if disaffected towards the monarch, could
shut themselves within their impregnable fortresses,
and set at nought his royal authority.

---

* These remarks on the age of Elizabeth are somewhat anticipa-
tory, as they refer to the period when the Greek and Roman Architecture had been revived in England.

To the castle succeeded the spacious hospitable mansion, embattled only for ornament, containing vast combinations of ill-matched rooms, put together without any discoverable principle. Though these mansions were insufficient to sustain a violent attack from an enemy, they were built with moat and drawbridge, tower and battlement, thick stone walls and numerous small windows.

Of these embattled mansions, one of the most perfect and most curious now remaining, is Haddon House, in Derbyshire, belonging to his grace the Duke of Rutland, a description of which will serve to give a correct idea of the style of that class of buildings.

"The high turrets of this mansion stood proudly towering on a rock, in the midst of thick woods and in a beautiful situation, looking down on the river Wye, which winds along the valley at a great depth beneath. It has undergone," says Mr. King, " fewer alterations, and retains more curious vestiges of the residence of an old English baron, and exhibits more manifest indications of the ancient mode of life, than any other building I ever saw."

Haddon House consisted of a continuous range of buildings, surrounding two open courts. Both of these have embattled walls, turrets, projecting windows, &c. The principal court was encompassed by various domestic offices, or small apartments on two sides, the chapel at a corner, the ladies' apartments on another side, and the great hall on the fourth. On the left side of the hall were four large doorways, with high Gothic arches. The first of these still retains its ancient door of strong oak, with a little wicket in the middle, just big enough to put a trencher in or out; and was clearly the butler's station; for the room within still retains a vast old chest of oak, with divisions for bread; a large old cupboard for cheese, and a number of shelves for butter. A passage down steps leads from this room to a large apartment, which is arched with stone, and supported by pillars, similar to the crypt of a church; this was the *beer-cellar*. The second doorway is an entrance of a long narrow passage, leading with a continued descent to the great *kitchen*, where are two vast fire-places, with irons for a prodigious number of spits, stoves, great double ranges of dressers, large chopping-blocks, and a massy wooden table, hollowed out into a sort of basins, by way of kneading-troughs for pastry. The third doorway opened to a very small vaulted room, which was clearly the *wine-cellar*, for when wine was considered merely as a cordial, the stock was not very large. The fourth great arch conducted, by a great steep staircase, to a prodigious variety of small apartments, which, from their number and situation, seem to have been designed for the reception of guests and numerous retainers; there being others of still inferior sort in the rest of the house, for servants. Facing these arches, was a large carved wooden screen with two doorways which opened to the *great hall* or dining-room. This occupied the whole height of the building; at the upper end was a raised floor or platform, where the table for the lord and his principal guests was placed. Over one side of the hall, and also above the screen at the lower end, is a gallery supported by pillars.

From the reign of King Edward the First to that of Henry the Seventh, the houses among the middling class of people, were built of wood. They generally had large porches before their principal entrances. The framework was constructed of timber, of such enormous size, that the materials of one house would make several of equal size, according to the present mode of building. The common method of making walls was to nail laths to the timber frame, and strike them over with a rough plaster, which was afterwards whitened and ornamented with fine mortar, and this last was often beautified with figures of men and animals, and other curious devices.

The houses in cities and towns were built, each story jutting forth over the former story, so that when the streets were not very wide, the people at the top, from opposite houses, might not only talk with each other, but even shake hands together. The houses were covered with tiles, shingles, slates, or lead, excepting in the city of London, where shingles were forbidden.

Oxburgh Hall was erected by Sir Edmond Bedingfeld, A. D. 1482, and has ever since belonged to his descendants, being now the property of Sir Richard

Bedingfeld, Bart.   In a turret projecting from the east
tower is a curious hiding-place in the wall.   A door is
formed of a wooden frame filled with bricks, (the
whole building is constructed of brick,) thus looking
exactly like the face of the wall.   This door turns on
an iron axle fixed across the middle and inserted firmly
into the wall; by a forcible pressure on the lower end,
it turns, and discloses a solitary den, or cell, in the
turret.   It would never be discovered without previous
exact knowledge of its situation.   Another hiding-
place of equal ingenuity has been discovered beneath
a fire-place, at Oxburgh Hall.   "I apprehend," says
Lady Bedingfeld, "this hiding-place to have been
formed during the persecution of Catholic priests, as
many such places are to be found in old Catholic mansions."*

The rage for building in England, during the
fifteenth century, led to immense extravagance.   To
defray the expense of their splendid and capacious
mansions, noblemen sold or mortgaged large estates.
During this whole period, farm-houses and cottages
were mostly wretched hovels, hardly sufficient to protect the poor depressed serfs from the inclemencies of
cold, wet, and snow, to which the English climate is
subject.

---

* Britton's Architectural Antiquities of Great Britain.

CHAPTER XV.

EARLY in the fifteenth century, the genius of classic literature awoke from the long slumber of "the
dark ages." Classic Art was once more seated upon
her ancient throne, and northern taste was soon reduced into complete subjection to her imperial sceptre.

While the Florid Gothic was still carried to luxuriant
extravagance in England, the ancient Roman Architecture began to be studied by men of genius in Italy.

Fellippo Brunileschi, a Florentine, of an ardont
temperament and much original genius, is said to
have been delighted with the remains of ancient buildings at Rome. From careful study of them, he was
led to imitation, and in the Cathedral of Florence,
evinced his power of adapting the principles he had
learned from ancient art.

The examples of his works and the perusal of the
writings of Vitruvius, created a general taste for Classic Architecture. These circumstances were prepa-
ratory to the undertaking which fixed the epoch of this

revival, and gave to the world a temple, which, in magnitude and variety of parts, far surpasses every Grecian and Roman temple—the celebrated St. Peter's at
Rome. (Plate XX.) It would require a large volume for
a full description of this modern wonder of the world.

St. Peter's is situated on the ancient site of the circus
and gardens of Nero, where that tyrant massacred
numbers of Christian martyrs. Tradition says, that
the bodies of these martyrs were buried by their faithful friends, in a grotto near the circus, and that among
those who were thus buried here, was the crucified
Apostle, St. Peter. In 306, Constantine founded a
church over the reputed grave of the holy Apostle.
This edifice remained for eleven centuries, when Pope
Nicholas V., in 1450, demolished it, and laid the foundation for the present St. Peter's. At the death of this
Pope, the structure had been elevated only four or five
feet above the pavement. The work was suspended,
or made but little progress, till the time of Julius II.,
who, in 1503, employed the celebrated Bramanté to
carry on this great undertaking. This architect
formed the original plan of the cupola, and caused
four stupendous pillars, or piers, two hundred and
nine feet in circumference, to be raised to support it.
The patron and the architect both died and left it in
this state.

Leo X. employed architects to carry on the work,
among whom was the celebrated painter, Raphael
d'Urbino, who strengthened the basis of the pillars,

Plate XX

ST PETER'S CATHEDRAL ROME.

which he deemed too weak to support the stupendous
cupola.   Various other architects were employed by
the pontiffs who succeeded Leo, until at last, Paul III.
committed the edifice to the incomparable genius of
Michael Angelo Buonarotti, who designed the dome
and cupola as they now stand.   He wished to make the
front like the Pantheon, but death removed him from
his labours, and the sublime idea was abandoned.
Michael Angelo, "left it an unfinished monument of
his proud, towering, gigantic powers; and his awful
genius," seemed to watch over his successors for a
long time.   Many other artists were employed upon
this stupendous edifice, until it was finished, under
Paul V., by Carlo Maderno.   Three centuries and a
half this church was being built; and 'in 1694, the
cost was estimated to have been 11,000,000 pounds
sterling, or about 49,728,000 dollars!

This edifice contains the best specimens of design
of the ablest architects who flourished during a period
in which the revived Classic style was carried to the
highest perfection which it reached in Italy.   The
extreme length of St. Peter's is seven hundred and
twenty feet; breadth, five hundred and ten feet; height,
from the pavement to the top of the cross upon the
cupola, five hundred feet.

The magnificent front is entirely of *travertino*.
Beautiful colonnades of white marble, fifty feet high,
encircle a paved court in front, in the centre of which
stands an Egyptian obelisk, and on each side a foun-

tain.   These colonnades are finely proportioned to the
church, and form a grand enclosure, which serves as a
screen to exclude all ignoble objects.   There rises the
lofty façade, composed of eight Corinthian pillars and
four corresponding pilasters; five doors, seven balconies, six niches, an entablature with its frontispiece,
and an attic, terminated by a balustrade, over which
are thirteen colossal statues, representing Jesus Christ
and the twelve Apostles.   The columns appear small
at a distance, but on a near approach are found to be
nine feet in diameter, and including pedestal, base,
and capital, one hundred feet high.   The great cupola,
and two smaller ones, (large enough for the single
cupolas of elegant churches,) at the sides, accord well
with the front.   The five grand doors, with marble
columns and entablatures, open into an immense porch
decorated with marble pilasters.   The central door is
of bronze, adorned with bas-relief, representing the
martyrdom of St. Paul and St. Peter.   One of the
doors is opened only on the day of the Grand Jubilee;
that is, once in twenty-five years, and is hence called
Porta Santa, or Holy Door.   The columns of this door
are of rare antique marble, and those of the others are
of violet and other beautiful marbles.   Nothing can be
more striking, than the perfect harmony and just proportions which prevail throughout this complicated
edifice.   When we consider how many pontiffs or-
dered, and how many architects planned, it is wonderful that the structure should have kept its proportions

inviolate, even to the meanest ornament. Forsyth, a severe critic, has remarked upon the attic, the front, and the Latin cross, as contrary to what he calls "the sacred unity of the master-idea;" but less acute, or less fault-finding critics, are willing to pass over the trifling defects which probably exist in some of the subordinate parts. We now come to the interior. This is in the form of a Latin cross, but has *three* naves. Corinthian pilasters of white marble, seventy-seven feet high, support an entablature around the whole interior. Arches, niches, statues, pictures, gilt-stucco, bronze, marbles of all colours, porphyry, alabaster, mosaics, in short, all that wealth can furnish, or art employ, have been used in decorating this splendid temple. "The nave is infinitely grand and sublime, without the aid of obscurity ; but the eye, having only four pillars to rest on, runs along it too rapidly to comprehend its full extent."

Upon these stupendous pillars reposes the incomparable dome. This is the concave of the wonderful cupola, planned by Michael Angelo, one of the boldest attempts of architectural skill. Its base is two hundred feet above the surface of the earth, and then it rises, with its lantern and cross, about three hundred feet higher. The diameter of this dome is only two feet less than that of the Pantheon ; the walls are double, (twenty-two feet thick,) and between the two walls are stairs leading to *the ball* on the top, which seems from the ground the size of an orange, but is in reality nine feet in diameter, and can hold sixteen persons, at the same time.	This staircase is lighted by small dormer windows, pierced through the outer wall of the dome. The cupola is decorated with thirty-two Corinthian columns, in pairs, between which are sixteen windows. There are beautiful chapels attached to this mighty building, and grottoes and tombs under its pavement.

St. Peter's nowhere so strikingly unfolds its dimensions, as on the roof.	Here are houses, one might almost say streets, occupied by various persons employed about the building, and in keeping it in repair. Here rise four cupolas, besides the great cupola, which, seen from the roof, seems itself an immense circular temple, ornamented with rich sculpture, seen usually by no eye but that of the passing bird.

No architecture ever surpassed, in effect, the interior of this pile, when illuminated at Easter, by a single cross of lamps, suspended from the centre of the dome. All travellers dwell with enthusiasm upon the glory of this scene.	Forsyth exclaims : " What fancy was ever so dull, or so disciplined, or so worn, as to resist the enthusiasm of such a scene!	I freely abandoned mine to its illusions!"

> " But lo! the dome—the vast and wondrous dome,
> To which Diana's marvel* was a cell—
> Christ's mighty shrine above his martyr's tomb !
> I have beheld the Ephesian's miracle,—

---

* The Temple of Diana at Ephesus.

Plate XXI

Its columns strew the wilderness, and dwell
The hyæna and jackall in their shade ;
I have beheld Sophia's* bright roofs swell
Their glittering mass i' the sun ; and have surveyed
Its sanctuary the while the usurping Moslem prayed.

But thou, of temples old, or altars new,
Standest alone—with nothing like to thee—
Enter ; its grandeur overwhelms thee not,
And why ? it is not lessened ; but thy mind,
Expanded by the genius of the spot,
Has grown colossal.—

Thou movest, but increasing with the advance,
Like climbing some great Alp, which still doth rise,
Deceived by its gigantic elegance—
Vastness which grows—but grows to harmonize—
All musical in its immensities :
Rich marbles—richer painting—shrines where flame
The lamps of gold—and haughty dome which vies
In air with earth's structures, though their frame
Sits on the firm-set ground, and this the clouds must claim.

St. Paul's Cathedral, in London, (Plate XXI.) though inferior in size and richness to St. Peter's, is a magnificent edifice. " The first stone," says the architect, Sir Christopher Wren, " was laid in 1675, and the works carried on with such care and industry, that by the year 1685, the walls of the choir and the side aisles were finished, with the north and south

---

* The mosque, formerly the church of St. Sophia, at Constantinople.

porticoes, and the great pillars of the dome brought to the same height; and it pleased God, in his mercy, to bless the surveyor (architect) with health and length of days, and to enable him to complete the whole structure in the year 1710, to the glory of his holy name, and promotion of his divine worship, *the principal ornament of the imperial seat of this realm.*"

"Thus was this mighty fabric, the second church for grandeur in Europe, in the space of thirty-five years, begun and finished by one architect, and under one Bishop of London, Dr. Henry Compton."

St. Paul's is five hundred feet in length, two hundred and fifty in breadth, and its height, from the pavement to the top of the cross, is three hundred and sixty-six feet. Height of the central nave to the top of the arch, eighty-five feet. Height from the pavement to the top of the interior dome, two hundred and eighteen feet.

The Grecian orders of architecture are mingled in St. Paul's. The principal columns on the exterior are Corinthian; then there are composite columns and pilasters. St. Paul's is decidedly an imitation of St. Peter's, and it is considered a successful one, producing upon the beholder the emotion of beauty and sublimity.

Brunileschi and Bramanté, fully imbued with enthusiasm inspired by the arts of the ancients, of which they had so many examples before them that are lost to us, established a style, as perfectly pure and consistent in all its parts, as it was distinct from either the Gothic or all that we know of the Roman. This was the style called the *cinquecento*. With all the great models of antiquity before them, these great architects only took such features as were in accordance with the buildings they erected; they were not seduced by the splendour of those noble columns, with their glorious acanthus crown, to insert them where they were not required; they did not imitate the portico, nor were they led away by the grandeur of the noble pediment. Full of the poetic feelings of the great artist, their models only served them to form new and original combinations.

The entrance and the windows were made the principal vehicles for ornament; and since palaces were no longer required to be fortresses, the window assumed its proper dimensions, and admitted that light freely into the apartments of a dwelling, which the fierce character of earlier times had long obliged them for safety, to exclude. The example in the margin, of one of the graceful windows of Bramanté, is from the Palazzo Giraud, Rome. (Fig. 32.)

Fig. 32.

Their works might serve, with some alterations, as models for our own times. Raphael and Giulio Romano, painters as well as architects, although they adopted the *cinquecento* style, reduced it to greater severity.

Michael Angelo introduced the first confusion into this style, by employing Corinthian or Ionic columns with their entablatures, for supports of a cornice and pediment above a window. One improvement he made upon the cinquecento, by the introduction of a rich cornice as a final crown to a building,—a feature which Gothic architects never understood; and this feature forms one of the leading ornaments in street architecture at the present day.

In France, a change was effected from the Gothic by the introduction of classical features, which produced a mode known as "la goût de la renaissance." This style approximated to the Roman in all its features, and was much admired afterwards both in England and on the continent. "*La Renaissance,*" as it is called, is again a favourite among architects, although considered unequal in purity to the cinquecento. About the same period, the first innovation was made upon the Gothic in England, which gradually produced the Elizabethan, which will be more particularly described hereafter.

Sir Christopher Wren subsequently introduced into England some works of a domestic character, which possessed claims to originality.

In France too, Le Brun, the painter, designed some buildings in what has been termed the Louis Quatorze style. It is capable of great richness of decoration, though its ornamental details possess little claim to

good taste or distinct meaning.   The architecture of
the reign of William and Mary, and that of the reign
of Anne, contained a strong admixture of the taste of
the Louis Quatorze.*

---

* Architectural Magazine, Vol. V.

CHAPTER XVI.

PRESENT STATE OF ARCHITECTURE IN EUROPE.

WE shall not enter into a minute investigation of the present state of the art in Europe; a few remarks on this part of our subject must suffice. "It is pretty generally admitted, among those who can boast of freedom from prejudice, that Paris outstrips London in the taste and magnificence of its public buildings. The *Arc de Triomphe*, the *Hôtel des Ministres*, the *Madeleine Church*, and the *Bourse* (in Paris), are fearful odds against that strange pile of waste and folly, Buckingham Palace, and the National Gallery in Charing Cross (in London). There are few Frenchmen who do not feel strong emotions of pride and enthusiasm, as he views these monuments, which, in addition to their individual interest, contribute to his national glory. Can an Englishman feel similar exultation as he surveys the public edifices of his capital? Undoubtedly he can, if he go back to the days of Wren; but his food for self-congratulation will be small indeed, if he confine himself to the structures that have risen up in his own day. The truth is, the genius to conceive, the patience to execute, and the mental culture to value *grand* architectural designs, seem dead in England.

"The few buildings raised of late years are not only deficient in the grand, but they are for the most part built in a style remarkable for its violation of established rule, and correct taste.   Many of the new churches that *adorn* the streets of the British metropolis vie with each other in curious absurdity.

"One of the most important principles in architecture, is, that a building should be adapted in its form and internal economy to its uses, and harmonize in its ornaments with the spirit of its destination.   Yet how utterly has it been lost sight of, in the construction of those modern churches! If an extravagantly grotesque and ludicrous exterior be adapted to the solemnity of such duties as are performed within their walls, their architects have succeeded marvellously well; if the internal arrangement of our churches should be such that a large portion of those assembled within them, to listen to the word of God, hear no more of it than they would in a Turkish mosque, then the designers are admirable artists.

"But we are told, these are imitations from the antique; they are copied from structures that have borne the brunt of critical severity for ages.   True, they *are* imitations, but in this is 'the very head and front of their offending.'   Can it rationally be supposed, that the light, airy style of architecture which suited the cloudless sky, and burning sun of Greece, should be fitted for the eternal rain, and the harsh clouds of a northern land? This want of keeping between the character of the architecture, and the physical condition of the country is, perhaps, its gravest fault.

" We shall not stop to inquire into the *cause* of the architectural degeneracy in England, (we believe its *existence* a fact that cannot have escaped the notice of the most dull-witted philanderer of the streets of London,) nor to refute the ingenious, but sophistical reasoning of a London periodical, which attributes it to the vitiating influence of the aristocracy. But without ascribing undue weight to the masses, we may venture to predict, that so long as popular indifference on the subject exists, the architecture of the metropolis will pursue its downward course to insignificance. It is by an *appeal to the people*, that the removal of the evil is to be hoped for."*

Great efforts are, however, being made at present in England, to effect improvement in the art. A writer in the Westminster Review, Vol. XL., in an able article, entitled " Practical Considerations for the Promotion of British Architecture," remarks as follows:

" We rejoice to notice the disposition evinced in the higher classes to extend the cultivation of the Fine Arts among all classes of people, by means of national education. This is beginning at the right end. In

---

* Edinburgh Magazine.

the useful arts we have not our equals; but set a country carpenter to sketch a plan for a rustic lodge, and the result would scarcely be a production which a native of New Zealand could not excel.

"Great opposition has been made in the majority of our free schools to the introduction of drawing classes for teaching the elementary principles of design. Ignorant persons suppose they are required only as accomplishments unsuitable for the poor; but who can calculate the influence upon the progress of a national architecture, from conferring upon every poor lad the ability to sketch a picturesque cottage, such as he might one day be able to build for himself, as an improvement upon his father's cabin? And, after all, how small, comparatively, is the effect produced upon the general aspect of a country by a few elegant villas or mansions, although erected in the most correct taste! For any one of these, we see, perhaps, fifty small houses springing up almost in a night for working men and humble tradesmen, possessing no one architectural feature upon which the eye can rest with pleasure. We must change the character of these structures, before we can boast of a national architecture."

The Church Extension Society has done much towards improving ecclesiastical edifices. All over England, churches, most of them in the Gothic style, have been recently erected. The new church at Reigate, Surrey, is a fair specimen of these modern Gothic structures. The octagonal tower and spire are remarkable for simplicity and lightness. The church is in all respects most substantially built. Throughout the building, the architect has adopted, for the most part, the forms which began to prevail early in the fifteenth century. (Plate XXII.)

The people of England are manifesting at present great interest in public schools,—parish schools especially. They are improving their school-houses in convenience and beauty. The writer last quoted says the rage for the Elizabethan style is such, that "if a school-house were not erected in this style, it would with many persons go far to prove that the Bible was not taught there." He gives as one of the most pleasing structures of these fashionable Elizabethan school-houses, one of the Brompton schools. Judging from the exterior, the interior arrangement might be rendered very convenient. "The architecture of the period of Elizabeth has strictly no style of its own. But by Elizabethan forms are generally understood those which began to prevail in the century preceding the Reformation and the dissolution of the monasteries by Henry VIII.," belonging to what correctly should be called the early Tudor style, or Perpendicular Pointed Gothic.

In Germany architecture has become a regal amusement, at least we infer the fact, from the following description of the Palace of the King of Bavaria, at Munich.

Plate XXII

"The exterior of the building is plain, but has an air of grandeur even from its simplicity and uniformity. It reminds me of Sir Philip Sidney's beautiful description. 'A house built of fair and strong stone; not affecting so much any extraordinary kind of fineness as an honourable representing of a *firm stateliness*; all more lasting than beautiful, but that the consideration of the exceeding lastingness, made the eye believe it was exceeding beautiful.'"

When a selfish despot designs a palace, it is for himself he builds. He thinks first of his own personal tastes and peculiar habits, and the arrangements are contrived to suit his exclusive propensities.

Thus, for Nero's overwhelming pride, no height, no space, could suffice, so he built his "Golden House" upon a scale which obliged its next possessor to pull it to pieces, as only fit to lodge a Colossus. George the Fourth had a predilection for low coilings, so all the future inhabitants of Pimlico Palace must endure suffocation. The commands which the King of Bavaria gave De Klenze, (the architect,) were in a different spirit. "Build me a palace, in which nothing within or without shall be of transient fashion or interest; a palace for my posterity and my people, as well as myself; of which the decorations shall be durable as well as splendid, and shall appear one or two centuries hence as pleasing to the eye and taste as they do now." "Upon this principle," said De

Klenze, looking round, "I designed what you now see."

On the first floor are the apartments of the king and queen, all facing the south; a parallel range of apartments behind, contains accommodations for the ladies of honour, chamberlains, &c.; a grand staircase on the east leads to the apartments of the king, another on the west to those of the queen, the two suites of apartments uniting in the centre. All the chambers allotted to the king's use are painted with subjects from the Greek poets, and those of the queen from the German poets.

We began with the king's apartments. The staircase is beautiful, but simple, consisting of a flight of wide, broad steps of the native marble; there is no gilding; the ornaments on the ceiling represent the different arts and manufactures carried on in Bavaria. Over the door which opens into the apartments, is the king's motto, "JUST AND FIRM." Two caryatides support the entrance; these figures are colossal.

1. *The first antechamber*, is decorated with great simplicty.

2. *The second antechamber*, is less simple in its decoration. The frieze around the top of this chamber is about three feet wide, and represents the Theogony, the wars of the Titans, &c., from Hesiod. The figures are in outline and tinted, but without relief, in the manner of some of the ancient Greek paintings on vases.

3. *A saloon* or reception-room, for those who are to be presented to the king. On this room, which is in a manner public, the utmost luxury of decoration is to be expended, but it is yet unfinished.

4. *The throne-room.* The decorations of this room combine in an extraordinary degree, the utmost splendour with the utmost elegance. The whole is adorned with bas-reliefs in white stucco, raised upon a ground of dead gold. The gilding of this room alone, cost 72,000 florins.

5. *A saloon or antechamber.* The ceiling and walls admirably painted, from the tragedies of Æschylus.

6. *The king's study;* painted with subjects from Sophocles. In the arch at one end of this room are seven compartments, in which are inscribed, in gold letters, the sayings of the seven Greek sages.

7. *The king's dressing-room.* Painted with subjects from Aristophanes.

8. *The king's bed-room.*

No description could give an adequate idea of the endless variety and graceful and luxuriant ornament, harmonizing with various subjects and the purpose of each room, and lavished on the walls and ceilings even to infinitude.

The queen's apartments are equally numerous, rich, and beautiful.

The dining-room is exceedingly elegant. Now it must be remembered that these seventeen rooms form the domestic apartments of the royal family; and magnificent as they are, a certain elegance, cheerfulness, and propriety has been more consulted than parade and grandeur; but on the ground floor, there is a suite of state apartments, prepared for the reception of strangers on great and festive occasions, and these excited my admiration *more than all the rest together.* This suite of apartments is ornamented with a series of splendid paintings in fresco, the subjects of which are taken from a German epic poem called the Nibelungen Lied. The walls of the apartments are immensely high, and upon the sides and ceilings ample space is left for these splendid paintings.

The unfinished chapel adjoining the new palace reminded me, in the general effect, of the interior of St. Mark's, at Venice; but of course the details are executed in a grander feeling and in a much higher style of art. The pillars are of the native marble, and the walls will be covered with a kind of Mosaic of various marbles, intermixed with ornaments in relief, in gilding and in colours—all combined and harmonizing together. The ceiling is formed of two large domes, or cupolas.

I learn that the king's *passion for building,* and the forced encouragement given to the enlargement and decoration of his capital, have been carried to an excess, and, like all extremes, has proved mischievous, at least for the time. *He has rendered it too much a fashion among his subjects, who are suffering from rash speculations of this kind.* A suite of beautiful unfurnished apartments, and even a pretty house in the finest part of Munich, may be hired for a trifle. Some of these new houses are enormous. Madame M—— told me that she has her whole establishment on one floor, but then she has *twenty-three rooms*. This is indeed the extravagance of architecture; and it appears, after all, from the foregoing description, that the splendour of the interior of German buildings is mostly produced by painting and gilding. The immense size and the comparative simplicity of the buildings prove, however, the great superiority of the art in Germany to its present state in England. It is, perhaps, the "golden age" of art in Germany, to which England has not yet arrived.

No order has yet been added to Architecture by modern Europe. The three Grecian orders, and the variations from them, called the Roman orders,—the Tuscan and Composite, remain the sole established orders. Almost all buildings of any pretension are built according to these orders, or follow the Gothic style.

In Russia, the beautiful Gothic style has never been prevalent. But few traces of it are to be seen in Moscow, of a later date than twenty years; and there is not a single fine building in this style in St. Petersburg.

For many years past, both Moscow and St. Petersburg have been well supplied with the most able Italian architects. The numerous models they have given of elegant taste and style, have drawn forth the eulogies of travellers, especially in these capitals of Russia, two of the noblest cities on the globe.

The *Græco-Italian* style must at first have been modified by the climate of Russia. But the architects, having acquired the art of counteracting severe cold by extremely thick walls, and excellent stoves, were left to the free exercise of taste, as in the more genial clime of Italy. In these days, the interior of the mansions of the nobles is so arranged that the visiter might conceive himself at Rome.

For ecclesiastical architecture, the Grecian style, modified and ornamented afterwards by the Italians, has ever prevailed, and still prevails in Russia. A few exceptions, of edifices which are not reducible to any known style, cannot affect this general conclusion. One ornament of the Russian churches, which is almost universal, has excited the attention and curiosity of all travellers. We allude to their *bulbous domes*, or domes of the shape of an *onion*. Dr. Lyall thinks these domes came from the East, where they are very common ornaments at present, and is of opinion that their *pagan* derivation is extremely plausible. The learned doctor's conjecture with regard to their origin seems more amusing than satisfactory. He says, "The Egyptians worshipped *onions*, and perhaps the same practice may have been common among others of the oriental nations; and as it is natural to elevate any object to which reverence or adoration is paid, it is probable that onions, and these onion-shaped bodies, may have been placed upon pillars to receive homage, and afterwards were continued merely as ornaments, in consequence of their agreeable figure, and their adaptation as the summits of towers; and from thence became the embellishment of sacred temples."

A popular traveller from our own country writes of the famous Kremlin at Moscow, as follows: "I had thought of it as the rude and barbarous palace of the Czars; but I found it one of the most extraordinary, beautiful, and magnificent objects I ever beheld. Its high and venerable walls; its numerous battlements and towers, and steeples; its magnificent and gorgeous palaces; its cathedrals, churches, monasteries, and belfries, with their gilded, coppered, and tin-plated domes; its mixture of barbarism and decay, magnificence and ruins; its strong contrast of architecture, including the Tartarian, Hindoo, Chinese, and Gothic; all together exhibited a beauty, grandeur, and magnificence, strange and indescribable. The Kremlin is two miles in extent, and is in itself a city. I shall not attempt to describe the palaces of the Czars. They are a combination of every variety of taste and every order of architecture, Grecian, Italian, &c., &c.; rude, fanciful, grotesque, gorgeous, magnificent, and beautiful." The same traveller says: "I do not believe that Rome, when Adrian reared the mighty Coliseum, and the Palace of the Cæsars covered the Capitoline Hill, exhibited such a range of noble structures as the Admiralty

Quarter, (St. Petersburg.) The Admiralty itself is the central point, and has a façade of marble, with ranges of columns, a quarter of a mile in length. A beautiful golden (gilded) spire shoots up from the centre, towering over every other object, and seen from every other part of the city, glittering in the sun; and three principal streets, each two miles in length, radiate from this point. In front is a range of boulevards, ornamented with trees, and an open square, at one extremity of which stands the great church of St. Isaac, of marble, jasper, and porphyry, upon a foundation of granite. On the right of the façade stands the well-known equestrian statue of Peter the Great. The huge block of granite forming the pedestal is fifteen hundred tons in weight."

The great Alexandrine column, on the other side of this splendid square, is described as rivalling those magnificent monuments in the Old World, whose ruins now startle the wandering traveller, and towering to the heavens as if to proclaim that the days of architectural greatness are not gone by for ever. It is a single shaft of red granite, exclusive of pedestal and capital, eighty-four feet high. The pedestal contains the simple inscription, "To Alexander I. Grateful Russia." Surrounding this, is a crescent of lofty buildings, having before it a majestic colonnade, of the Corinthian order. In the middle is a triumphal arch, which with its frieze reaches nearly to the upper part of the lofty edifice, having a span of seventy feet. Next, on a line with the Admiralty, stands the first of a long range of imperial palaces, extending in the form of a crescent for more than a mile along the Neva. The Winter Palace is a gigantic and princely structure, built of marble, with a façade of seven hundred and forty feet. Next, are the two palaces of the Hermitage, connected with it, and with each other, by covered galleries on bold arches. Next, the stately Grecian Theatre of the Hermitage. Beyond this are the barracks of the guards; then, the palace of the French Ambassador; then the marble palace built by Catherine II., for her favourite, Prince Orloff. This magnificent range, presenting an uninterrupted front of marble palaces upwards of a mile in length, is unequalled in any city of the world." Thus much, for the present state of architecture in Russia.

In Italy, Spain, and Portugal, no recently built edifices can compare in beauty and magnificence with those of former ages.

14

CHAPTER XVII.

PRINCIPLES OF ARCHITECTURE.

THE leading principle in Architecture is fitness for the end designed. Utility, convenience, and propriety are included in the term fitness.

In order to carry out this principle in the erection of any edifice, several things must be taken into consideration; namely—

To what purpose the building is to be devoted.

How it may be constructed at the least expense.

How it may be rendered strong and enduring.

How it may be made beautiful.

Every edifice should have a distinctive character, derived from the use to which it is to be applied. For example, in a building for large public assemblies, the main objects to be gained are the following:

To contain within a given space the greatest number of individuals, conveniently placed for seeing and hearing.

That ingress and egress be effected without difficulty.

That a free circulation of air be enjoyed.

That it be sufficiently lighted.

That it be constructed strongly and of durable materials, that no danger ensue from weight and pressure.

If any one of these conditions be neglected, the building is faulty.

In every dwelling-house, the main objects are as follows:

That a given number of persons be accommodated with convenient apartments for eating, sleeping, bathing, &c.

That these apartments be rendered warm in winter, and cool in summer.

That they be well lighted and ventilated.

That access to these apartments be easy and convenient.

From the cottage to the palace, these are essential requisites in every building designed as a habitation for man. In order that fitness be complete, all the subordinate parts of a building,—doors, windows, fireplaces, staircases, chimneys, &c., must be well distributed and arranged. When a building is thus constructed, the effect of the whole will be, that it is *fit* for the end in view.

But, in addition to this kind of fitness, Architecture goes farther, and produces what is termed *expression* of fitness; that is, it gives a definite character to every building, so that it appears to be what it really is. A dwelling-house should not be so constructed that its *expression* should be that of a bank or a state-house;— a stable should not resemble a dwelling-house for man;

—a church should not look like a barn—neither should a barn be ornamented with Gothic windows, battlements, and turrets. A jail should not have the light and airy expression of a place of amusement, but a heavy, sombre, gloomy expression. "The beauty of truth is so essential to every other kind of beauty, that it can neither be dispensed with in art nor in morals." Architecture has become an ornamental art when expression is thus given by it to every kind of building.

A church should be characterized by noble and sublime simplicity, inspiring awe and devotion.

We have no *royal* residences in the United States, but the President's house, belonging, as it does, to the nation, should have an expression of magnificence, inspiring admiration and respect.

A monument, designed to transmit to posterity memorable events in history, or the high deeds of heroic men, ought to indicate, independent of its sculptures and inscriptions, the purpose for which it is designed. A dwelling-house should have its peculiar character expressed; the city mansion—the villa—the ornamented cottage—the farm-house, should each befit the station of its occupant, and convey the idea of propriety, neatness, and home-enjoyment.

When *fitness for the end in view*, and the *expression of appropriateness* are effected, a building may be considered complete. In order to accomplish this result, and, moreover, to render it perfectly pleasing to the eye, it must have *proportion* and a due degree of *orna-*

ment. Without *proportion,* (which, if analyzed, might be found to result from *fitness,*) the richest and most elaborately ornamented building can never be pleasing to the eye; and a building entirely unornamented may be so perfectly symmetrical in its proportions as to excite the emotion of beauty.

" Proportion," says Vitruvius, " is a due adjustment of the size of the different parts to each other, and to the whole: on this proper adjustment symmetry depends. This is as necessary to a building as to a well-formed human figure."

Walls should be proportioned in thickness and height to the weight they have to support; windows to the size of the building; columns to the entablature; colonnades to the edifice; porticoes to the doorway; height should be in proportion to the breadth. If a building is one among a row of other buildings, it will bear to be narrow in comparison with its height, because its width does not appear, and because it seems supported by the adjoining buildings. These, and many other things, go to make up *proportion,* and produce the impression of symmetrical beauty.

Ornament must be suited to the general character of a building, or it destroys the proper expression. It has been questioned whether ornament can be beautiful, unless it convey the idea of utility. The only utility that we can discover in many things, is the pleasure given to the senses. Ornament in architecture, is not always associated with utility, yet who can doubt that it is pleasing to the eye of taste? But, the ornamental parts of a building must be perfectly symmetrical, or they do not add to its beauty.

The different orders of architecture, have different characters, requiring each its peculiar ornaments.

"The Tuscan is distinguished by its severity; the Doric by its simplicity; the Ionic by its elegance; the Corinthian and Composite by their lightness and gaiety. To these characters their ornaments are suited with consummate taste. Change these ornaments; give to the Tuscan the Corinthian capital, or to the Corinthian the Tuscan, and every person would feel, not only a disappointment from this unexpected composition, but a sentiment also of impropriety, from the appropriation of a grave or sober ornament, to a subject of severity."*

Several very important considerations render the rectangular form most suitable for buildings in general. Contrasted with the straight lines and right angles of an edifice, the flowing and curved lines of ornaments have a pleasing effect. Such are volutes, foliage, and mouldings. In the earliest specimens of Grecian Architecture, the exterior of buildings was but little ornamented; the Doric order was only relieved from the entire sameness of straight lines and right angles, by the bold ovolo that forms the capital. Sculptured figures of men and animals, oxen's heads, and vessels used in sacrifice, appear upon the metopes and pedi-

---

* Alison on Taste.

ments of Doric edifices of a later period. The Ionic is varied with numerous flowing and curved lines; and an exuberance of foliage and flowers ornaments the Corinthian. These exquisite forms complete the beauty of a building.

" A magnificent and appropriate edifice," says the learned Britton, " is the noblest, the most important, and the most transcendent work of man: when nearest to a state of perfection, it exhibits his genius, science, and talents, in a proud and dignified point of view; for such a building is the master-piece of human invention and elaborate operation."

The economy and strength of buildings depend mostly upon the materials of which they are composed: these should be chosen with judgment, used with care, and put together with skill.

An architect should understand perfectly before he commences a building, what sum of money is to be devoted to it; then he must employ it in the best possible manner. For this purpose he must know the quality and force of all building materials; these are stones of all kinds, (natural and artificial,*) woods, metals, and cements.

If the *means* afforded him will allow him to build of granite, without sacrificing size or convenience, he would be, not only unwise, but dishonest, to build of wood. Granite, however, might not be as suitable for

---

* Brick and tiles, may be called artificial stones.

the required purpose, as marble or freestone. The diversity of circumstances, for which an architect's skill is put in requisition, will enable him in time to judge of the resources of his own country, and apply them to the best possible advantage.

The architects of this country, or rather their employers, have shown a great want of true economy, in employing perishable materials for large buildings. An architect might better refuse to build at all, than to sacrifice his reputation, by constructing a *plaster model* for a building, instead of a building, properly so called. His duty to himself, as well as to his country, demands that the public edifices that he plans and builds should not, in the course of ten or twenty years, be in a ruinous condition, and the laughing-stock of the community. A fault into which architects in this country are in danger of falling, is *affectation*. An ostentatious display of *simplicity* in style, often produces affectation.

But a more common kind of affectation arises from a close and literal imitation of a grand style for ordinary buildings. This has been amusingly described by an old writer as follows: "One builder, smitten forsooth with the beauty of the old Roman manner, raises himself a house, having the outward semblance of a temple of some pagan god; and to accomplish this whimsy, he shows a door only in its best front, and it is well if a pair of windows is to be seen in any of the others; and these, mayhap, so placed, as if he were ashamed to show to the passers by that he must have the sweet light of heaven to enliven some pendicle of his dwelling. Another, humbler withal, but equally touched with the leprosy of affectation, aping his betters, must needs garnish his thatched grange with battlements. A third, will so beplaster his mud walls with griffins and lions, and stick crockets on pinnacles, and pinnacles on juttings, that it were a hard matter to find a space ample enough to write *fool* upon, in letters no bigger than those of the good Bishop Latimer's Bible. And a fourth, who, like the mole, seems to live in the world without eyes, is contented to burrow in a house so bare of becoming and seemly ornament, that when we behold it, we cannot stay feeling ' that, in truth, the affectedness of plain building is as noisome as any of the others.'

" There are some buildings which are calculated only for a distant view ; for though, when beheld afar off, they may please, yet no sooner do we come up to them, than we discover them to be greatly inferior to what they first promised to be. The spell is broken, nor is it to be renewed ; because, when we again look at them from a favourable distance, we are aware of the illusion. There is no further any room for imagining beauties in store for us on nearer examination, which we already know do not exist.

" The power of architecture, as a fine art, manifests itself only in æsthetic effect. Effect is its alpha and omega. The first requisite in the art, is effect; the second, is effect; the third, is effect.   It is necessary, therefore, that an architect should understand the æsthetic department of his art thoroughly, be master of its picturesque power, and be able to combine and invent; and also, that he should be well versed in all that comes under the head of decoration.

"Like the bee, an architect should be able to extract his nutriment, that is, the *hyle* or material of his art, from the most varied sources, afterwards concocting it into something altogether his own.   He should study not only what is acknowledged to be beautiful, but the contrary also, and that for a double purpose; first, that, by understanding deformity, he may know how to avoid it, and so profit by the bad taste of others; and secondly, that he may search whether there be any latent germ of beauty concealed beneath ugliness.   Even as the ' toad wears a precious jewel in his head,' so will many a barbarous design be found to contain something valuable; valuable at least to him who knows how to turn it to account, and to purify and exalt the base ore into sterling metal.   Plagiarisms of this kind are not only excusable, but glorious; they constitute the triumphs of art.   In such a process lies its genuine alchemy."*

---

* Architectural Magazine, 1838.

CHAPTER XVIII.

QUALIFICATIONS FOR AN ARCHITECT.

In order to rise to eminence in art, *genius* is indispensable. By study and practice, a man of ordinary talents may become a good *builder;* he may understand his art, so far as it relates to the necessaries and conveniences of life; but something more is requisite to raise him to the rank of an artist,—on the same level with the poet, painter, sculptor, and musician.

In ancient times, men of royal birth and of noble parentage became architects. This only proves the estimation in which the art was held; they who were neither royal nor noble by birth, were raised by genius to equal dignity and honour with those who possessed this adventitious superiority. Genius is true nobility. In our country we *profess* reverence for no superiority, but that which every man may acquire, by his virtues and his talents. It is ridiculous pretension for a man who has had just education and "calculation" enough to scrape together, "by hook or by crook," some thousands or millions of dollars, to look down upon the man of genius and education, who plans his spacious mansion, adorns its walls with glowing landscapes, or lays upon his drawing-room tables

"Thoughts that breathe and words that burn."

Such pretension could only be tolerated among a people but half-refined, where Mammon is the idol.

A man who intends to be an architect, should possess *ingenuity* and *mathematical talent,* and should receive an education with direct reference to the practice of his art.

He should be *ingenious.* Without this qualification, he might study the works of the most eminent artists, and become thoroughly imbued with a correct taste, but he would never be able to apply his knowledge and exercise his taste according to the varying wants of his own age and country. A man may have a certain dexterity of hand, which will enable him to perform skilfully some work of art, which another has planned for him, or given him an exact model to copy; but he is then only performing manual labour, and exercising the one faculty of imitation; if he can go no farther, he never will become a complete artist; he will never produce any work which will acquire for him a reputation, for his is not the master-mind. Architecture, through all its progress from infancy to perfection, is an *inventive* art.

An architect must be *practical.* He cannot live in a world of fancy, like the poet; he cannot copy nature in her loveliest aspects, like the painter; nor perfect nature in forms of surpassing beauty and grace, like the sculptor. He must render tasteful and beautiful that which is essential. In doing this, he must not speculate and theorize till he has lost sight of the main object in all his works, utility. Practical knowledge must make him acquainted with all that is best adapted to insure convenience, strength, and durability; and a constant regard to the end in view prevent him from sacrificing the substance to the shadow—fitness to factitious ornament. He must be practical, too, in order to gain respect and confidence. A theorist may be expert in drawing plans, and fill his studio with an endless variety, when only one good plan is needed; his own mind will wander amid this variety, without being able to make a choice. If this choice is at length made by another, the theorizing man has so many alterations and additions to make in carrying on the work, that he puzzles and vexes the men whom he employs, and loses their confidence, by seeming to have no plan at all in his own mind. He will not be an economical artist. In following out a favourite theory, little regard will be paid to expense, and probably, he will not be able to make an exact estimate, as he never knows when his plan is fixed; and besides, he has not the patience to examine into minute details.

A complete architect should be thoroughly educated, with special reference to his art. He should gain a good knowledge of arithmetic, mensuration, geometry, trigonometry, and algebra. He should be well acquainted with the history of mankind and the history of the arts. Drawing, he should learn with almost as much eagerness as if he were to be a painter. The most eminent architects have often been the best painters and sculptors of the age in which they lived. Perspective and projection he should carefully study, that he may know how a building will appear from every point of view. A knowledge of mechanical philosophy is indispensable—chemistry and mineralogy very desirable acquisitions, that he may know the relative strength and durability of all building materials.

Beside these acquirements, an architect should have his taste improved and refined by poetry and classic literature.

" Proficiency in the French and Italian languages," says Sir William Chambers, " is also requisite to him ; not only that he may be able to travel with advantage, and converse without difficulty, in countries where the chief part of his knowledge is to be collected, but also to understand the many books treating upon his profession, the greater part of which have never been translated."

With a due deference to the genius of the ancients, and a suitable admiration of their works, an American architect must possess the power to adopt what is suitable to our soil, climate, manners, civil institutions, and religion, without servile imitation.

An architect, who would produce beautiful works,

must be himself a severe critic upon his own designs; he must admit nothing definitely, without having submitted it to the most vigorous examination. His ingenuity and skill must not be entirely employed upon the exterior for self-glorification, while the interior is left inconvenient and ill-proportioned. In short, an architect should be governed by the strictest principles of integrity and rectitude.

From these few hints on the qualifications for an architect, it will be inferred, that his education should be commenced in boyhood, with special reference to the noble art which he is to practice. A lasting benefit would be conferred upon the country, if some of our young men, as soon as they evince talents for artists, were regularly and thoroughly educated for that purpose. Many young men, who now make the tour of Europe without any definite object in view, and with little advantage to themselves, thus prepared by previous education, might study the *chef-d'œuvres* of art in the cities and galleries of Europe, and return home with correct taste and skill in the Fine Arts, and moreover, with enthusiasm, which would render them admirable artists.

A report from the Select Committee on Arts, of the (British) House of Commons, thus terminates: "It will give your committee the sincerest gratification if the result of their inquiry, (in which they have been liberally assisted by the artists of this country,) tend in any degree to raise the character of a profession,

which is said to stand much higher among foreign
nations than our own; to infuse, even remotely, into
an industrious and enterprising people, a love of Art,
and to teach them to respect and venerate the name of
artist."

On the continent of Europe, there are "Schools of
Art," where young men are educated with special
reference to some particular branch of art. They
have nothing of the kind in England, neither have we
at present in this country. The sagacious statesman
Burke, long since regretted this deficiency in England. "If there be any one," says a writer in the
Edinburgh Review, "who, for the most effectual pro-
secution of his profession, requires the highest mental
cultivation, it is the artist. This would give rank and
honour to the profession. The known learning of
some of the professors has already, we think, been
beneficial."

In Bavaria there are no less than thirty-three schools
of Art. In France there are about eighty schools of
Art.

"The School of Art at Lyons, originated in a decree
of Bonaparte, dated from Warsaw. Its object was to
give elementary instruction in Art, with a view to the
improvement of the silk manufactures of France. But
its field of usefulness has widened from time to time,
and it is now divided into six principal departments;
1. Painting. 2. Architecture. 3. Ornament, and
mise en carte, (which is arranging patterns upon paper

for all kinds of fabrics.) 4. A Botanical Department.
5. Sculpture. 6. Engraving."

These schools in France are assisted by the state.
At Paris, 60,000 francs are yearly given to the Royal
School of Design. The course of study lasts for three
years, and the students pay five francs, (one dollar!)
for the first year, and ten francs, (two dollars!) for
each of the second and third. The schools of art in
Switzerland are regulated in a similar manner. At
Geneva the students pay the same as in Paris. Dr.
Bowring mentions that he found a *Chinese* at Geneva,
who had studied there three years in one of the schools
of art.

Why should not such schools be established in the
United States? If not supported, they might be aided
by the States where they were instituted. Like other
schools, they might in time sustain themselves; but at
the outset the expenses would be such, that a grant of
money from the Legislature would be needed, or aid
from patriotic men of wealth.

Something of this kind has been attempted in the
Academy of the Arts of Design, in New York, but on
a very different plan from the schools of art in Europe.

In our higher schools and academies, some elementary instruction in art might be introduced with great
advantage to pupils generally. In an enlightened
and refined nation, every man and woman should
know enough of the principles of architecture to en-

able them to order their houses to be built with due
reference to comfort and good taste. "The prize, as
well as the race, is set before us," says an able American writer, "and we have everything that can give
us hope. Whatever labour it may impose upon our
architects, to all other persons the means of success
are the easiest possible. We need scarcely more than
wish for it (good taste), and it will come. I will point
out the way. The artist who loads our edifices with
ornament, or multiplies the parts more than is necessary, is either ignorant of his art, or means to slight his
work and throw dust in our eyes, so as to blind us
to its defects. Let us begin, then, with requiring *simplicity* in our buildings. We shall soon have it; and
its immediate effect will be a powerful and favourable
action on our taste. Let us look for a moment at the
effect our demand for it will have on the architects
themselves. Finding it impossible to dazzle or bewilder the mind by factitious helps, they will from
necessity attempt beauty and power of design; their
taste will thus begin a course of discipline, and will
again act on ours. Mind will continue to operate on
mind; and then will arise among us men of pure and
lofty conceptions, who will scorn all tricks of art, and
whose taste will be content only when it makes each
object it touches an image of itself."

The same able writer says that an architect must
possess "a *taste* so well *disciplined* as to be able to
judge with instinctive certainty as regards beauty of

form ; and this taste must be exercised with unceasing industry in combining such forms and in trying their combinations. The Greeks were like other men, and came to perfection in architecture as men have come to perfection in other matters. We err most egregiously if we suppose them architects *by nature,* or that they gained their mighty power by folding their hands and waiting for hints in a happy dream, or even by profuse but idle admiration of the efforts of men from other countries. *They took the powers which nature gave them, and by unceasing culture brought them to the very highest perfection ; these they applied, and they succeeded ; others will succeed when they do all this, and not till then.*"

CHAPTER XIX.

ARCHITECTURE IN THE UNITED STATES, FROM
THE FIRST SETTLEMENT OF THE COUNTRY.

IN tracing the progress of the art in the United States, we are upon almost untrodden ground, where only a few faint footsteps can be discovered.

Although the first adventurers from England brought with them the knowledge of the arts of civilized and refined society, their situation for years was such as to preclude the exercise of these arts.

When the first colonists of Jamestown set sail for a harbour in Virginia, A. D. 1607, of the one hundred and five on the list of emigrants, there were but twelve labourers, and very few mechanics. "They were going to a wilderness, in which as yet not a house was standing, and there were forty-eight gentlemen to four carpenters." Their first employment was to fell timber for the erection of places of shelter, houses they could scarcely be termed. They might have received some hints for their rude architecture from the imperial residence of Powhatan.* Captain Newport,

---

* This native chieftain has been styled the "Emperor of the Country."

Captain John Smith, and twenty other colonists, soon after their landing at Jamestown, visited the principal residence of this renowned chieftain, near the site of the present city of Richmond; it consisted of twelve wigwams.

As might have been expected from the predominance of gentlemen over working-men, the colony was soon in a miserable condition. At first they were all compelled to labour; as Captain John Smith says, " Now falleth every man to worke; the Councell contrive the fort, the rest cut down trees to make place to pitch their tents; some provide clapboard to relode the ships, some make gardens, some nets, &c.;" but soon they became exceedingly idle.

Various calamities beset the colonists. Not long after they were established, an accidental fire destroyed nearly the whole of Jamestown. Smith says, " The towne, which being but thatched with reeds, the fire was so fierce as it burnt their pallisados, (though eight or ten yards distant,) with their armes, bedding, apparell, and much private provision. Good Master Hunt, our preacher, lost all his liberary, and all he had but the cloathes on his backe; yet none never heard him repine at his losse. This happened in the winter, in that extreme frost, 1607."

Famine followed, and continued dread of their savage foes.

Their scanty provisions had become spoiled on the long voyage. " Our drink," say they, " was unwholesome water; our lodgings, castles in the air." Despair of mind ensued ; so that, in less than a fortnight after the departure of the homeward-bound fleet, hardly ten of them were able to stand ; the labour of completing some simple fortifications was exhausting; and no regular crops could be planted. During the summer, there were not on any occasion five able men to guard the bulwarks. The fort was filled in every corner with the groans of the sick, whose outcries night and day for six weeks, rent the hearts of those who could minister no relief.*

Disunion and strife among the colonists, completed the scene of misery. Nothing but the favour of God, through the instrumentality of the brave and enterprising Smith, saved the colony from entire destruction.†

It was a long time before sad experience taught the mother country the necessity of sending colonists who were hardy men, skilled in mechanical arts, and accustomed to labour.

" When you send againe," wrote the indefatigable Smith, "rather send but thirty carpenters, husband-men, gardeners, fishermen, blacksmiths, masons, and diggers-up of trees-roots, well provided, than a thousand such as we have ; for except wee be able both to lodge them, and feed them, the most will consume with want of necessaries, before they can be made good for anything."

---

* Bancroft.

† His friend, the youthful Pocahontas, who saved his life, is called by one of the early historians, the Numparell (nonpareil) of Virginia.

Thus, struggling with ten thousand difficulties, the indomitable spirit of Smith at length succeeded in placing the colony upon a firm, enduring foundation. The gentlemen, compelled by stern necessity, could wield the axe like accomplished wood-cutters; for after two years of disasters, it was enacted as a law, " That if any man would not work, neither should he eat."

But like most public benefactors, Smith was sorely beset by enemies; notwithstanding his entreaties for efficient colonists, they continued to send broken-down tradesmen, dissolute gallants, &c., men more fitted to corrupt, than to found a commonwealth. These gave him infinite trouble, yet he resolutely maintained authority over them. At last an accidental explosion of gunpowder disabled him, by inflicting wounds, which the surgical skill of Virginia could not relieve. Delegating his authority to Percy, he embarked for England. Extreme suffering from his wounds, and the ingratitude of his employers, were the fruits of his services. He received for his sacrifices and his perilous exertions, not one foot of land, *not the house he himself had built*, not the field his own hands had planted, nor any reward but the applause of his conscience, and the world.* Smith at his departure left more than four hundred and ninety persons in the colony; in six months, indolence, vice, and famine, reduced the number to sixty.

The arrival of Lord Delaware, in June, 1610, saved

---

* Bancroft.

the colony from entire destruction. "It was," says the elegant historian of the United States, "it was on the tenth day of June, that the restoration of the colony was solemnly begun by supplications to God. After the solemn exercises of religion, Lord Delaware caused his commission to be read; a consultation was immediately held on the good of the colony, and its government was organized with mildness but decision. The evils of faction were healed by the unity of the administration, and the colonists, excited by mutual emulation, performed their tasks with alacrity.

"At the beginning of each day they assembled in *the little church, which was kept neatly trimmed with the wild flowers of the country ;* next they returned to their houses to receive their allowance of food. The settled hours of labour, were from six in the morning till ten, and from two in the afternoon till four. The houses were warm and secure, covered above with strong boards, and matted on the inside, after the fashion of the Indian wigwams."

Blessed little church in the wilderness ! Would that we could minutely describe that rude structure, decorated with wild flowers, the first edifice erected to the worship of God in the United States ! There, prayer and praise daily ascended to the Almighty, and thus was a permanent foundation laid, for the noble State of Virginia.

When afterwards Sir Thomas Gates, A. D. 1611, assumed the government of the colony, and employed religion as the foundation of order and of laws, "Good," said the colonists, "are the beginnings where God thus leads."

Gates built a new town, and called it Henrico. He environed it with a palisado; then he built at each corner of the town, "a high commanding watch-house; then a church and store-houses; which, being finished, he began to think upon convenient houses for himself and men, which, with all possible speed he could, he effected, to the great content of his company and all the colony."

Here then, was the first regularly built town in the United States. "It hath," says the quaint old historian, "three streets of well-framed houses, a handsome church, and the foundation of a better laid, to bee built of bricke, besides store-houses, watch-houses, and the like."

Jamestown, at this time, is described as having "two rows of houses of framed timber, and some of them two stories and a garret higher, and three large store-houses joined together in length." This was in 1611.

Thus we see, from what humble beginnings, the most useful and the most superb of all arts takes its rise.

From an old work on Virginia, published in London in 1722, "by a native and inhabitant of the place," we extract the following chapter, which shows the progress of the art in the colony.

"OF THE BUILDINGS OF VIRGINIA.

" There are three fine buildings in this country, (Virginia,) which are said to be the most magnificent of any in the English America. One of which is the College, another the Capitol, or State House; not far from this is also built the public prison for criminals, which is a large and convenient structure, with partitions for the different sexes, and distinct rooms for petty offenders; besides a large yard for the prisoners, and a separate prison for debtors.

" The house for the Governor, though not the largest, is by far the most beautiful of all. It was granted by the Assembly, begun in President Jennings his time, but received its beauty and conveniency for the many alterations and decorations of the present Governor, Colonel Spotswood, who, to the lasting honour and happiness of the country, arrived there while the house was carrying up. In his time was also built a new brick church, and brick magazine for arms and ammunition, and the streets of the towne altered from the fanciful forms of W's and M's, to much more conveniences. These are all built of brick, and covered with shingle, except the debtors' prison, which has a flat roof covered with slate.

" The private buildings are also very much improved, several of them there having built themselves large brick houses of many rooms on a floor, but they don't covet to make them lofty, having extent of ground enough to build upon; and now and then they are visited by high winds, which would incommode a towering fabric. They love to have large rooms, that they may be cool in summer. Of late, they have made their stores much higher than formerly, and their windows larger and sasht with crystal glass. Their common covering for dwellings is shingles, which is an oblong square of cypress or pine wood. Clapboards are used to cover the tobacco-houses."

Thus we see, that improvements were slowly made for the space of one hundred years.

THE PLYMOUTH COLONY.

On the memorable 11th of December, 1620, the Pilgrim Fathers stepped upon the Plymouth Rock, and on the 22d, their families were landed, and the May Flower was safely moored in the harbour. It was an inclement season; the colonists were grievously afflicted with consumption and lung fever; nevertheless, it was agreed that each man should build his own house.

"The sounding aisles of the dim woods rang,"

at one time with the voice of prayer and praise, and at another with the colonists' axe and the crash of the trees of the forest.

Sorely were they hindered by sickness, storms, and frost; the miserable shelters they erected were insufficient to protect them from the bitter cold and driving snow of that inclement winter. The living were scarcely able to bury the dead; the well, not sufficient to take care of the sick. At the season of the greatest distress, there were but seven, able to render assistance.

Ten years after the settlement of Plymouth, the colony of Boston was in a situation somewhat similar. "Every hardship was encountered. The emigrants lodged at best in *tents of cloth*, and in *miserable hovels*." For religious worship they assembled under the shade of a spreading tree.

Hitherto, the colonists of New England had built their houses in a very rude manner, without having their towns laid out according to a regular plan.

NEW HAVEN COLONY.

In 1638, a colony was founded at New Haven, Connecticut, by Theophilus Eaton, John Davenport, and other men of education and wealth. They laid out the beautiful city of New Haven in nine equal squares, with the streets crossing each other at right angles. The centre square was the public "Green." Upon it their first meeting-house was commenced in 1639. "The cost of the building was to be £500. The house was fifty feet square. It had a tower surmounted with a turret. On the floor of the house there were neither pews nor slips, but plain seats. That humble edifice,—humble in comparison with the spacious and beautiful structures that now adorn the same ' Green,'—was built and maintained in repair with an honourable zeal for public worship. There, assembled men and women who had been accustomed to the luxuries of wealth in a metropolis, and to the refinements of a court. There, were ministers who had disputed in the universities, and preached under Gothic arches in London."*

The dwelling-houses of the principal colonists were large and convenient structures. They are even said to have been "fair and stately." Governor Eaton "maintained a port," says an old writer, "in some measure answerable to his state." His plate was worth £700; and his house must have been large, to accommodate the immense quantity of furniture mentioned in an inventory of his estate. There was " the green chamber," with its "tapestry, Turkey-work and needle-work cushions, down bed, green curtains, fringed and laced," &c. &c. &c. Beside " the green chamber," there was " the blue chamber," with nothing of " blue laws" in the furniture;—" the hall," a stately apartment, with "drawing table" and "round table," "green cushions," "great chair with needle-work," "high chairs" and "high stools," "low chairs" and "low stools," " Turkey carpet," "high wine stools," "great brass andirons," &c. &c. Then there was " the par-

* Bacon's Historical Discourses.

lour," less considerable than the hall, " Mrs. Eaton's chamber, with abundant furnishing," and numerous other apartments, proving that the Governor's house must have been, for those days, a very stately dwelling, suitable for a man of his wealth and station.

NEW YORK.

In 1623, a block-house was built by the Dutch on the island of Manhattan, and a few rude cabins were clustered around it.   This was the foundation of New Amsterdam—now New York.   In a short time a more substantial fort was built, and Governor Klieft had the charge of the colony.

Within the walls of the fort, adjoining the Governor's house, a church was built.   It was a Dutch edifice, with some kind of cupola or spire ; and it had a bell brought from Holland, which was not alone a "church-going bell," as it was rung on all occasions of alarm, or of assembling the people for secular business.   Beneath this venerable first church of New York, the Dutch and English Governors were for many years interred.

When New Amsterdam passed into the possession of the English, the old Dutch church was honoured with the new name of "King's Chapel."   In 1691 it was repaired and remodelled, and thus remained until 1741, when it was accidentally destroyed by fire.   A view of the second church built in New Amsterdam, called the Garden Street Church, has been preserved.

Many of the emigrants who flocked from the Netherlands to New Amsterdam, brought their houses with them; i. e. they brought tile, and brick, timber and wainscoting, glass and putty; and soon their houses, with high sloping roofs, and gable end to the street, were irregularly scattered about the island of Manhattan. "The government of New Netherlands had formed just ideas of the fit materials for building not only houses, but a commonwealth. They desired farmers and labourers, foreigners and exiles, men inured to toil and labour. New Amsterdam in a few years could boast of stately buildings, and almost vied with Boston."

PHILADELPHIA.

"In August, 1683, Philadelphia consisted of three or four little cottages, (or log cabins;) the deer fearlessly bounded past blazed trees, unconscious of foreboded streets; the stranger who wandered from the river bank was lost in the thickets of the interminable forest; and two years afterwards the place contained about six hundred houses, and the schoolmaster and the printing-press had begun their work." Philadelphia was regularly planned and laid out by its founder, William Penn. A distinguished English author,*

---

* Dr. Prideaux.

who wrote in 1715, has the following note in the margin of the page where he describes the ancient city of Babylon :

" Much according to this model, (Babylon,) hath William Penn, the Quaker, laid out the ground for his city of Philadelphia, in Pennsylvania ; and were it all built according to that design, it would be the fairest and best city in all America, and not much behind any in the whole world. For it lieth between two navigable rivers, at the distance of two miles from their confluence, and consists of thirty streets, ten of which, being drawn from river to river, are two miles long, and the twenty others, being drawn across the said ten, and cutting them at right angles, are a mile long. In the midst of the whole, is left a square of ten acres, and in the middle of the four quarters of the town, into which it is equally divided, is a square of five acres ; which said places are designed for the building churches, schools, and other public buildings, and also to serve for the inhabitants to walk, and other ways to divert themselves in them, in the same manner as Moorsfields do in London. Above two thousand houses are in this place already built, and when it shall be wholly built according to the plan above mentioned, it will be the glory of all that part of the world ; and if the country round it comes to be thoroughly inhabited, the great conveniency of its situation for trade, by reason of the two navigable rivers on which it stands, and the great river Delaware, into which

Plate XXIII

SWEDE'S CHURCH.

both fall, will soon draw people enough thither not only to finish the scheme, which hath been laid of its first founder, but also to enlarge it by such additions on each side, as to make its breadth answer its length, and then, barring the walls and greatness of Babylon, it will imitate it in all things else, and in the conveniency of its situation, far exceed it. But this is to be understood as a comparing of a small thing with a great; for though Philadelphia were built and inhabited to the utmost I have mentioned, that is, to the full extent of two miles in breadth, as well as in length, yet fifty-six of such cities might stand within those walls that encompassed Babylon."

The neat and beautiful "City of Brotherly Love," has more than realized this prospective plan, and Dr. Prideaux's prophecy, that "it will be the glory of all that part of the world," is fully accomplished.

The Swedes Church at Wilmington, Delaware (Plate XXIII.), is one of the oldest ecclesiastical edifices remaining in the United States.

STYLE OF BUILDING.

The meeting-houses of New England, excepting in cities, were, (down to the present century, and even in some places at a later period,) built of wood. They were huge structures, filled with plain, oblong win-

F̲ɪɢ. 33.

HOOPER.Sc

dows, and looking like immense lanterns. When they had arched windows, they were Episcopal churches; that was in fact for a long time the external distinction between an Episcopal church, and the churches of other denominations. The meeting-houses (Fig. 33) had slender spires, or dumpy cupolas, stuck upon four, six, or eight posts, which stood upon a square tower, that was placed in front of the meeting-house, which it joined to the top of the roof. They often stood upon an elevated situation, and though truly grateful and even beautiful from association, to the eye of piety, they were outrageous deformities to the eye of taste.

Court-houses and academies were built in the same uncouth style. Happily, they were all of such perishable materials, that they will not much longer remain to annoy travellers, in "search of the picturesque," through the beautiful villages of New England.

Dwelling-houses, in the English colonies of this country, were built after the style then prevailing in England, as nearly as circumstances would permit. Gradually, home-bred artisans were employed, and all resemblance to English mansions of the better sort, entirely disappeared. The best houses in New England were built of wood, with two stories in front, and a high roof, which sloped down almost to the ground behind; or at least so low, that the eaves were just over the back door. In some instances they were only one story, with large dormer or dormant windows upon the roof, and a piazza in front, with slender octagonal or square posts. Red was a favourite colour for these wooden enormities, although some very tasteful persons preferred a bright yellow, with red doors and roof. Often they were left without paint, and became a dingy brown, deepening every year.

School-houses in the country were usually built in an unenclosed place, where two or more roads met. No trees shaded them from the mid-day sun, no shrubbery adorned the play-ground. The buildings themselves were erected at the least possible expense; dark, cold, and dreary in winter, and hot and uncomfortable in summer. "The young idea," however, was under these disadvantages, "taught to shoot," among the hardy sons of New England. The schoolmaster was reverenced, though the school-house was considered of little consequence. Are there not some of these miserable school-houses, even at the present day, used for common schools? Modern improvement has not so entirely demolished them, that the present generation cannot find specimens enough of the rude architecture of the infant Colonies. Surely, it is not veneration for antiquity that has preserved these mean temples of science.

CHAPTER XX.

ENGAGED for a long time in a struggle for very life, the colonists were in no condition to cultivate anything but the soil upon which they trod. Scarcely had they a breathing-time, after their Indian foes were subdued, or driven from their immediate neighbourhood, before the French war again exhausted the strength of the infant nation.

Once more at peace, had they been dependent upon their own resources, manufactures and arts must have been encouraged and cultivated. But it was the policy of England to keep her colonies dependent upon her for all articles of manufacture that could be imported. Although boundless forests spread around them, they often imported the wood-work of their houses;* and

---

* A building that was thus brought over before the Revolution, still remains at New Haven, Conn. It has been repaired by the present owner, and is now a fine spacious English cottage. The wainscoting of the wide hall, the balusters and staircase, and even some of the floors, are of polished cherry, and black walnut.

although clay for bricks was abundant, they too were often brought over from England. Skill was not acquired in the mechanical arts; genius was not elicited. Yet the latter could not always be repressed. Benjamin West, with no model but his sleeping sister, and no instrument but an old pen, was a painter; still, at home he could not be patronised, and soon England claimed him as her own.

The manacles which England had thus imposed upon the Colonies began to be galling. The latent, but gigantic energies of the nation were aroused; these energies were at first employed in throwing off the manacles and fetters. Why should hands strong to labour, guided by ingenious minds, not be free to work their will?

In the struggle for freedom, (civil, religious, commercial, manual, mental,) political and military genius were developed of the highest order.

The contest was won; yet minds the most powerful must for a long time exert their loftiest energies in settling a new form of government. Subordinate minds must be employed in the accumulation of wealth. And for this object, no one doubts the industry and ingenuity of the people!

No sooner was genius free to act, than its power was applied to the immediate wants of the community. Mechanical inventions, *equal* (it would not be presumptuous to say *superior*) to any in the world, have been thus elicited; and bridges, aqueducts, canals, railroads, viaducts, steamboats, telegraphs, together with thousands of patent labour-saving machines, bear witness to the acuteness, ingenuity, and skill, of the free Yankee.

Look at the contrast between the condition of this wide continent at the beginning of the seventeenth century, and its present state in this nineteenth. Then, " Man, the occupant of the soil, wild as the savage scene, was in harmony with the rude nature around him; his knowledge in architecture surpassed, both in strength and durability, by the skill of the beaver; bended saplings the beams of his house; the branches and rind of trees its roof; drifts of forest leaves his couch; mats of bulrushes, his protection against the winter's cold."

Now, man, civilized, intellectual, refined, through the mysterious guidance of Providence, occupies the same soil. " For him, the rivers that flow to remotest climes, mingle their waters; for him, the lakes gain new outlets to the ocean; for him, the arch spans the flood, and science spreads iron pathways to the recent wilderness; for him, the hills yield up the shining marble and the enduring granite; for him, the forests of the interior come down in immense rafts; for him, the masts of the city gather the produce of every clime, and libraries collect the works of genius of every age."

Wealth has poured its golden showers. Emigration has rolled a tide of population upon the shores of this country, that threatens its destruction.

How are this wealth and these many hands to be

employed? Is luxury to enervate and demoralize the nation? Are poverty, idleness, and crime to render the people desperate, and lead to anarchy and ruin? Let us hope better things.

"It has been well ascertained that there are few things so productive of civilization and refinement, or *so conducive to the tranquil happiness of communities,* as the cultivation of the fine and liberal arts." Should not the attention of the statesman and the political economist be directed to this matter?

The useful arts alone cannot employ the genius and industry of this whole people. It has been the wise policy of all refined nations to stimulate and reward genius for the fine arts, and to employ multitudes of the people in accomplishing enduring works of art. Such should be the policy of an enlightened republic, where the people are ever in danger of becoming restless and discontented. We have seen the unrivalled excellence to which Greece exalted the fine arts during her republican might. No nation has yet surpassed her; but it is not impossible that this may yet be done by the United States; for since the decline of Greece, no people have ever been more favourably situated for the accomplishment of great designs.

In order that the fine arts may be successfully cultivated, *taste* must be universally diffused among the higher classes of the community. It has been judiciously remarked by a late writer, that "the fine arts have ever been the *consequences* of the teaching of the intellect—never its teachers. Necessity is the mother of invention; and the fine arts, whenever they have truly attained excellence, have, to use a familiar expression, *followed the lead of society*, rather than acted as a promoting cause."

The number of persons who go abroad to visit the beautiful creations of foreign genius may be expected to bring home a desire for those embellishments which they have enjoyed in the old world.

Among the arts of design, Architecture must precede Painting and Sculpture : they are but the handmaidens who decorate her palaces, her capitols, her churches.

CHAPTER XXI.

MATERIALS FOR ARCHITECTURE IN THE UNITED STATES.

NEVER was a country more bountifully furnished with the materials for architecture than the United States. Majestic mountains of granite lift their heads above the clouds; marble of the purest white, and of every beautiful hue, veins the earth. Sandstone, slate, limestone, trap-rock, offer imperishable materials, that may be used to prove to distant generations that the present age consulted not alone selfish and temporary interests.

The trees of the yet interminable forests yield every variety of wood to beautify interior architecture. Metals hide themselves beneath the surface of this wide territory, awaiting the call of science and industry.

Useless were all these treasures, without the creative power of art. Already have they been summoned from cave and from mountain-top, from forest and valley, and far down in the deep mines, to do the bidding of a genius more potent than he of Aladdin's lamp, whose creations are not "the baseless fabric of a vision," but real, beautiful, permanent.

Granite, a primary rock, may be called the *foundation-stone* of the earth. Its constituent parts are quartz, feldspar, and mica. It is a hard and brittle stone, but with much labour may be worked into capitals and other ornamental parts of a building. It abounds in the New England States, especially in New Hampshire and Massachusetts. A beautiful white granite is there quarried, and employed in building at home, and sent to distant parts of the Union. The United States Bank is of this white granite; the market-house at Boston, some fine dwelling-houses in New York, and many other edifices there and elsewhere.

Sienite is often called granite, from its resemblance to it; feldspar and hornblende predominate in its composition. It is even more difficult than granite to chisel into ornamental work. The fine quarry of this stone at Quincy, near Boston, has given it the name of Quincy stone, by which it is extensively known. The Astor House in New York is built entirely of sienite, and in Boston, there are many structures which have now been standing for some years; showing that it bears exposure to the air, without injury to its appearance. The Bunker Hill Monument is of this stone.

Marble is one of the most durable of stones. The beautiful Pentelic marble of the Parthenon, has stood the storms of more than two thousand years, without injury. Happily for us, this fine material abounds in almost every part of the country. The black, gray, and white marble of Vermont are extensively known.   Massachusetts furnishes specimens of various kinds.   The splendid columns of the Girard College, were brought from Sheffield, in Berkshire county, in that State.   New Hampshire has several quarries.   In Connecticut, near New Haven, green marble abounds, resembling the verde antique.   Many specimens of this marble have been sent to Europe, and been much admired in the cabinets of the curious and scientific.   Near the same place another quarry is found, in which yellow predominates.   White marble abounds in Pennsylvania.   In short, marble is so abundantly supplied, that taste and durability may be combined by the use of this material in elegant edifices.

The United States Mint, Custom-House, and Pennsylvania Bank in Philadelphia, are all of Pennsylvania marble; the Washington Monument, Baltimore, is also of white marble.

Sandstone, usually called freestone, is found of various colours, from gray to red, and dark brown.   It is easily wrought and much used in building.   Extensive quarries of red freestone are worked at Chatham, in Connecticut.   The Potomac freestone is extensively used; the President's House, the Capitol at Washington, and St. Paul's Church, Boston, are built of it.   Sometimes it is employed without smoothing, and is thus a durable and economical material for cottages, stables, &c.   It is in general use for the basement, window-sills, and caps, of brick buildings.

Gneiss, a stone containing a large proportion of

mica, splits with ease, and affords a beautiful paving-stone.

Slate is found in great abundance in this country; it is used for covering roofs, and should be universally substituted in cities for shingles or other combustible materials.

Sand for glass is found on the banks of the Delaware, and some other localities. Sand for mortar abounds in almost every state in the Union.

Clay for bricks is also abundant. It is generally impregnated with oxide of iron, and this causes it to turn red in burning.

Metals of all kinds are found in the United States. Gold mines have been opened in Virginia, North Carolina, South Carolina, Alabama, Tennessee, and Georgia; those of North Carolina, have hitherto been the most productive.

Silver has been found, but not frequently, nor to any great amount, in this country.

Copper has been found, but till recently no mines of sufficient value to repay the labour of working them.

Iron is found in all the Northern and Northwestern States, in great abundance. The Connecticut and Virginia iron is extensively known as of a superior quality, and New York, Pennsylvania, and New Jersey afford iron equal in quality to any in the world.

Lead abounds in Missouri and Illinois. In the latter State the mines are very extensive and pure, furnishing vast quantities for manufactures. This metal is also exceedingly abundant throughout the North-western Territory.

No country in the world is more abundantly supplied with wood of every variety than the United States.

The *white oak* grows to a great height in the Middle States and in Virginia. It is strong and durable, and although sometimes employed in domestic architecture, is more generally used for ship-building. The black oak rises to a still greater height, but is not so large in circumference. Several other kinds of oak abound, all of them durable, and some of them excellent for timber.

The *black walnut* is a beautiful wood for the interior, being susceptible of a fine polish, and not liable to warp, nor to split. In Ohio and Kentucky, this wood is used for the shingling of houses, and occasionally for timbers. It is admirably adapted for doors and window-frames.

Maple, of several varieties, is also susceptible of a fine polish. The curled and bird's-eye maple, are very handsome for interior finishing. Maples grow in almost every part of the Union; they are numerous and luxuriant in the Western States.

Pine is a soft wood, easily worked, and has for this reason been hitherto quite too much used for building. It is, however, a valuable wood, and will long continue to be used for the interior, after more durable materials are substituted for the exterior of buildings. From

Maine to Florida, pines of various kinds abound, and are exported in large quantities to Europe and the West Indies.

The *white ash* is a strong and durable wood, which sometimes grows to the height of eighty feet. It splits straight, and is not apt to warp or shrink. It abounds most in the Northern States.

Birch is not much used in building, although it abounds in New England and the Middle States.

The *black birch* furnishes a hard, dark-coloured wood, that receives a fine polish, and is very handsome for interior finishing.

The *cypress* grows to a great size in the Southern States, and is frequently used for building.

The *white cedar* grows abundantly in the Middle and Southern States, and being a soft light wood is used for shingles and interior finishing. The *red cedar* is a durable wood, used for posts and fences.

Chestnut is a coarse-grained wood, not suitable for buildings. It is liable to warp, and if used for timber, often stains the outer covering to buildings. It is durable when exposed to the air, and therefore much used for common fencing, in New England and New York, where it is abundant.

The *elm* is a beautiful ornamental shade-tree, which grows to a great size in many parts of the United States; it is seldom used in building.

The natural facilities for transportation, (by rivers, lakes, and oceans,) render the rich materials for buildings with which our country abounds, accessible to almost every part of it; these, together with the railroads and canals which intersect it, bring to every inhabited spot, the productions of its remotest territories and a tribute from foreign climes. In New England, almost every farm is furnished with stone for fences and buildings. Instead of cutting down and wasting the trees, comfortable and durable farm-houses might be constructed of the stones that now encumber the soil. A little more labour than what is now employed to pile them in heaps, might lay them up in walls. There has hitherto been a great want of economy in this respect, and it is therefore the more earnestly urged upon the attention of the community. As the present wooden edifices decay and gradually disappear, it is hoped that everywhere more enduring ones may take their place.

CHAPTER XXII.

PRESENT STATE OF ARCHITECTURE IN THE UNITED STATES.

A NEW era in art has commenced in our country. American painters and sculptors are already favourably known abroad and admired at home. A few scientific architects have arrived at eminence in their profession. It is impossible to mention the names and works of all architects who have thus distinguished themselves. If they were to give descriptions of the buildings upon which they are employed, with plans and elevations, they would essentially benefit the community. A beautiful volume of this kind was published at Boston, in 1830, entitled "A Description of Tremont House, with Architectural Illustrations, by J. Rogers, Architect."

The limits of the present work will allow us merely to mention a few of the principal public edifices in the United States. It is not presumptuous to believe that the time is not distant when our native architects will rival those of Europe.

BOSTON.

The State House, 173 feet long, 61 wide. It has a fine dome, 52 feet in diameter, upon which is a circular cupola, or lantern. Under this dome stands a statue of Washington, by the English sculptor, Chantrey.

King's Chapel, built of rough stone, finished in 1754. It has a Corinthian colonnade in front; and although faulty in style, is superior to most of the edifices that were built in New England during the 18th century.

Trinity Church, in Summer Street, a Gothic edifice, of granite, was built in 1829.

The Tremont House is a large and beautiful building, of granite, with a fine Doric portico in front. J. Rogers, architect.

The Market House, of granite.

The Masonic Temple.

The Massachusetts General Hospital.

The United States Bank.

The Boston Athenæum.

Two beautiful Gothic churches, of freestone, were built in 1847. Billings, architect.

A modern traveller,* who was not over fond of praising anything American, says: "There is in Bos-

---

* Hamilton's "Men and Manners in America."

ton less of that rawness of outline, and inconsistency of architecture, which had struck me in New York. The truth is, that the latter has increased so rapidly, that nine-tenths of the city have been built within the last thirty years, and probably one-half of it within a third of the period. In Boston, both the wealth and population have advanced at a slower pace. A comparatively small portion of the city is new, and the hand of time has somewhat mellowed even its *deformities*, (unfortunately there are many such,) contributing to render that reverend which was originally rude. A considerable number of buildings are of granite, or, more properly speaking, of sienite; but brick is the prevailing material, and houses of framework are now rarely to be met with in the streets inhabited by the better orders. There is an air of gravity and solidity about Boston, and nothing gay or flashy in the appearance of her streets, or the crowds who frequent them. New York is a young giantess, weighing twenty stone;—Boston the matron of staid and demure air, a little past her prime, (a great mistake!) yet showing no symptoms of decay."*

The Library Edifice of Harvard University, at Cambridge, is a Gothic building, of granite, recently erected.

The Bunker Hill Monument, at Charlestown, is a beautiful granite obelisk, two hundred and twenty feet high.

---

* " Among the monuments at Mount Auburn, near Boston, are many of great beauty; we were struck with a plain black marble obelisk, of exquisite polish, ornamented by a single cross in relief;

NEW YORK.

There are in New York more than two hundred churches, or places of worship, belonging to different denominations. Some of these are spacious and well built; others are incongruous, unsymmetrical buildings, exhibiting great want of taste and skill.

St. Paul's, near the Park, is considered one of the finest of the older churches.

The Church in Washington Square, belonging to a

---

several granite obelisks, of plain and almost severe simplicity, which are admirably suited to the place and the purpose; several fine monuments of white marble, among which are an unfinished column and a cenotaph, erected by the mechanics of Boston to the memory of a young man who died at a distance from his home. This cemetery stands in complete and honourable contrast with most resting-places of the dead. We cannot but hope that this example will be followed. The community at large have yet to learn the right feeling of respect for the dead. That respect is not shown only by the care which guards the sepulchre from violation, nor by setting up ghostly monuments, covered with tales of idle vanity or unmeaning affection. The true respect for the dead will be shown by making their resting-place such that the stranger shall not retreat from it in disgust and scorn, by employing the decorations of nature, which are always at hand, and by appointing persons of taste to superintend the laying out and ornamenting of these solemn habitations of the dead. Every village in New England might and ought to do this, that instead of the dreary desolation that now renders them tenfold more gloomy, they may present a melancholy but pleasing appearance.

Plate XLVII

Plate XXIV

TRINITY CHURCH.

congregation of the Dutch Reformed denomination, is said to be one of the most perfect Gothic structures in the United States. Le Fevre, architect.

Trinity Church (Plate XXIV.) was commenced in 1841, on the site of the old church in Broadway, and completed in 1846. It is built of a beautiful fine-grained freestone, in the Perpendicular Gothic style. It is one hundred and ninety-two feet long, and eighty-four wide. Its graceful, symmetrical spire is two hundred and sixty-four feet high. It is by many considered the finest specimen of ecclesiastical architecture in this country. Mr. Upjohn, architect.

Grace Church, on Broadway, is built in the form of a cross, in the Gothic style, and is of white marble. The windows are of stained glass, and the edifice cost $145,000. It was completed in 1845. Mr. Renwick, architect.

The University Buildings.

The Hall of Justice, in Franklin Street, in the Egyptian style.

The Merchants' Exchange is built of marble, and is eighty-five feet long, fifty-five in width, and forty-five in height to the dome, from which it is lighted.

The Masonic Hall, in Broadway, has a Gothic front, of gray granite.

The Custom House, in Wall Street, is a beautiful Doric building, one hundred and seventy-seven feet long, and fifty-nine wide. The architects were Ithiel Town and Alexander J. Davis.

The Astor House is built of sienite, (commonly called Quincy granite.)   It is a massive building which has been much admired.

Many other public buildings might be mentioned, that are worthy of high praise.   There are also some beautiful dwelling-houses, built in a chaste and simple style, of enduring materials, and others that are truly magnificent.   New York may well be proud of her splendid Broadway, which, though possessing too much uniformity, is allowed to be one of the finest streets in the world.   Much regard has been paid to architectural style of late in New York, and a successful effort is being made to redeem the character of the commercial emporium from the imputation of sameness and bad taste.   They may, in attempting too much style, become extravagant and affected for a time; but these errors will be corrected, and beautiful buildings will be the final result of the present mania for the art. "The recent evidences of improving taste and public spirit of the citizens, offer the most certain promise that at some future day New York will equal in splendour the proudest cities of the old world."*

* Architectural Magazine, London.

PHILADELPHIA.

Of this neat and pleasant city an English traveller remarks, "that it possesses an interior almost unrivalled in the world," although its exterior, when seen from a distance, is not imposing. The streets are broad, and many of them have rows of trees, forming a delightful shade, and taking away the glare of the brick buildings. The stranger is struck "with the air of simplicity, yet strength and durability which all the public edifices possess, while the private dwellings, with their neat white marble steps and window-sills, bespeak wealth and respectability. The churches which adorn this beautiful city, are not many of them fine edifices."

The United States Bank, now the United States Custom House for the port of Philadelphia, is one of the most beautiful buildings in this country. It is closely copied from a perfect model, the Parthenon. Its length is one hundred and sixty-one feet; its breadth eighty-seven feet. The fine massive Doric columns of the portico stand upon a platform of white marble, the ascent to which is by a high flight of marble steps. Thus lifted up away from the street, it has a very imposing appearance. The banking-room is eighty-one feet long and forty-eight feet wide.

The new Bank of Pennsylvania is copied from the Ionic Temple of the Muses, upon the Ilissus; it is built of marble, and is a large and handsome edifice.

The Asylum for the Deaf and Dumb is an extensive, commodious building, without much claim to architectural beauty.

The Pennsylvania Hospital occupies a large extent of ground, and is exceedingly well arranged for the purpose for which it was designed.

The United States Mint is of the Ionic order, and copied after a fine Grecian model.

The Eastern Penitentiary at Cherry Hill, near the city of Philadelphia, is an imposing structure: the walls, of granite, are thirty-five feet high, with towers and battlements. A space of ten acres is enclosed for the use of this institution, which is designed to carry into effect the plan of solitary confinement.

The Girard College (Plate XXV., Frontispiece) is situated about one mile and a half northwest of the centre of the city of Philadelphia, on a tract of land containing forty-five acres; the whole of which was appropriated by Mr. Girard, exclusively to the purposes of the institution.

" The main building, which is the subject of this description, is composed in the Corinthian order of Grecian Architecture: it covers a space of one hundred and eighty-one feet by two hundred and thirty-nine and one-half feet, and consists of an octastyle peripteral superstructure, resting upon a basement of eight feet in height, composed entirely of steps extending around the whole edifice; by which a pyramidal appearance is given to the substruction, and a means of approach afforded to the porticoes from every side.

The dimensions of the stylobate (or platform on which the columns stand), are one hundred and fifty-nine feet on the fronts, by two hundred and seventeen feet on the flanks; and the cell, or body of the building, measures one hundred and eleven feet, by one hundred and sixty-nine feet. The whole height, from the ground to the apex of the roof, is one hundred feet.

" The columns are thirty-four in number; the diameter of the shaft at the top of the base is six feet, and at the bottom of the capital, five feet; the height of the capitals, including the abacus, is nine feet, and the width, from the extreme corners of the abacus, ten feet; the whole height of the column, including capital and base, is fifty-five feet. The entablature is sixteen feet three inches high, and the greatest projection of the cornice, from the face of the frieze, is four feet nine inches; the elevation of the pediment is twenty feet five inches, being one-ninth of the span. The capitals of the columns are proportioned from those of the monument of Lysicrates at Athens: they are of American marble, and were wrought upon the grounds of the college.

" The corners of the building are finished with massive antæ, having bases and capitals composed on the principles of Grecian Architecture.

" The doors of entrance are in the centre of the north and south fronts; they are each sixteen feet wide in the clear, by thirty-two feet high.

" The building is three stories in height, each of which is twenty-five feet from floor to floor : there are four rooms of fifty feet square in each story. Those of the first and second story are vaulted with groin arches, and those of the third story with domes supported on pendentives, which spring from the corners of the rooms at the floor, and assume the form of a circle on the horizontal section, at the height of nineteen feet. These rooms are lighted by means of skylights of sixteen feet in diameter. All the domes are terminated below the plane of the roof; and the skylights project but one foot above it, so as not to interfere with the character of the architecture.

" The roof is covered with marble tiles, so nicely overlapping each other as to defy the most beating storms.

" Beside the main edifice, there are four other buildings belonging to the institution, each fifty-two feet wide, one hundred and twenty-five feet long, and four stories high." Thomas U. Walter, architect.

The Athenæum (Plate XXVI.) has a front of freestone, with a fine balustrade of stone. The windows are richly ornamented. This building is a beautiful specimen of street architecture. Where the space for an edifice in the city is necessarily very limited, the best possible way of rendering it ornamental, is to decorate the doors and windows, the cornice and balustrade. John Notman, architect.

Plate XXVI

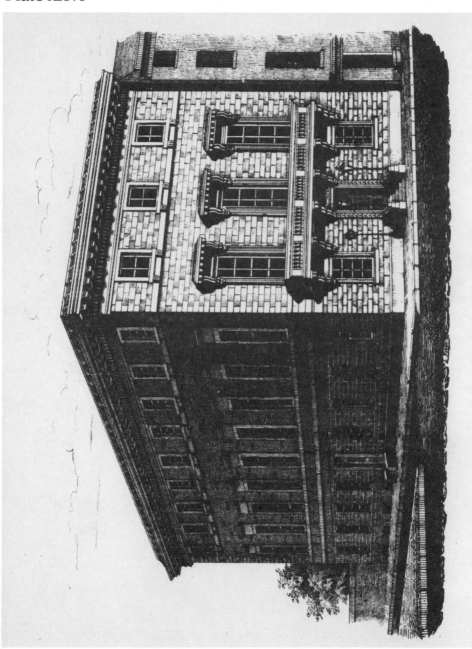

THE ATHENÆUM AT PHILA.

WASHINGTON.

The President's House, is of Potomac freestone. It has two fronts with porticoes, and is one hundred and eighty feet in length by eighty-five in width.

The Patent Office is still unfinished; it is designed when completed, to surround the square on which it stands. It is of the dark freestone of the Potomac. The building already completed has a superb portico of the Doric order.

The General Post Office, of white marble, is a magnificent building, ornamented with pilasters, and an entablature of the Corinthian order. The edifice already occupies the front and part of two other sides of a square. It is unfinished, but when completed will be one of the most splendid buildings in the United States.

The Treasury Department edifice is of the Potomac freestone. Its long Ionic colonnade is much admired.

The buildings for the other Departments are large and commodious.

The Capitol is finely situated, commanding a view of the city, with the surrounding country, and the River Potomac. It is three hundred and fifty-two feet long in front, and its greatest height one hundred and forty-five feet. The Hall of the Representatives is of a half-circular form. The dome rises above an entablature, supported by twenty-four Corinthian columns of variegated marble, (sometimes called pudding stone,) from the banks of the Potomac. This is said to be one of the finest representative halls in the world. Architectural critics have detected some things which they consider faults, but it is generally allowed to be very beautiful.

BALTIMORE.

The Roman Catholic Cathedral was planned by Latrobe. It is of the Ionic order; one hundred and ninety feet in length, one hundred and seventy-seven feet wide, one hundred and twenty-seven feet high, to the top of the dome.

The Washington Monument is a column of white marble resting upon a high quadrangular pedestal. The shaft of the column is about one hundred and twenty feet high; the whole height of the monument one hundred and sixty-three feet. On the summit is a colossal statue of Washington. This is considered the finest commemorative structure in the Union.

Battle Monument is not so large, nor so fine as the Washington Monument. It is of white marble, fifty-five feet high, and was erected in memory of the defenders of the city, who fell on the 12th and 13th of September, 1814.

The Merchants' Exchange is a spacious, fine structure.

Plate XXVII

THE ATHENÆUM AT HARTFORD CONN.

INDIANAPOLIS.

The Capitol of Indiana is a large Doric building, and does great honour to the taste and liberality of the State. It is one hundred and eighty feet long and eighty wide. Ithiel Town and A. J. Davis, architects.

HARTFORD, CONNECTICUT.

The Athenæum (Plate XXVII.) is a Gothic edifice, of rough freestone. It is a symmetrical and effective building. The interior arrangements are remarkably convenient, and admirably adapted for the accommodation of the library and other departments of the institution. Henry Austin, architect.

Christ Church. A Gothic church, of sandstone. This is a fine symmetrical building, planned by Ithiel Town and the Rev. Nathaniel Wheaton. The ornaments, both on the exterior and within, are well executed, and perfectly in keeping with the " Perpendicular Gothic" style. Few churches in the United States offer so good a model for a church of the same size.

NEW HAVEN, CONNECTICUT.*

Yale College Library is built of rough freestone, and is a symmetrical, effective building, in the Gothic

* As early as 1815, President Dwight describes New Haven as follows: " The area occupied by New Haven is probably as large as that which usually contains a city of six times the number of inhabitants, in Europe. A considerable proportion of the houses have court-yards in front, and gardens in the rear. The former are ornamented with trees and shrubs, the latter are luxuriantly filled with fruit-trees, flowers, and culinary vegetables. The beauty and healthfulness of this arrangement needs no explanation. The houses in this city are generally decent, and many of the modern ones handsome. The style of building is neat and tidy. Fences and out-houses are also in the same style, and being almost universally painted white, make a delightful appearance to the eye; an appearance not a little enhanced by the great multitude of shade-trees; a species of ornament in which this town is unrivalled. Most of the buildings are of wood, and may be considered as destined to become the fuel of a future conflagration. Building with brick and stone is, however, becoming more frequent. (The erection of wooden buildings has been forbidden by law in the populous parts of the city, since January, 1817.) The mode of building with stone, which seems not unlikely to become general, is to raise walls of whin-stone, broken into fragments of every irregular form, laid in strong mortar; and then to overcast them with a peculiar species of cement. The corners, frames of the doors, arches and sills of the windows, cornices, and other ornamental parts, are of a sprightly-coloured freestone. The cement is sometimes divided by lines at right angles, in such a manner as to make the whole resemble a building of marble, and being smooth and white, is very handsome.

[Plate LXVII.]

Plate XXVIII

YALE COLLEGE LIBRARY.

style (Plate XXVIII.) The main building is devoted to the hall for the library of the college; the wings to rooms for the society libraries. The interior of the hall is beautifully arranged; the windows of the clerestory and the large windows at the end let in the light from above, upon the clustered columns and well-filled alcoves. This beautiful edifice was completed in 1847. Henry Austin, architect.

A foreign traveller remarks as follows: " In the United States there are many splendid temples for

---

Several valuable houses have been lately built in this manner; and the cement, contrary to the general expectation, has hitherto perfectly sustained the severity of our seasons. This mode of building is very little more expensive than building with wood; and will, I suspect, ultimately take the place of every other. I know of no other equally handsome, where marble itself is not the material. Both these kinds of stone are found inexhaustibly at a moderate distance. All the congregations in New Haven voted, in 1812, that they would take down their churches, and build new ones. Accordingly, two of them commenced the work in 1813, the others in 1814. The first was finished in 1814, the others soon after. They are all placed on the western side of Temple Street, in a situation singularly beautiful, having an elegant square in front, and stand on a street one hundred feet wide. The Presbyterian churches are of Grecian architecture. The Episcopal church is a Gothic building, the only correct specimen it is believed in the United States. Few structures, (many have since that time been erected in every part of the country,) devoted to the same purpose, on this side of the Atlantic, are equally handsome, and in no place can the same number of churches be found, within the same distance, so beautiful, and standing in so advantageous a position."—*Dwight's Travels in New England and New York.*

religious worship, not on a scale of magnificence to equal the St. Peter's of Rome, or the St. Paul's of London, nor the ancient Abbeys or Minsters of this country, yet, generally speaking, on a par with many or most of the modern religious edifices throughout the United Kingdom. There are numerous superior specimens of architecture in the United States, which, although neither antique nor original, are highly creditable to the genius and generosity of the American people. Many instances might be enumerated in Boston, New York, Philadelphia, Baltimore, Washington, and other cities, of different public buildings.

" The United States Banking-House at Philadelphia, built on the model of the ancient Parthenon, excels in elegance, and equals in utility, the edifice not only of the Bank of England, but that of any banking-house in the world.

"The Exchange Hotel of New Orleans, in St. Charles Street, is probably the largest of its kind in the world; the cost of the ground and building has amounted to upwards of $600,000. The hotel is two hundred and twenty-eight feet in front by one hundred and ninety-six feet throughout or square. The front view is elevated on a plain basement, fourteen feet high, in the centre of which is a portico containing six columns, projecting from the main building, with four also on either side, receding inward, all in the Corinthian order, and forming an elegant colonnade along two-thirds of the front, the other third being solid and ornamented with pilasters. It is six stories high. From the basement to the top of the cornice the height is seventy-one feet, but there is an octagon in the centre of the building, seventy feet in diameter, which is raised fifty-three feet above the roof, and surmounted by a dome; above this is an observatory; the whole height from the ground being one hundred and thirteen feet.

" The theatre of New Orleans is on a similar scale of magnificence and magnitude."

We are far from having named all the public buildings worthy of note in the United States. This list is necessarily very limited.

CHAPTER XXIII.

DOMESTIC ARCHITECTURE IN THE UNITED STATES.

DOMESTIC architecture in this country must be adapted to the circumstances and condition of the people. As it is an art originating from necessity, the progress of society must change the architecture of every country, from age to age. As wealth and refinement increase, taste and elegance must be consulted, without destroying convenience and appropriateness. We can no more adopt the style of architecture than the dress of a foreign people. We acknowledge the flowing robes of the Persian to be graceful and becoming; they suit the habits and climate of the country. The fur-clad Russian of the north has conformed his dress to his climate, and made it rich and elegant; yet, as he approaches his neighbours of Turkey, his dress becomes somewhat assimilated to theirs. France is said to give the law of fashion in dress to the civilized world; and the absurdities that have resulted from following her dictates, have produced ridiculous anomalies in other countries.

In adopting the domestic architecture of foreign countries, we may be equally ridiculous. England, our fatherland, from some resemblance in habits and institutions, might furnish more suitable models for imitation than any other country; yet they would not be perfectly in accordance with our wants. Our architecture must, therefore, be partly indigenous.

FIG. 34.

Our associations of convenience, home-comfort, and respectability are connected with a certain style of building, which has been evolved by the wants, manners, and customs of the people. Any great deviations from a style that has been thus fixed, cannot be perfectly agreeable. We must improve upon this style, so that domestic architecture may in time be perfectly American. Fig. 34 is decidedly English.

" Nationality is founded in a great degree on feelings and prejudices inculcated and aroused in youth, which

Fig. 35.

grow inveterate as long as its views are confined to the
place of its birth. The love of country will remain
with undiminished strength in the cultivated mind;
but the national modes of thinking will vanish from
the disciplined intellect. Now as it is only by these
mannerisms of thought that architecture is affected,
we shall find that the more polished the mind of its
designer, the less natural will be the building; for its
architect will be led away by a search after a model of
ideal beauty, and will not be involuntarily guided by
deep-rooted feelings, governing irresistibly his heart
and hand. He will therefore be in perpetual danger
of forgetting the necessary unison of scene and climate,
and, following up the chase of the ideal, will neglect
the beauty of the natural. We must not, therefore, be
surprised if buildings, bearing the impress of the exercise of fine thoughts and high talent in their design,

should yet offend by perpetual discords with scene and climate." Fig. 35 is an English cottage.

"Again, man in his hours of relaxation, when he is engaged in the pursuit of mere pleasure, is less national than he is under the influence of any of the more violent feelings that agitate every-day life."*

Hence it is that in our country there is danger that our villas will be anything rather than national. The retired professional man, the wealthy merchant and mechanic, wish to build in the country. Instead of consulting home-comfort and pleasurable association, they select some Italian villa, Elizabethan house, or Swiss cottage, as their model. Ten chances to one the Italian villa, designed for the border of a lake, will be placed near a dusty high-road; the Elizabethan house, instead of being surrounded by venerable trees, will raise its high gables on the top of a bare hill; and the Swiss cottage, instead of hanging upon the mountainside, will be placed upon a level plain, surrounded with a flower-garden, divided into all manner of fantastic parterres, with box edgings.

We trust the following caricature, taken from the London Architectural Magazine, is not particularly applicable to our country:

"The architect is requested by a man of great wealth, nay, of established taste in some points, to make a design for a villa in a lovely situation. The future proprietor carries him up stairs to his study, to give him

---

* Architectural Magazine, London.

what he calls his 'ideas and materials,' and, in all probability, begins somewhat thus: 'This, sir, is a slight
note: I made it on the spot: approach to Villa Reale,
near Pozzuoli. Dancing nymphs, you perceive; cy-
presses, shell-fountain. I think I should like something like this for the approach; classical, you perceive,
sir; elegant, graceful. Then, sir, this is a sketch made
by an American friend of mine; Whee-whaw-Kanta-
maraw's wigwam;—King of the—Cannibal Islands,
I think he said, sir. Log, you observe; scalps and
boa-constrictor skins: curious. Something like this,
sir, would look neat, I think, for the front door; don't
you? Then the lower windows I've not quite decided
upon; but what would you say to Egyptian, sir? I
think I should like my windows Egyptian, with hieroglyphics, sir; storks and coffins and appropriate mouldings above: I brought some from Fountain Abbey the
other day. Look here, sir; angels' heads putting their
tongues out, rolled up in cabbage leaves, with a dragon
on each side, riding on a broomstick. Odd, I think—
interesting. Then the corners may be turned by
octagonal towers like the centre one in Kenilworth
Castle, with Gothic doors, portcullis and all, quite perfect; with crop-slits for arrows, battlements for mus-
ketry, machicolations for boiling lead, and a room at
the top for drying plums; and a conservatory at the
bottom, sir, with Virginian creepers up the towers;
door supported by sphinxes, holding scrapers in their
forepaws, &c. &c.' "

The English writer says, " This is no exaggeration ; we have contemplated the actual illustrious existence of several such buildings, with sufficient beauty in the

Fig. 36.

management of some of their features, to show that an architect had superintended them, and sufficient taste in their interior economy, to prove that a refined intellect had superintended them ; and had projected a Vandalism, only because fancy had been followed, rather than judgment."

Our country, containing as it does, in its wide extent, hills and mountains, sheltered dells and far-spreading valleys, lake-sides and river-sides; affords every possible situation for picturesque villas ; and great care should be taken that appropriate sites be chosen for appropriate and comfortable buildings ; comfortable, we say, for after the novelty of the exterior has pleased the eye of the owner for a few weeks, if his house wants that half-homely, but wholly indis-

F<small>IG</small>. 37.

pensable attribute, comfort, he had better leave it to ornament his grounds, like an artificial ruin, and build himself another to live in. Cottages are at present quite " the rage" in many parts of the United States. Some outré enormities are styled Swiss cottages, (Fig. 37,) quite unlike the cottage described as follows:

" Well do I remember the thrilling and exquisite moment when first I encountered, in a calm and shadowy dingle, darkened with the thick spreading of tall pines, and voiceful with the singing of a rock-encumbered stream, and passing up towards the flank of a smooth green mountain, whose swarded summit shone in the summer snow, like an emerald set in silver; when, I say, I first encountered in this calm defile of the Jura, the unobtrusive but beautiful front of the

Swiss cottage, I thought it the loveliest piece of architecture I had ever had the felicity of contemplating; yet it was nothing in itself,—nothing but a few mossy fir trunks, loosely nailed together, with one or two gray stones on the roof; but its power was the power of association; its beauty, that of fitness and humility." In fact, the cottage of the Swiss peasant is a genuine log-hut,—the picturesque châlet. The larger and better kind of Swiss cottages are built with roofs projecting from five to seven feet over the sides; these projections are strengthened by strong wooden supports, that the heavy snow which falls upon the roofs need not crush them. Utility and beauty are thus combined; but there is no beauty in such a cottage in a sunny vale, where the snow falls seldom or lightly. On the Green Mountains, or among the White Hills, it might stand as gracefully as it does among its native Alps. Walnut and chestnut trees are always beautiful accompaniments to the Swiss cottage.

The same care should be taken to render the cottage comfortable, as the villa; and in this point, unfortunately, there is often a complete failure. There is no absolute need that this should be the case. A cottage or a farm-house may be picturesque without sacrificing one tittle of its convenience. The great and leading object should be utility, and where that is absolutely sacrificed in architecture, whatever may be substituted in its place, it cannot be considered beautiful. The sameness of town-houses destroys the picturesque ap-

Fig. 38.

pearance of the streets; this might be remedied in part; but in general it arises so much from the necessity of the case, that glaring departures from regularity are oppressive to the eye.   Much, however, might be done to improve street architecture, as is demonstrated by some of the beautiful dwelling-houses lately erected in the city of New York.

The few examples here given,. of the cottage, villa, and town-house, merely afford a hint of the kind of dwelling-houses now being erected in various parts of the United States.

Fig. 38, a Grecian cottage, New Haven, Connecticut. It has five rooms and a hall or entry on the first floor, very conveniently arranged.   The whole expense of the building was not more than two thousand five hundred dollars.   H. Austin, architect.

F<small>IG</small>. 39.

Fig. 39. A cottage in the modernized Gothic style. H. Austin, architect. The centre of the building is occupied by two large parlours; on the sides are three other convenient rooms, beside bathing-room, pantries, and entries. In the upper story are five bed-rooms, two dressing-rooms, and four closets. It is suitable for a rural city, a village, or for the country. If of wood, the colour should be light brown,—the colour of oak ;—if of brick or stone, cemented, it should be of a yellowish hue, like the English Portland stone. It was, however, a favourite opinion of Sir Joshua Reynolds, that the colour of houses should be the same as the colour of the materials for buildings, furnished by the locality where they are erected. He says they would then be always in harmony with the landscape.

Fig. 40.

Fig. 40. An Elizabethan villa, the country-seat of Gerard Halleck, Esq. It stands by the water-side, near the shore of New Haven harbour. The observatory commands an extensive and beautiful prospect. The interior of the villa is arranged with reference to comfort and convenience, as well as elegance. The large conservatory on the southern side, with its range of Gothic windows, adds much to the beauty of the exterior. Sydney M. Stone, architect.

Plate XXIX. Bute Cottage, at Roxbury, near Boston, is a beautiful specimen of rural architecture, designed by William B. Lang, Esq.

Plate XXIX

BUTE COTTAGE.

FIG. 41.

Fig. 41. A truly New England house, the residence of Roger Sherman Baldwin, Esq. It has four
large rooms upon the first floor, and a wide hall
through the centre. Neatness, simplicity, and elegance, are happily combined in this edifice. It is in
perfect keeping with the elms and evergreens of the
city of New Haven, and the design is well suited for
the neighbourhood of larger cities, where space could
be allowed for ornamented grounds. Sydney M. Stone,
architect.

Glenn Cottage, (Plate XXX.,) Roxbury Highlands, is another of the beautiful designs of Mr. Lang. It is small, but exceedingly well arranged for convenience and for effect. The large bay-window in front opens into the main parlour, which is a fine, spacious apartment; back of this is a dining-room, separated from the parlour by an entry and stair-case. The small addition to the main building is for a library; the larger one is the kitchen, &c. The vicinity of Boston is remarkable for its romantic and beautiful scenery; and no locality in that neighbourhood is more strikingly picturesque than the Roxbury Highlands.

All the needful buildings about a country-house may be rendered picturesque, without great expense. Figs. 42, 43, 44, and 45 are designs, by Mr. Lang, for the smaller buildings on the grounds about one of the Highland cottages.

Fig. 42, a play-house for children.

FIG. 42.

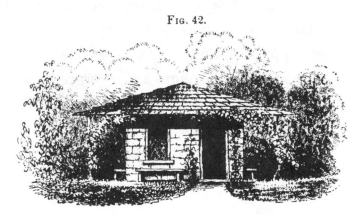

Plate XXX

GLENN COTTAGE.

Fig. 43. A small Garden House.

FIG. 43.

Fig. 44. A Rustic Arbour.

FIG. 44.

Fig. 45.   A Pump House.

Fig. 45.

The specimens of domestic architecture already given, have been mostly of a rural character.

Plate XXXI. is a perspective view of the mansion of James Dundas, Esq., in Philadelphia.   It is seldom that a city-house can be embellished with grounds so extensive, and thus command "ample room and verge enough" for every convenience and elegance of life. The plainness of the front is relieved by a beautiful Ionic portico, of white marble; the colour of the edifice is yellow, so delicate that the ornamental parts, though of a pure white, are not in glaring contrast.   It is, moreover, a symmetrical building, very pleasing to the eye.   Thomas U. Walter, architect.

Plate XXXI

MANSION OF JAMES DUNDAS ESQ. PHILA.

CHAPTER XXIV.

USE OF THE GRECIAN ORDERS AND GOTHIC STYLE IN PUBLIC BUILDINGS.

THE appropriate use of the Grecian orders, in the architecture of the United States, is a subject demanding nice investigation. This topic has been ably discussed in an article in the Journal of Science for 1830–31, and from it a few extracts will be made, although in some things, we take the liberty to differ from the very able writer.

The Roman Doric is frequently employed in our country. It differs from the Grecian in having a base; in the height of its shaft, which is eight diameters instead of six; in the capital, which is richer than the Grecian; in the disposition of the triglyphs; in the admission of a variety of decorations; in the metopes, and in a more richly-moulded frieze. Its characteristic is a cheerful dignity, which is often very agreeable, and for which we could perhaps find no substitute in the other orders.   I should be far from desiring its exclusion; but wish to have its proper character, and the danger to which we are exposed in using it, clearly understood.   The latter arises from the inherent richness of the order, seen in the numerous mouldings, and in the variety of ornament which it admits.   A flower, an ox-head,* a fillet, or something of this kind, is almost universally employed upon the metopes, and seems, indeed, to be requisite that the frieze may be in keeping with the architrave and cornice as well as the column.   By this minute attention to ornament, *the expression as a whole* may be sacrificed.   Here is the most difficult part of an architect's labours, and the most important, the part, indeed, in which his genius is chiefly shown.

"If I can convey my idea," says Sir Joshua Reynolds, "I wish to distinguish excellence of this kind by calling it, *the genius of mechanical performance.* This genius consists, I conceive, in the power of expressing, (in painting or architecture,) *the object as a whole;* so that the general effect and power of the whole may take possession of the mind; and for a while suspend the consideration of the subordinate and particular beauties or defects.   I do not mean to

---

* This most inappropriate ornament for a Christian edifice, may be seen upon the metopes of a Congregational church at New Haven, in the Grecian Doric or Tuscan style ; otherwise a fine building.

prescribe what degree of attention ought to be paid to the minute parts; this is hard to settle. We are sure that it is expressing the general effect of the whole, which alone can give to objects their true and touching character, and wherever this is observed, whatever else may be neglected, we acknowledge the hand of a master."

Beside the danger into which the Roman Doric is apt to lead, of neglecting this expression *as a whole*, in attention to minute parts, there are many purposes to which its powers are unequal. In most large edifices we wish to express grandeur, or solemnity, or both united. We shall find these in the true *Doric*. The Bank of the United States, at Philadelphia, is an example of this: and I know of no instance in which it has been employed, in which its pure, chaste, and noble character has not been at once appreciated. There is in it so much of true grandeur, united with great simplicity; such boldness, joined with delicacy in the outlines; such apparent recklessness of effect; such disregard to everything extraneous, and seeming confidence in its own inherent merits; in short, such consonance in all its parts with the principles of beauty with which we have been familiar in nature, that every one feels immediately a charm to which he has not been accustomed in architectural objects. In large banks, custom-houses, houses for legislation, or for the administration of laws, and for all edifices where grave and simple majesty is requisite in the expression, *the Doric* should be employed. It is an order, however, that will admit of no dallying; and he who uses it must be careful not to vary from the perfect proportions given it by Grecian skill, in the best days of Grecian art.

The *Ionic* has hitherto been much employed in our country, in the façades of churches and dwelling-houses. The ancient Ionic, uncorrupted by Roman invention, is light and graceful. The Roman Ionic, which is often substituted, has not the same fine expression, as a whole, (the point which an architect must ever keep in mind.) The Ionic is suitable for a high-school, or academy of art, and for the interior of legislative halls, and other large halls for public assemblies. It is peculiarly appropriate to suburban villas and fine country mansions. The *Composite*, which is a union of the Ionic and Corinthian, is not in good taste, and should seldom be employed.

The Corinthian was passionately admired, as we have seen, by the Romans, and has been much used in modern Europe. It is a favourite already in our own country. Its rich and elaborate ornaments are apt to delight the popular fancy. Here is its greatest danger; and if it should become the favourite order, it is predicted that we shall never rise to any eminence in architecture. "It can never be used for churches with any propriety." It certainly does not possess the

requisite solemnity, or gravity of expression. It is
well suited for light and tasteful edifices of a gay character. To recapitulate:

The Doric. The highest effort of the art, characterized by grandeur and majesty. To be employed in
all buildings where such an expression is desired.

Roman Doric, or *Tuscan.* Its character, a cheerful
and pleasing dignity. To be used where this expression may be desired, but to be used with caution.

Grecian Ionic. Gracefulness its characteristic.
Suited to the smaller kind of banks, to edifices for
the exhibition of the arts, sometimes for collegiate and
academic edifices, and for the larger kind of private
dwellings.

Roman and Modern Ionic. To be used in subser-
vience to the preceding, in order to keep it from being
made common, and for the sake of variety.

Corinthian. Gay and showy. To be used where
such is the expression desired.

The *Gothic* style has been considered too expensive
for general adoption, even for churches. But where
is our liberality, where our devotion? Should we not
set a noble example for those who are to come after
us? Should we not strive to erect lasting monuments
of the religion we profess? We complain of the want
of time-hallowed structures, consecrated by historic
and holy associations. Let us leave behind us some
sacred edifices, which the hearts of distant generations

will love and venerate, and farther, such as they will admire, that both the religion and the taste of the nineteenth century may command their respect.

It has been objected too, that the form of Gothic cathedrals (a cross) is unsuited to Protestant worship. Very true; but that does not preclude the employment of the Gothic style. A rectangular church, divided into aisles, is perfectly suitable, or rather, well adapted to the clustered pillars, and numerous arches of the vault. An edifice with Gothic windows on a smooth wall, both at the sides and above, is a burlesque upon the style. It is better not to adopt it at all, unless it can be carried out in all the subordinate parts. But this has been done successfully in our country. Christ Church, at Hartford, is an example of this. The style has been preserved even to the minutest details. The buttresses break up the smoothness of the exterior; and the interior is happily relieved from stern and naked simplicity by the galleries. These have been considered an evil. They doubtless would disfigure a cathedral. But, says the author to whom we have so often referred, the case is different with us. The form of our churches must be simple, a quality entirely at variance with this style, and without something to conceal and draw attention from this plainness, their interior will appear meagre and bare. Galleries assist in doing this; but the edifice should be accommodated to them, and they to it, more than is

now usually done. The windows should be so constructed, that we may feel that the gallery is not con-
cealing their beauty from our view; and on the other
hand, the gallery should not be carried in a straight
horizontal line from pillar to pillar, in the manner of a
Grecian entablature, but should be supported by low
arches, and thus made to preserve their Gothic character throughout. The great variety of arches and of
ornaments admitted by the style, will easily allow the
architect to do this. The cathedral form is represented by fresco painting upon the wall of the new
church in Washington Square, and the effect is considered by many as very fine; the deception complete.
Whether it is well to attempt such deception, is ques-
tionable.

The windows of a Gothic church should be of
stained, or ground glass; the former is in all cases to
be desired where it is not too expensive. Variety in
the designs, is in unison with this style. Uniformity
and variety seem paradoxical, yet they are most happily united in the true Gothic. The spire had its
origin with the Gothic style, but towers are generally
used with it in this country. Some architectural critics
object strenuously to the mode with us in common
use, of placing the tower and spire in the front of the
church. They contend, that the unity and beauty of
the façade are destroyed by this mode. Yet, to those
whose taste has not been formed by familiarity with

European churches, this objection does not suggest itself.

"But where shall it be put? The question is a perplexing one." Surely it is, and in most churches it would be a defect, rather than a beauty, to have the tower placed upon the other end of the church, and not in front. "In Gothic churches, a tower at each angle of the front is preferred. In this situation they will be powerful helpers to the façade; they give it breadth and richness, and it acquires the importance it deserves."

Where we employ the spire, I think we generally err in giving it too little height in proportion to the tower. The highest spire in England is one hundred and fourteen feet in height, the diameter of its base being nineteen; the tower on which it rests is seventy feet high, and twenty-two feet square.

One word more;—let us banish all fishes, arrows, and everything of the kind, everything resembling a vane, from the top of our spires. They are no ornament; a stranger would think us wonderfully anxious about the wind. If we must have them, let them be put in some other place.

Public edifices in almost every part of our country are now being built of durable materials; and they will stand as monuments of the taste and skill of the present age. We wish those who come after us to respect our memory; and, what is of far more consequence, to respect our laws and institutions. Let us then endeavour to have the objects associated with these laws and institutions,—(state-houses, colleges, academies, churches, &c.,)—such as to heighten reverence. The architect's work stands out in the broad light of day, where all see, where all judge, where all may applaud, and where all may sneer. They should then form their plans with careful deliberation.

Where expensive and lasting edifices cannot be built, it is still important to have churches in good taste.

Fig. 46.

The little church, Fig. 46, is a neat edifice for a small country parish, designed by Mr. Arthur Gilman, of Boston. This church is heavily framed, and covered with unplaned plank. The proportions are allowed by good judges to be beautiful. But the most striking feature of this church is the interior. It has an open timber roof. One of the advantages of this form of construction is, that a lofty interior can be had in a building with posts not over eighteen or twenty feet in length. The whole cost of this church, completely furnished, was less than $3000.

CHAPTER XXV.

IT has already been remarked, that it would be a great improvement to our cities, if more variety could be introduced into the houses that line the long streets. There is a sameness that is tiresome, in the uniform rows of doors and windows in an unbroken range of buildings. Although some general resemblance, in size and form, will, of necessity, prevail, the details may be endlessly varied.

The grave and majestic Doric will rarely be employed for dwelling-houses; they should have tho expression of cheerfulness, to be pleasing; yet, if it be true, as has been asserted, " that the character of a family, will generally be found to have some resemblance to the house in which they live," some grave and sober citizens will, here and there, rear a majestic front of granite, with Doric columns at the entrance, and an entablature, with its appropriate triglyphs and metopes.

The graceful and cheerful Ionic of the Greeks, is adapted to dwelling-houses, where white marble can be used for the building material.

Plate XXXII. The mansion of Matthew Newkirk, Esq., in Philadelphia. The front is of white marble. The beautiful portico is copied from the Erectheum; the Ionic columns and richly-ornamented capitals of that celebrated temple have been universally admired as perfect models in classic architecture. Thomas U. Walter, architect.

Where this order is employed upon the building as a whole, some of the smaller parts, especially in the interior, may be of the Roman Ionic. In small porticoes and fire-places, the modern Ionic is also extremely appropriate. The Corinthian, gay and beautiful as it is, can be seldom used to advantage, yet it should by no means be entirely excluded from the domestic architecture of large cities. A row of buildings in one of our cities has a Corinthian colonnade, with the columns so near to each other, that the weight they support appears quite too small, or rather the columns seem of little utility, and the houses behind them, appear only placed there that something may be attached to this elaborate colonnade.

The Roman Doric, or Tuscan, may occasionally be introduced with good effect, and the general expression is not unsuitable to large city mansions.

There has been for many years in our country a perfect mania for the Grecian orders. Every building, from the shop of the tradesman to the church and the capitol, must be Grecian.

In some instances houses appeared to be built merely

Plate XXXII

to accommodate a portico; or rather the Grecian porticoes stood elevating their bold fronts, with a mean house sneaking behind them.

An English writer severely criticises one of our public buildings as follows, namely: "Imagine an Ionic hexastyle, with fluted columns, stuck up against a two-storied house, and you have the image of it at once. Really, such a thing is enough to make one wish Grecian architecture buried ten thousand fathoms deep, beyond the possibility of resuscitation, and the very name of it obliterated for ever. It is *the very doggerel of architecture.* Why, if such things are allowed to pass for Grecian, there is no reason why apothecaries' Latin should not pass for Ciceronian. Taking this building as a sample of its architecture, I should say that America must be the paradise of builders and the purgatory of architectural connoisseurs."

Happily a better taste is now prevailing. The Grecian mania has passed by, and some caution is necessary that the people become not as rabid with the Gothic and Elizabethan mania, that has now seized them.

In the country, where a selection of the site of a house can be made, it is always best to choose one where fine trees are already grown.*

---

* "The first thing done in the new parts of our country, when a spot is determined on for a house, is to cut down all the trees within many rods of it; and then, year by year, the work of destruction goes

The Gothic style for dwelling-houses, although often censured, may be used with a happy effect. It can be made light and cheerful, and (admitting of much irregularity) extremely convenient.

Pugin, one of the best architectural writers on the

---

on, as if the very sight of a forest tree were odious. The house stands alone in the clearing, its inmates, and particularly the children, roasted and browned under the hot summer's sun ; but by and by the nakedness and dreariness of the situation are felt, and then are planted some *Lombardy poplars*, reminding us of Pope's couplet :

> ' A little house, with trees a row,
> And, like its master, very low.'

Now, the trees which we cut down with such an unsparing hand are the very kind which English gardeners cultivate with the most persevering diligence, and are planted here, just as they labour most to plant. And we too shall cultivate them before long, and shall then think with the most bitter regret of the sad destruction which we and our ancestors have made, but in vain ; for all the art of man will not be able to restore, in any length of time, such glades, and thickets, and lawns as we now possess. When about to build in a new country, we should save, *near our house, an acre or two of the forest*, and should guard it with the most watchful care. Morning, noon, and evening, it would be an agreeable retreat ; its shade would be refreshing in our scorching heats ; it would connect us in some measure with ages long since gone, and would bring before us the wild but high-souled Indian, his council-fire, his battle-song, the war, the chase, the feast, and the dance. A noble grove would gratify our taste ; it would raise our thoughts to Him who is ' a shadow from the heat, a strength to the needy in distress.' I say again, let us spare our noble forest trees."

Gothic style, says: "In designing or adapting Gothic edifices, it is of primary importance to calculate on the size, proportion, object, and situation of an intended building, and to select a style applicable to these points. The next requisite is to preserve harmony or consistency of style throughout all the members and details of the work. Disregarding this, or ignorant of its principles, many *builders*, miscalled *architects*, have committed egregious blunders, and have jumbled together in one design, not only the style of different ages, but mixtures of *castellated*, *domestic*, and *ecclesiastical* architecture. Indeed, it is to the tastelessness of persons who occasionally compose, or rather build such edifices, *without well-planned and well-digested designs*, that modern Gothic has been treated with sneers and contempt, and has been sarcastically termed ' Egyptianized, Castleized, Abbeyized,' &c. Whether a design is for a mansion, a cottage, or a church, does not appear to have entered into the calculations of many builders. They blunder on, with some confused notions of pointed arches, slender columns and embattled parapets; and at length produce a nondescript building, which cannot degrade them, *because they have no reputation to lose*, but unfortunately excites a prejudice against, and erroneous opinions of, a class of architecture which is susceptible of great beauties and impressive combinations."

It is lamentably true with regard to the Gothic style in our country, that awkward buildings, having no pretensions to rank under any known style, have disgusted the public.   Better success will attend those who employ men skilled in their art, and the capabilities and beauties of it will be made to appear.

As the mania for the Elizabethan style is actually raging, some remarks on the principles to be observed in the erection of Elizabethan villas will not be inappropriate.   This style is said to be peculiarly appropriate to a " woody or green country."

First. The building must be either quite chaste or excessively rich in decoration.   Every inch of ornament short of a certain quantity will render the whole effect poor and ridiculous; while the pure perpendicular lines of this architecture will always look well if left entirely alone.   The architect, therefore, when limited as to expense, should content himself with making his oriels project boldly, channelling their mullions richly, and, in general, rendering his vertical lines delicate and beautiful in their workmanship; but if his estimate be unlimited, he should lay on his ornament richly, taking care never to confuse the eye.   Those parts to which, of necessity, observation is especially directed, must be finished so as to bear a close scrutiny, that the eye may rest upon them with satisfaction; but their finish must not be of a character which would have attracted the eye by itself without being placed in a conspicuous situation; for, if it were, the united attraction of form and detail would confine the contemplation altogether to the parts so distinguished, and render it impossible for the mind to receive any impression of general effect. Consequently, the parts that project, and are to bear a strong light, must be chiselled with infinite delicacy ; but those parts which are to be flat, and in shade, should be marked with great sharpness and boldness, that the impression may be equalized. When, for instance, we have anything to do with oriels, to which attention is immediately attracted by their projection, we may run wreaths of the finest flowered-work up the mullions, charge the terminations with shields, and quarter them richly, but we must join the windows to the wall, where its shadow falls, by means of more deep and decided decoration.

Secondly. In the choice and design of his ornaments, the architect should endeavour to be grotesque, rather than graceful, (though little bits of soft flower-work here and there, will relieve the eye ;) but he must not imagine he can be grotesque by carving faces with holes for eyes, and knobs for noses ; on the contrary, whenever he mimics grotesque life, there should be wit and humour in every feature, fun and frolic in every attitude ; every distortion should be anatomical, and every monster a studied combination.

Thirdly. The gables must, on no account, be jagged into a succession of right angles, as if people were to be perpetually engaged in trotting up one side and down the other. This custom, though sanctioned by authority, has very little apology to offer for itself, based on any principles of composition.

In street effect, indeed, it is occasionally useful, and where the verticals below are unbroken by ornament, may be used in the detached Elizabethan, but not when decoration has been permitted below. They should then be carried up in curved lines, alternating with two angles, or three at the most, without pinnacles or hip-knobs. A hollow parapet is far better than a battlement in the intermediate spaces; the latter, indeed, is never allowable, except when the building has some appearance of having been intended for defence, and therefore is generally barbarous in the villa, while the parapet admits of great variety of effect.

Lastly. The garden of the Elizabethan villa should be laid out with a few simple terraces near the house, so as to unite it well with the ground.

Fig. 47 is a beautiful English villa, in the Elizabethan style. It has not the awkward, outré character of many of those buildings styled Elizabethan, which are blotting the fair face of our country,—those dark-brown deformities, with as many high, pointed gables as can be contrived by the skill of the ignorant artisan, in lieu of anything else to distinguish them as Elizabethan. This villa may serve as a model for a spacious country-house in the Northern, Middle, and Western States.

FIG. 47.

ELIZABETHAN VILLA.

CHAPTER XXVI.

A RANDOM CHAPTER, ON WALLS, CHIMNEYS, WINDOWS, ETC.

To build a "house upon the sand," is considered the extreme of folly; every wise man builds upon a firm foundation. If it is not upon a rock, it must be made firm by artificial means, such as driving timber into the loose soil or mud. Thus the Hollanders have built their cities, robbing old ocean of his rightful domain. Various kinds of walls have been used in ancient and modern times. The immense oblong stones employed by the Etruscans and Romans, were made perfectly smooth, and laid up without mortar, the courses overlaying each other so as to "break joint," as it is technically termed. A double wall was in some instances constructed, and the space between, filled in with broken bricks, rubbish, and mortar. The walls of the Pantheon were of this kind, and time has so consolidated the whole mass, that unless destroyed by an earthquake or volcano, they may stand as long as "the great globe itself." In some of the cities of the United States, walls for large buildings are only a brick and a half in thickness. Fearful consequences may result;—they have already resulted from this mistaken economy. Lives have been lost by their falling in.

Wooden walls of timber and boards do well for a new country, where forests are abundant, and men must build in haste; but as soon as they have more leisure and more wealth, they should build of less perishable materials.

In warm climates, flat roofs afford a pleasant retreat, where families gather with their books, work, &c., as in cold climates they do by the ingle-side; but where the snow must have an easy slide, or else encumber the roofs, they are high and steep.

The brightly polished floors of wood, and the beautiful cool marble, are for warm climates; in colder regions we are glad to be made comfortable by covering them with carpets.

Windows and doors may be made highly ornamental. They form the most important features in the architecture of the houses of a city. That the ancients had windows to their dwellings is quite certain, yet they must have been small and unornamented. Houses of one story were lighted from the roof. In the Lombardic period, windows began to be a conspicuous ornament, and in the Gothic style, they are *the*

Fig. 48.

ornament *par excellence.* The bay-windows (Fig. 48), or as they are often erroneously called, bow-windows, give beauty both to the interior and exterior of Gothic buildings. The windows of a city may be varied ad infinitum. Fig. 49, a rich style from the Palazzo Medici, Rome.

Fɪɢ. 49.

The question arises, cannot our architects furnish us with a truly American style? Will not something original in time be produced? Or rather, will not modifications grow out of former styles, suited to our climate, customs, and mode of life?

Doors in ancient edifices were of brass, bronze, and other rich materials; plates of gold and silver were used for their covering, and the finest sculpture was lavished upon them. In modern times, the portal constitutes the leading feature in the front of most buildings. For a dwelling-house, care should be taken that it be not too large; and yet, this is not a common defect. A wide, lofty entrance gives a hospitable expression to a dwelling-house, and besides, affords ample space for rich ornament.

Chimneys have almost invariably been ugly appendages to all kinds of buildings in our country. It is said by a tasteful architect, that "a chimney can properly be an *ornament* to nothing but a cottage." We like to see the curling smoke gracefully rising from the secluded cottage in the valley or on the mountain-side; it is associated with home-comfort. And a most important matter it becomes, that the smoke should arise "without let or hindrance." It may do so as well through a handsome as an ugly form, and therefore attention should be specially directed to it.

Fig. 50.　　　　　　　Fig. 51.

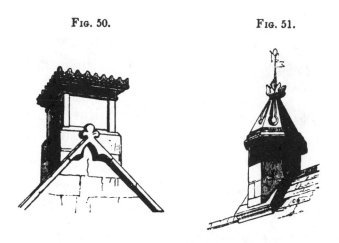

Decoration has been considered out of place upon a chimney, the main object being only to make them *not ugly*. Yet variety of form may be given, and this is desirable; and they should be kept in unison with the style of the edifices upon which they must appear. After all, generally the less conspicuous they are in a city the better; in the country they can be made picturesque. (Figs. 50 and 51, old English chimneys.)

In interior architecture, *fire-places* are among the most ornamental features. The introduction of furnaces and stoves, it is hoped, will not expel them from modern dwelling-houses. Marble of every variety is employed for fire-places in the United States, and many beautiful specimens of sculpture have been brought from Italy and France to decorate the mansions of the wealthy. The skill of native artists now renders it unnecessary to employ foreign aid for this or any other part of American buildings. Greenough, Powers, Clevenger, Augur, Brackett, Ives, Hughes, and many other sculptors, are known to every lover of national art. A long list of architects might be named, who have a right to claim commendation and confidence; to verify this, enter our large cities, and "look around."

To build without the aid of a skilful and scientific architect is presumptuous. It is a narrow-minded and short-sighted economy, which brings its own punishment. Let the artisan and the artist each have his own part assigned, and not trespass upon each other's ground. "We conclude," in the words of another, "with exhorting all house-builders (owners) to 'fling away ambition;' to contrive their houses with a view to comfort, rather than show; and to take special care that the proportions be not so great, and the cost so extravagant, as to gain for their edifices the unenviable name of 'Follies.'"

> "Art thrives most
> Where commerce has enriched the busy coast;
> He catches all improvements in their flight,
> Spreads foreign wonders in his country's sight,
> Imports what others have invented well,
> And stirs his own to match them, or excel."
>
> COWPER.

FIG. 52.

Fig. 52, an English school-house of the Elizabethan style. It is one of the famous Brompton school-houses, described at page 200. It is admirably adapted for the purpose designed, having separate entrances and apartments for girls and boys, and above them convenient recitation rooms. Surrounded by large shade trees, it would have a picturesque appearance.

CHAPTER XXVII.

ARRANGEMENTS OF A CITY, AND THE BEAUTI-FYING OF TOWNS AND VILLAGES.

THE Italian architectural writer Milizia, has given the following hints on the founding and arrangement of a city.

"In the case of founding a new city, the most advantageous position should be selected."

"1. The neighbourhood of marshy and low land should be avoided, because the air is thereby rendered unwholesome. 2. Plenty of good water is indispensable, either below the ground, that wells may be digged in any part of the city, or in the vicinity, that it may be brought in abundance by aqueducts and pipes to every house. 3. Nearness to the sea, or to a navigable river, for commercial advantages. 4. An eminence should be chosen, if possible, for the site, both for beauty of appearance, and for keeping the streets well drained. The form must be in a measure adapted to the location. The circular form and polygon have been recommended, but in general the square form will be found to offer the greatest advantages."

Some cities in the Western States have been laid out in a circular form, with a space in the centre for public edifices; the principal streets diverge from this open space, like the radii of a circle. These streets would be beautiful and convenient, but the cross-streets must be unpleasant, and the public buildings not sufficiently distributed for convenience. Perfect regularity produces disagreeable monotony.

" A city requires squares of various sizes, and streets cutting each other in various directions, and differing from each other in size and decorations. In this arrangement there should be quantity, contrast, even some disorder, to produce beauty and elegance. Extreme uniformity is an essential fault in a city." Of this fault we are at present not much in danger, in the United States. The builders of New York, followed " a cow-path," as tradition has it, for their principal streets. The settlers of Boston, says Dr. Dwight, "appear to have built where a vote permitted, or where danger or necessity forced them to build. The streets strike the eye of a traveller as if intended to be mere passages from one neighbourhood to another, and not as the open, handsome divisions of a great town. It deserves to be remembered, that almost all the great cities in the world have been formed in a similar manner. London, Paris, Madrid, Vienna, Moscow, Constantinople, Aleppo, &c., are all principally built on wretched streets, and with a deplorable confusion. The founders of Nineveh and Babylon seem to have been the only ancients who understood this subject. Whence these men acquired such largeness of heart, it will be difficult to determine, unless we suppose Nineveh to have derived its noble form from traditionary remains of antediluvian improvement, and Babylon to have been a copy of Nineveh. Why the Greeks, who readily adopted the improvements of other countries, and originated so many of their own, neglected a thing of so much consequence, it is not easy to explain." Doubtless they preferred variety to such perfect uniformity. "The plan of a city should be so arranged as to subdivide the whole into an infinity of particular beauties, each so widely differing from the other, that something new should be continually presenting itself to the eye. Four things are requisite to form a beautiful city, namely: 1. Its entrances. 2. Its streets. 3. Its squares. 4. Its edifices. 1. The entrances should be free, numerous in proportion to the size of the enclosure,* and sufficiently ornamented within and without. On the exterior should be a long road, with rows of trees on each side, and fountains, terminating in a square before the gate, which should be a superb triumphal arch, giving admittance to another noble square, surrounded by noble buildings, with several majestic

---

* This has reference to a city surrounded, like most European cities, with walls.

streets, branching off to various parts of the city, all terminated by some particular (imposing?) object."

Happily, we have no need of walls to surround our cities, but the suggestion of a broad road, with rows of trees on each side, is one that should be followed. It would thus form a delightful drive, or promenade, sheltered from the sun.

"2. The streets are for the purpose of rendering communication easy, they should therefore be numerous, straight, and wide. Their width must correspond not only with the size and population of the city, but also with the height of the edifices, and their own length. The greatest width should be in the centre, where there is the greatest thoroughfare. The streets should be planted with trees, when they are first laid out; some in regular rows, others at various places in groups.

"The squares should be numerous, and varied in figure and size, not only for the use of the people, but for the salubrity, and to give a more spacious effect."

The citizens of New York have at length become aware of the beauty and salubrity of public squares. St. John's Park, Washington Square, Union Square, and several others in recently-built parts of the city, are tastefully ornamented with trees and shrubbery, affording sweet green spots for the eye to rest upon, as a relief from the glare of brick walls and dirty pavements.

Every city should make ample provision for spacious public squares.   Trees of every variety, shrubs, flowers, and evergreens, should decorate these grounds, and fountains throw up their sparkling waters, contrasting their pure, white marble with the deep green foliage.   Here, beneath the shaded walks, the inhabitants might enjoy the sweet air, the children sport upon the fresh grass, and all be refreshed and cheered by the sight of beautiful natural objects.   Here the young and the old might meet to "drive dull care away," and lose for a few brief moments the calculating, money-making plans that almost constantly usurp American thought and feeling.

The Boston Common is the most spacious public pleasure-ground in the United States.   Seventy-five acres were appropriated by the early "fathers of the town" to this purpose, on the condition that it should ever remain devoted in this way to public convenience and comfort.   The same venerable elms which shaded the patriots of the Revolution, still wave over the heads of their successors, and fresh young trees are planted from year to year by the side of the new-gravelled walks, rendered necessary by the rapidly increasing population of the city.   The undulating ground of the Common gives it a pleasing diversity of hill and vale, and the little lake or pond near the centre, adds to its picturesque beauty.

The New York Battery, though much smaller, is very delightful, affording a view of the magnificent

harbour, gemmed with its beautiful islands.   Convenient seats are placed about the Battery, that its numerous visiters may quietly enjoy the cooling breezes from
the ocean, beneath the grateful shade of the trees.   It
is one of the loveliest spots in the world.

The public squares of Philadelphia, are incalcula-
bly important to the health of the city.   Beneath the
dense foliage of Washington Square, crowds of merry
children enjoy, unmolested, their healthful sports.
Within the enclosure of Independence Square, was
first promulgated the Declaration of Independence.
Franklin Square has in the centre a fountain, falling
into a handsome, white marble basin.   Penn, Logan,
and Rittenhouse Squares are also ornamental to the
city.

The New Haven Green has been justly celebrated
as one of the most beautiful public squares in this
country.   Its elms are remarkably fine; it has recently been enclosed with a light and tasteful iron
railing, which adds much to its beauty.

Many of our large cities are entirely destitute of
such green retreats.   Gardens and squares are so
necessary to the health, as well as the enjoyment of
those who are shut up in the close streets of a city,
that it should be considered an imperative duty to
provide them for all classes of the inhabitants.   It may
be urged, that if left open and free, the decorations
would soon be destroyed by the populace; some few

rude hands might occasionally make sad havoc among them, but when the people had once learnt how much such places of resort contributed to their health and pleasure, they would carefully protect them from injury.

" 4. The beauty of the edifices constitutes the principal beauty of the streets, squares, and city in general. And who should preside over this department? Every city should have its Academy of Architecture, without whose approbation nothing should be erected." (The independence of American taste would not submit to such dictation.) " The height of the houses should never be more than three stories, their façades regular and well proportioned, all equally simple, but differing in their style and ornament. Uniformity should be admitted in the squares only."

The public edifices should be so placed as to suit public convenience. The university, colleges, and high schools, should stand upon commanding situations, with squares and courts about them, planted with trees and ornamental shrubbery, excluding as much as possible the noise and dust of the city. A correct taste would thus be early implanted in the minds of the young, and a love of the beautiful "grow with their growth and strengthen with their strength." Banks, exchanges, and custom-houses, should be built where " men most do congregate;" and have the expression of richness and durability.

Markets, with abundant space about them, should be as near the suburbs as convenience permits, and should stand at the termination of some of the principal streets. The Boston market-house is finely situated, and is a beautiful building.

Hospitals, manufactories, and magazines, should be without the city, in open elevated places, where they can enjoy a free, fine atmosphere. Cemeteries should be laid out with taste; planted with suitable trees and evergreens, and kept with scrupulous neatness. Architecture ought to be displayed with the greatest sublimity in churches, which neither on the exterior nor within, should have anything mean or inelegant. They should stand upon an open square, or at the termination of a street, presenting the whole façade to close the vista.

The exterior of a church should be of one single order, simple and imposing. The Gothic is doubtless the most appropriate style for large churches; all the associations with that noble style are of a *Christian* and not of a Pagan character; or, in other words, it has always been appropriated to Christian worship. The Episcopal Church of the Holy Trinity, at Brooklyn, New York, is one of the finest specimens of Gothic architecture in this country. A citizen of Brooklyn, with a munificence above commendation, has erected this noble edifice, at a cost of about one hundred and fifty thousand dollars. Lefevre, architect.

VILLAGES.

Bad judgment and bad taste have prevailed in the laying out of many of the villages in the United States. The New England villages have been much admired for their neatness and beauty. An observing and venerated author,* whom we have once or twice quoted, thus contrasts the villages, or towns, in the Connecticut Valley with those on the Hudson River:—"They are not, like those along the Hudson, mere collections of houses and stores, clustered round a landing, where nothing but mercantile and mechanical business is done; where the inhabitants form no connexions nor habits beside those which naturally grow out of bargains and sales; where the position of the store determines that of the house, and that of the wharf often commands both; where beauty of situation is disregarded, and every convenience, except that of trade, is forgotten. On the contrary, they are villages destined for the reception of men busied in all the employments existing in this country. The settling in them is not merely to acquire property, but to sustain the relations, perform the duties, and contribute to the enjoyments of life. Equally, and, to my eye, happily, do they differ from most European villages. The villages on the other side of the Atlantic are exhibited as being generally clusters of houses, standing contiguously on the street;

* President Dwight.

built commonly of rough stone, clay, or earth, and roofed with thatch, without court-yards or inclosures, and of course incapable of admitting around each house the beautiful appendages of shrubs, trees, gardens, and meadows.

" New England villages, and, in a peculiar degree, those of the Connecticut Valley, are built in the following manner.

" The local situation is pitched on, as a place *in itself desirable;* as a place, not where trade compels, but where happiness invites to settle. Accordingly, the position of these towns is usually beautiful." One wide street, planted with trees, generally passes through the whole length of the village. " The town-plot is originally distributed into lots, containing from *two to ten acres*, (not twenty by fifty feet!) In a convenient spot, on each of these, a house is erected at the bottom of the court-yard, often neatly enclosed, and is furnished universally with a barn and other convenient out-buildings. Near the house there is always a garden, replenished with culinary vegetables, flowers, and fruits, and very often also, prettily enclosed. The lot on which the house stands, universally styled the home-lot, is almost, of course, a meadow, richly cultivated, and containing generally a thrifty orchard. It is hardly necessary to observe, that these appendages spread a singular cheerfulness and beauty over a New England village, or that they contribute largely to render the house a delightful residence."

These villages have been the models of many in the western part of New York, and still farther west. The buildings in some of these villages, especially in the State of New York, are superior to those of New England. Who has not admired the beautiful location of Canandaigua, Geneva, and Skaneateles, upon their lovely lakes? The refined taste exhibited in their style of building too, has excited the surprise and pleasure of travellers. We have been accused of a want of patriotic and generous feelings as a nation; of possessing strong individuality of feeling and interest, amounting to absolute, controlling selfishness. This accusation may, or may not be true; it is perhaps as difficult for us to know ourselves as a nation, as the wise Milesian considered it for each one to be acquainted with himself. It is certain that we have too few objects of common interest. Every state, county, and even village, is divided into innumerable jarring and contending parties and sects. Though a prosperous, we are not a cheerful people. Anything that would contribute to unite public feeling, by bringing men to act together for the general good, would be a great benefit to a community. Suppose it to be a public garden and promenade, open and free to all. Every villager contributes according to his means to this object. Some suitable persons are chosen to lay out the grounds, others to keep them in order. It belongs to the village, it must be beautiful, for the good of the village. It is a common object of thought, feeling, and action. The moral influence of it will soon be felt. The men, instead of going to the tavern for the news, may walk out at the sweet hour of summer twilight, and beneath spreading trees enjoy the society of his neighbours, and at the same time have his children under his eye.

"Who can say enough in praise of the Pareo?* (The Prado, or place for the evening promenade.) It furnishes an amusement at once delightful and innocent, and from which not even the poorest are excluded; a school where the public manners, and the public morals are beautified and refined by social intercourse, and by mutual observation; where families meet families, and friends meet friends, as upon a neutral ground, inform themselves of each other's affairs, unrestrained by ceremonial, and keep alive an intimacy, without the formalities of a visit. In these delightful associations, persons of every rank and every calling forget their exclusive pretensions, whilst the softer sex, to whom belong the attributes of modesty and grace, banish indecorum, and shed a charm over the whole assemblage."

If this public garden or promenade were richly and tastefully arranged and ornamented, a desire for neat and pleasant dwelling-houses would naturally arise among the villagers. Lord Kames, in his " Elements of Criticism," remarks, that, " In Scotland, the regularity and polish even of a turnpike-road has some

---

* A Year in Spain, by an American.

influence of this kind upon the people in the neighbourhood. They become fond of regularity and neatness; which is displayed first upon their yards and little enclosures, and next within doors. A taste for regularity and neatness, thus acquired, is extended by degrees to dress, and even to behaviour and manners."

Two little girls from a city, had one day taken a long walk beyond the city, upon a public road. A sudden shower of rain threatened to drench them to the skin. Several houses upon the road offered themselves as places of shelter; the youngest girl proposed to enter the nearest one. " No," said the elder, " we will not go in here, nor into the next, but yonder is a neat, pretty cottage, with flowers in the front yard; I know they will be kind there." " But this is the biggest house," urged the younger sister. " Oh! but I am afraid to go in here, it looks so dirty and careless; hurry, hurry, sister! for I know they will treat us well where they take so much pains with their neat house and garden." And the girl's reasoning was correct. There was gentleness and kindness within, as well as neatness and taste without.

Would it not be well if some of our statesmen would condescend to pay more attention to this subject? How often might they become public benefactors, at a small expense of time and money, if they were men of cultivated taste and generous public spirit! Those beautiful avenues of elms in the city of New Haven, are they not graceful, magnificent monuments to the memory of the noble statesman who placed them there? Who can estimate the influence that his tasteful benevolence has exerted upon the community to which he was so great a benefactor?

On a review of this subject, it may be urged, that we are a business people, an industrious people; we have no time to devote to amusements; besides, we are a serious people, and such objects as are here proposed, are not in unison with our habits and feelings. Our cities must grow up and increase as they have done hitherto, without the fostering hand of taste; we are young, and not yet prepared for such improvements, if indeed they are improvements. With due deference to those who differ, and with becoming modesty, we must still urge that the purity of morals, the simplicity and sobriety of the citizens of the United States, would not be endangered by suitable attention to the cultivation of a taste for architecture, and the beautifying of cities and villages. It is as easy to plan a city, a village, or a building, in good taste, as in bad taste, and *as cheap too*, since that is an all-important consideration. Simplicity of style in architecture is in itself a beauty. A Doric temple is perfectly simple, yet what object of art is more imposing and beautiful? We have wealth enough, if we have only taste to use it, to render our country as superior in artificial, as it is in natural beauty, to almost any country in the wide world. When Athens was at the height of her glory and splendour, she had not one quarter of the population or the wealth that the State of New York now possesses. And New York is arousing herself like a giantess, and soon, we trust, will exhibit to the world buildings which, for "nobleness of design, vastness and grandeur of conception, proportion and harmony of parts," shall rival the decaying glories of republican Athens.

But this is not what we would mainly urge. There may, and ought to be taste, and even elegance, where there is but little wealth. Every town and village may appear beautiful, if proper attention be paid to the houses and grounds. A rustic farm-house may be convenient and picturesque. A turnpike gate, now a most unsightly object, might be made even ornamental. If we are not yet prepared for these things, we ought to be. Professing ourselves free, liberal, enlightened, *refined*, without any perception of beauty!

> " Beauty was sent from Heaven,
> The lovely ministress of truth and good,
> In this dark world; for truth and good are one,
> And Beauty dwells in them, and they in her,
> With like participation. Wherefore then,
> O sons of earth! would ye dissolve the tie?"

Does any one fear that our morality, nay, even our holy religion, may be endangered by the cultivation of taste?

" On virtue can alone a kingdom stand ;
On public virtue ; every virtue join'd.
For lost, this social cement of mankind,
The greatest empires, by scarce felt degrees,
Will moulder soft away, till tottering loose,
They prone at last, to total ruin rush."

What then must preserve the public virtue? In
the language of the poet just quoted, we answer :—

" Sweet-featured Peace ; fearless Truth ;
Firm Resolution ; Goodness, blessing all
That can rejoice ; Contentment, surest friend ;—
.   .   .   True-judging, moderate desires ;
Economy and Taste combined, direct
The clear affairs, and from debauching fiends
Secure the kingdom."

We can scarcely conceive of a more effectual check
to extravagance and licentiousness, than careful cultivation of the Fine Arts.   They may be a consequence
of luxury, but they do not produce it.   Luxury may
lead to sensuality and extravagance ; but it is not when
employed upon useful works of art, or in giving beauty
to objects of sight, that it endangers public morals.
We should be careful to separate the luxury and licentiousness from the fine arts which have been cultivated,
when and where they also have prevailed, and have
led to the final destruction of a nation.   It was not the

Parthenon, nor the Temple of Jupiter Olympus, that brought the Greeks to destruction. A false system of religion, war and a love of conquest, licentiousness and falsehood, effected what Darius and Xerxes were unable to accomplish.

CHAPTER XXVIII.

CEMETERIES.

THERE is one thing more to be mentioned—the cemetery. For too many years these places of solemn and mournful memories were merely places of quiet deposit. We seemed not to honour the departed even as much as the Mahomedans. Even the untutored Indian holds sacred the burial-place of his ancestors, and his vengeance is implacable against him who dares to violate their resting-place.

With the increase of civilization and refinement, a taste for the beautiful and sublime is induced; but the exalted principles of Christianity evoke a deeper sentiment, which leads us to hallow the grave where rest the remains of our beloved ones, till the last trumpet shall summon them to put on immortality.

"There is certainly no place, not even the church itself, where it is more desirable that our religion should be present to our mind, than the cemetery; which must be regarded either as the end of all things, or the last, melancholy, hopeless, resort of perishing humanity, the sad and fearful portion of man, which is to involve body and soul alike in endless night, or, on the other hand, as the gateway to a glorious immortality, the passage to a brighter world, whose splendours beam even upon the dark chambers of the tomb. It is from the very brink of the grave, where rest the mortal remains of those whom we have best loved, that Christianity speaks to us in its most triumphant soul-exalting words, of victory over death, and a life to come."* Every city and every town should have the cemetery placed at some distance from them, away from the bustle and distracting din of busy life, where the associations are of a soothing and elevating character. Appropriations of ground for this purpose have been made by most of our larger cities; and our villages are, with pious sentiment and refined taste, beautifying their burying-grounds.

"The grave should be surrounded by everything that might inspire tenderness and veneration for the dead, (says Washington Irving,) or that might win the living to virtue; it is the place, not of disgust and dismay, but of sorrow and meditation.

"Let us be careful, however, in our anxiety to escape from gloom and horror, not to run into the opposite extreme of meretricious gaudiness." The solemn realities of death are not to be shut out of sight by the paltry ornaments and misplaced conceits of "fashionable prettiness." The cemetery should be placed

---

* North American Review.

among venerable woods, shut out from the "working-day world," where no sound can reach the spot but the low murmur of the wind through the summer leaves, or the sighing of the storm through the wintry branches, realizing, if any situation could do so, the description of the poet:

> " There is a calm for those who weep,
> A rest for weary pilgrims found;
> They softly lie and sweetly sleep
> Low in the ground."

These chosen spots must be enclosed, and the aid of art is demanded for these enclosures and their gateways for chapels and monuments.

Enclosures.—Heavy walls have been erected in many places, where iron railings might have answered a better purpose for enclosures. But where the place originally selected has, through the increase of population, been brought into close proximity with the town or village, high walls may be needed to give the spot within, the air of seclusion and quietness most desirable for solemn meditation and mournful remembrances.

Gateways.—These may be built of sufficient size to accommodate the gate-keeper with a place of residence. The Egyptian style has been adopted in many instances for these ornamental entrances. Its massiveness may have recommended it, as conveying ideas of duration and strength; but what other association can it have, appropriate to a Christian cemetery? The emblems are such as paganism suggested; the form of the structure is that of the propylon which guarded the entrance to the temples of idolatry.

Grecian gateways are far more beautiful; but "there is no analogy between the classical style of architecture and a Christian burial-place." "But there is a style which belongs peculiarly to Christianity, and owes its existence even to this religion; whose very ornaments remind one of the joys beyond the grave; whose lofty vaults and arches are crowded with the forms of prophets, and martyrs, and beatified spirits, and seem to resound with the choral hymns of angels and archangels. But peculiarly are its power and sublimity displayed in the monuments it rears over the tomb— the architecture of Christianity, the sublime, the glorious Gothic."

Chapels.—These have usually been built in the Gothic style. Mount Auburn and Laurel Hill have appropriate edifices of this kind. The Monument Cemetery has a chapel, (Plate XXII.,) which answers the double purpose of a gateway and a place for religious services.

Architecture and sculpture have from time immemorial been employed to perpetuate the memory of the dead. *Monuments* are raised as memorials of the glory of the departed, far from the place where their

---

* Architectural Magazine.

remains are interred, or they are shrines or sepulchres for the dust of death. " The monument rejoices,—the sepulchre mourns." This beautiful sentiment would seem to forbid the erection of splendid monuments by private affection. " All *monuments* to individuals are, to a certain extent, triumphant."

Hence, there should be the proper expression, in these consecrated shrines. Simplicity,—pure, chaste simplicity, for the memento of private affection and grief, magnificence and beauty, when a nation perpetuates the glory of the departed.

Free scope should be given to individuals for the exercise of taste and feeling in selecting shrines for their loved ones. " They are instructive records for those who wander among them, musing on the mystery of their own existence," and care should be taken, that they be appropriate to the character of the departed; that the associations should all be harmonious.

" The grave must always have a home-feeling about its peace; it should have little connexion with the various turbulence which has passed by for ever; it should be the dwelling-place and the bourne of the affections."

" The dead, the dead! the precious dead,
O bear them from the noisy tread,
And crowded haunts of busy men,
To the sunlit mount and vine-clad glen;
Where the mourner, bending o'er the stone,
May pour her tears, and breathe her moan,

In the luxury of grief alone ;
And no profane step intrude,
Upon the silent solitude."

To carry out the expression, and appropriate associations of a monument erected by those who would
honour " the mighty dead," such localities should be
chosen as will best suit the character of the person
thus commemorated.

" The monument to the Swiss, who fell at Paris,
defending the king, in 1790, is in the very heart of
the land in which their faithfulness was taught and
cherished, and whose children they best approved
themselves in death ; it is cut out in their native crags,
in the midst of their beloved mountains. A tall crag
of gray limestone rises in a hollow behind the town of
Lucerne ; it is surrounded by thick foliage of various
and beautiful colour ; a small stream falls gleaming
through one of its fissures, and finds its way into a
deep, clear, and quiet pool at its base, an everlasting
mirror of the bit of bright sky above, that lightens
between the dark spires of the uppermost pines. There
is a deep and shadowy hollow at the base of the cliff,
increased by the chisel of the sculptor ; and in the
darkness of its shade, cut in the living rock, lies a
dying lion, with its foot on a shield bearing the fleur-
de-lis, and a broken lance in its side."

One of the most beautiful and appropriate sites
for the monument of a hero, may be seen on the banks

Plate XXXIII

ENTRANCE TO THE CEMETERY AT NEW HAVEN.

of the Hudson River. Amid the evergreens that crown the summit of the frowning Palisades, and where they are shaken by the cannon of West Point, rises the monument of Kosciusko.

It would be impossible in the brief space allotted to this topic, to name all the cemeteries in our country that challenge admiration.

Greenwood Cemetery near New York, is beautifully situated, and contains many magnificent monuments.

The "burying-ground" at New Haven, Connecticut, has long been celebrated for its beauty. It has recently been enclosed with a massive wall on three sides, and a bronzed iron fence in front. The entrance is of freestone, in the Egyptian style. (Plate XXXIII.) H. Austin architect.

Mount Auburn, near Boston, for its great extent, and the uncommon variety and beauty of its natural scenery, has been justly placed among the most beautiful. The hillside, with its verdant covering of fresh grass and aspiring trees; the sequestered glen, where the bright waters of the miniature lakes reflect the clear sky and passing clouds; the flowers, the birds, and the squirrels, all give to this lovely spot the character of sweet and tranquil rural retirement. It is rarely that a spot can be found so near a city, where nature has been left in primitive and beautiful simplicity, to receive the congregation of the dead.

Laurel Hill, on the banks of the Schuylkill, is another rural cemetery, consecrated to the repose of the dead, by the citizens of Philadelphia. "Every mind capable of appreciating the beautiful in nature, must admire its gentle declivities, its expansive lawns, its hill beetling over the picturesque stream, its rugged ascents, its flowery dells, its rocky ravines, and its river-washed borders."

In humble imitation of the Almighty Artificer, man becomes the creator of beauty; he decorates his earthly habitation, and his final resting-place. The sense of the beautiful, and the power to produce it, are among the gifts of his higher nature, to be perfected when the "mortal shall put on immortality."

> "Thanks for each gift divine!
> Eternal praise be thine,
> Blessing and love, O thou that hearest prayer!
> Let the hymn pierce the sky,
> And let the tombs reply!
> For seed that waits the harvest time, is there.

Plate XXXIV

BANK OF NORTH AMERICA PHILA.

CHRONOLOGICAL TABLE

B. C.

1400. *Trophonius* and *Agamades* are said to have been the sons of a Bœotian King. They built the renowned Temple of Apollo, at Delphos. Cicero relates, that after they had completed this magnificent work, they prayed the God to reward them with whatever was best for man; three days after, they were found dead.

1250. *Dædalus* was an Athenian of the royal family, who built the famous Labyrinth in the Island of Crete, and many other edifices in various places.

1200. *Hermogenes* built the Temple of Bacchus, at Teos, in the Ionic order, remains of which are still seen. Vitruvius calls him the father of pure architecture.

700. *Rhœcus* and *Theodorus*, of Samos, rebuilt the famous Temple of Juno, of the Doric order, at Samos. Theodorus was also a sculptor.

---

* Taken principally from Milizia. The chronology is not supposed to be perfectly acurate.

650. *Eupalinus*, of Megara, constructed a magnificent aqueduct at Samos, and other immense buildings, the ruins of which are remaining.

550. *Pteras* built a city in Crete, and adding a letter to his name, called it *Aptera*. *Spinthærus*, of Corinth, rebuilt the Temple of Apollo, at Delphi, which had been destroyed by fire. *Ctesiphon* designed and commenced the famous Temple of Diana, at Ephesus.

540. *Metaganes*, his son, carried on the Temple; he invented ingenious machines to carry the immense columns from the quarry, eight miles distant, safely to the temple. To this famous edifice all Greece, and her colonies, contributed for the space of two hundred years, when it was burnt by Erostratus.

500. *Gitiades*, of Sparta, constructed there the Brazen Temple of Minerva. *Chirosophus*, of Crete, built a number of temples at Tegea.

450. *Callimachus*, of Corinth, invented the Corinthian capital, and established the proportions of the Corinthian order. *Andronicus Cyrrhestes*, of Macedonia, built the Temple of the Winds at Athens. It was octagonal, representing on each side, in sculpture, the wind that blew from that quarter. *Clœtus*, an architect and sculptor, erected the barrier and Stadium, near Olympia, where the Olympic games were celebrated. *Pheacus* erected some splendid temples at Agrigentum,

in Sicily, the remains of which may still be seen. *Libon*, of Messena, erected the famous Temple of Jupiter, near Olympia, in which was the statue of Jupiter, by Phidias.

FROM THE TIME OF PERICLES, TO ALEXANDER THE GREAT.

Pericles, the munificent patron of the arts, was himself an architect. By continually observing the erection of so many magnificent works at Athens, by conversing with the most able architects, especially his friend Anaxagoras the philosopher, who was president of architecture, Pericles acquired the science; the design of the Odeum, at Athens, is attributed to him. *Ictinus* and *Callicrates* were employed by Pericles to erect a Temple to Minerva, called Parthenon or Virgin. *Phidias* was also employed upon this temple, both as sculptor and architect. A full description of it has been given under Grecian Architecture. These architects erected many other beautiful edifices in Greece. *Mnesicles*, by order of Pericles, built the famous Propylon, that magnificent portico which served as an entrance and façade to the citadel of Athens. At this time Greece abounded with treatises on Architecture; the artists were accustomed to give descriptions of the

edifices on which they had been employed.   Most
of these writings are now lost, but durable monuments remain to demonstrate the perfection to
which the art had attained in the days of Pericles.

420. *Polyclites* built a rotunda of white marble at
Epidaurus, and a theatre, which Pausanias says
were " of singular beauty."   *Demetrius, Peonius,*
and *Daphnis,* built some of the most magnificent
temples in various parts of Greece.   *Statyrus* and
Pytheus were employed upon the superb tomb,
which Queen Artimisia caused to be erected in
Halicarnassus, to the memory of her husband,
Mausolus, King of Caria.   The tomb was considered one of the seven wonders of the world,
and has given the name of Mausoleum, to monuments erected for a similar purpose.   *Pytheus*
built in Prienne a Temple to Minerva Polias, of
the Doric order, the remains of which are still to
be seen.   Pytheus described this temple in a written exposition.   He was so enthusiastic a lover of
his profession, that he asserted, " It behoved an
architect to excel more in all arts and sciences
than the individuals who carried each art and
science to the highest summit of reputation."

Scopas, of Paros, an island in the Ægean Sea,
celebrated for its beautiful white marble, was a
sculptor and an eminent architect.

FROM ALEXANDER THE GREAT TO AUGUSTUS.

B. C.

300. At the period when Alexander enriched Greece with the spoils of the various nations he had subjugated, architecture shone in its fullest splendour. It was then introduced into Macedonia, where there still exists an ancient temple, having more than one thousand columns of the finest marble, jasper, porphyry, &c. From thence it spread over the various countries which fell under the dominion of Alexander's successors. The beautiful ruins of Balbec and Palmyra may belong to this period, as their date is uncertain. Balbec, or Baalbek, stands in a delightful plain, at the foot of Mount Libanus, in Syria. It was anciently called Heliopolis, which signifies the same as Baal-bek, the city of Baal, or the Sun, the divinity to whom the splendid temples were consecrated, which now excite the wonder and admiration of the traveller. The Corinthian order predominates everywhere; and to grandeur of architecture is united the beauty of sculpture, of the most exquisite design and finish. The remains of Baalbek vie with the most stupendous works of Egypt, Athens, or Rome. The same may be said of Palmyra, in Syria, called Tadmor in the Desert, and believed by some writers to have been founded by Solomon. Amid the desolation of these splendid remains are

many high towers, of five or six stories, which were used as sepulchres for this city of the dead. Oblivion has for ever buried the names of the architects who planned these beautiful remains, and a solemn mystery enshrouds their works. This magnificent city of Palmyra was destroyed by the Emperor Aurelian, when he conquered Queen Zenobia, about A. D. 273; a piece of wanton barbarity, which disgraces the page of history.*
Dinocrates, an ingenious but neglected architect of Macedon, determined to attract the attention of Alexander. He clothed himself in a lion's skin, with a chaplet of poplar boughs on his head, and a club in his hand, like Hercules. His large stature, agreeable countenance, and dignified mien, suited well with this disguise; the king was attracted by the novelty of his appearance, and demanded who he was. "I am," replied Dinocrates, a "Macedonian architect, who come to thee with ideas and designs worthy of the greatness of thy fame; I have formed a design to cut Mount Athos into the statue of a man, in whose left hand shall be a large city, and in his right hand a basin, which shall receive all the rivers of the mountain, and discharge them into the sea." Alexander inquired if there would be sufficient country around the city in the giant's hand, to supply it with food. When answered that there would not,

---

* Wood's Balbec and Palmyra.

and that it must be supplied by sea, Alexander declined the proposition, but retained the architect in his service. The fame of the Emperor and the architect was more effectually perpetuated by the building of Alexandria, at the mouth of the Nile. Dinocrates planned this magnificent city; its walls, fortified with towers, its aqueducts, fountains, canals, temples, palaces, and streets; Cairo furnished an immense quarry, from which the new city was adorned. Few architects ever had the direction of a work so important.

300. *Sostratus*, one of the most celebrated architects of antiquity, was so esteemed by Ptolemy Philadelphus, that he was surnamed " The favourite of kings." His greatest work was the lighthouse in the Isle of Pharos, considered one of the wonders of the world. It was a tower 450 feet high, built upon a rock, and could be seen at a hundred miles distance. It consisted of several stories, decreasing in size; the ground story was a mile in circumference; at the top was an immense lantern, where fires were lighted at night to guide the mariner's course. On the lighthouse was the following inscription in Greek, " Sostratus of Cnidus, son of Dexiphanes, to the gods, the saviours; for the benefit of sailors." It has been said that Sostratus secretly covered this inscription with cement, and placed over it another in honour of Ptolemy, which in a few years mouldered away and showed the first.

200. *Cossutius*, one of the first Roman architects, who adopted the Grecian orders. It is remarkable that we have no previous notice of Roman architects, when it is known that the simple Doric was introduced very early into Italy, and that the Etrurians were skilled in the art. In their edifices they used stones of immense size, often fifty feet long, and thirty wide. The best artists employed in Rome, were, for a long time, brought from Etruria. *Hermadorus*, of Salamis, is supposed to have built the Temple of Mars, in the circus of Flaminius, at Rome.

Saurus and *Batrarchus* were Lacedemonians who built several temples at Rome, at their own expense. Not being allowed to inscribe their names upon their works, they perpetuated these by carving upon them a *lizard* and a *frog*, which their names signify. In the churches of St. Eusebius and St. Lorenzo, at Rome, may still be seen Ionic capitals with a lizard and frog carved in the eyes of the volutes. They doubtless were taken from some ancient temple built by these architects.

100. *C. Mutius*, constructed the Temples of Honour and Virtue, at Rome.

Valerius of Ostia, invented a manner of covering the theatres at Rome, which were before without roofs.

FROM THE REIGN OF AUGUSTUS TO THE DECLINE
OF ARCHITECTURE.

FROM THE FIRST TO THE FOURTH CENTURY.

A. D.

1. The reign of Augustus, was the golden age of science and the fine arts throughout the Roman empire. In the time of the Cæsars, fourteen magnificent aqueducts conducted whole rivers to Rome from a distance of many miles, and supplied one hundred and fifty public fountains, one hundred and eighteen immense public baths, besides the water which was necessary for those Naumachia or artificial seas in which naval combats were represented; 100,000 statues ornamented the public squares, the temples, streets, &c.; ninety colossal statues, raised on pedestals; forty-eight obelisks of Egyptian granite adorned various parts of the city. Nor was this stupendous magnificence confined to Rome; all the provinces emulated the capital. We have unfortunately but scanty memorials of the architects of that period, and amid the stupendous edifices we seek in vain for the names of those who erected them. However much the age of Augustus may be exalted, we cannot think it equal to the age of Alexander. The Romans cultivated the arts more from pride

and ostentation, than from refined taste. Domitian expended £7,000,000 in gilding the Temple of Jupiter Capitolinus, and caused several columns of Pentelic marble, that were extremely beautiful and of perfect proportions, to be recut and polished, thus depriving them of their symmetry and grace. Every country may still turn to unrivalled Greece for models in the fine arts.

Vitruvius Pollio, was born at Formiæ, in Italy. He may be regarded as the father of Roman Architecture. He wrote an elaborate treatise, giving the rules of Grecian Architecture, together with the names of many ancient architects and their works. He lived in the time of Augustus, his great work being dedicated to that Emperor. He built a basilica justiciæ, and probably planned many other edifices; but at length overcome by the jealousies of his contemporaries, he gave himself up more to study than to practice. If we can judge of an author's character by his works, he was a man of excellent morals.

Vitruvius Cerdo, erected at Verona a beautiful triumphal arch of the Corinthian order.

C. Posthumius and *Cocceitus Auctus*, were both freedmen and architects, at Rome.

Celer and *Severus* were employed by Nero in the construction of his " Golden House," which surpassed all that was stupendous and beautiful in Italy. The Emperor's statue, one hundred and twenty feet high, stood in a court ornamented with porticoes of three rows of lofty columns, each row a mile long. The gardens were so large, that a pond in them was converted into a miniature sea, surrounded by a city. Gold, gems, and other precious materials were used with reckless profusion. The most exquisite perfumes were shed from the vaulted ceiling of the banqueting hall, which represented the firmament constantly revolving, imitating the motions of the heavenly bodies. The Emperor Vespasian restored to the people the lands which Nero had taken from them, and thus the Golden House disappeared, like one of the enchanted palaces of Ariosto; in its place rose the mighty Coliseum and the magnificent Temple of Peace. Of these, and thousands of sumptuous edifices at Rome, the architects are unknown.

80. *Rabirius* was employed in many works by the Emperor Domitian. The Roman road called Via Domitiana was forty miles long, and constructed with such solidity that it seemed made for eternity. At the point where this way met the Via Appia, were a triumphal arch and a bridge both of white marble, very richly ornamented. Rabirius is believed to have been the architect of all these great works.

Julius Frontinus composed a work on the Roman

aqueducts of which he had the superintendence under the Emperor Nerva.

C. Plinius Secundus, the nephew and adopted son of Pliny the naturalist, though not an architect by profession, planned many edifices, which he has described with great ability. What does most honour to Pliny, is the excellent use he made of his riches, which every opulent man should imitate; he erected at Como, his native place, a library, and endowed it with funds for the maintenance of a professor and poor scholars.

Mustius erected a temple to Ceres, by order of and at the expense of the above-mentioned Pliny.

Apollodorus was born at Damascus, and by his rare talents acquired the favour of the Emperor Trajan. He is celebrated as one of the few independent architects. His most famous work was a bridge over the river Danube. The length of this bridge was a mile and a half, its height three hundred feet. The life of Apollodcrus was unhappily terminated. The Emperor Adrian built a temple to Venus and Rome; when it was finished, he sent a plan of it to the accomplished architect, to prove that it was in his power to build without assistance. Apollodorus, who was not a courtier, remarked, that if the goddess of the temple, who was represented in a sitting posture, should be inclined to rise and take an airing, she must break her head on the ceiling. Adrian perceived the irreparable error, and revenged himself upon Apollodorus, by taking off the too candid artist's head.

C. Julius Lacer flourished in the time of Trajan, in honour of whom he built a small but elegant temple at Alcantara in Spain. He also constructed a bridge over the Tagus, considered the most celebrated in all Spain.

100. *Detrianus,* more of a courtier than Apollodorus, cultivated the good opinion of Adrian, who confided to his management the greatest works that were done at Rome. This architect restored the Pantheon, the Forum of Augustus, and many other edifices that had been burnt or destroyed. No sovereign erected so many buildings in all parts of the empire as Adrian; doubtless many of them were from his own designs, as he was constantly journeying through the provinces.

Antoninus, a senator of Rome, was well versed in architecture.

150. *Hippias* was much esteemed for his peculiar ability in the construction of baths. *Nicon,* the father of the celebrated physician Galen, was a mathematician and architect.

250. The Emperor Alexander Severus, was a great lover of Architecture. Not content with employing the most able professors, he wished the science taught publicly to the youth destined to the pursuit. In times so happy for the art, it is

astonishing that the names of no architects should have reached us. After the time of this emperor, that is, about the middle of the third century, we may fix as the period of the decline of architecture, and from that time it became worse and worse, till it sunk into the lowest state of barbarism. The Emperor Constantine despoiled the whole Roman Empire of statues, pictures, bas reliefs, marbles, and bronzes, in order to decorate Constantinople, and make it a second Rome, but the architecture of his new city was as inferior to that of Rome, as its situation on the Golden Horn, was superior to that on the dark and troubled Tiber.

Metrodorus, a native of Persia, obtained immense wealth by his profession in India, and afterwards gained the friendship of the Emperor Constantine, and induced him, it is said, to carry the war into Persia in favour of Christianity.

363. *Alypius*, of Antioch, held many important offices under the Emperor Julian. It is said that he was commanded by that Emperor to rebuild the Temple at Jerusalem, and that when the workmen were employed in excavating for the foundations, fire issued from the earth and destroyed them.

Cyriades was employed by the Emperor Theodosias, as an architect, but evinced so strong a propensity to the passion of avarice, that he did not give the necessary solidity to the buildings for which he contracted.

450. *Sennamar*, an Arabian, built two palaces which the Arabs place among the wonders of the world ; they say that in each of these palaces one single stone unites the whole structure, so that if it were removed the whole would fall into ruin. This sounds like one of the stories of Schezerade. It is farther said, that the monarch, for whom these edifices were erected, fearful that the architect would make known the situation of the important stone, caused him to be drowned in a ditch.

Entinopus, of Candia, the first who contributed to the foundation of Venice.

490. *Aloïsus* was commissioned by Theodoric, prince of the Ostrogoths, and king of Italy, to restore several edifices in Rome, and the surrounding country. This king's formula to the prefect of Rome, on the architecture of the public edifices, is a curious document, commencing as follows : " The beauty of the Roman buildings requires a skilful overseer, in order that such a *wonderful forest of edifices* should be preserved with constant care, and the new ones properly constructed, both internally and externally. Therefore we direct our generosity, not only to the preservation of ancient things, but to the investing new ones with the glories of antiquity."

Cassiodorus, the greatest man of his time, secretary of state to Theodoric, was well acquainted with architecture.

500. *St. Germain*, Bishop of Paris, gave the design of the church which King Childebert, erected in honour of St. Vincent.

St. Avitus, Bishop of Clermont, built the church of Notre Dame du Port.

St. Agricola, Bishop of Chalons, was the architect of the church in his diocese.

Dalmatius, Bishop of Rhodes, ambitious of the honour of becoming an architect, undertook to rebuild his cathedral, but not succeeding, demolished and rebuilt it again so many times, that he died without finishing it.

550. *Anthemius*, of Tralles, in Asia Minor, and *Isidorus*, of Miletus, built by order of the Emperor Justinian, the church of St. Sophia, at Constantinople.   Justinian was desirous of making it one of the most superb edifices in the world.   When it was finished he exclaimed, " I have surpassed thee, O Solomon?"

Chryses, of Dara, was a Persian, skilled in the construction of moles, dikes, &c.

600. *Isidorus* and *Johannes*, built the city of Zenobia.

673. *Saxulphus*, Abbot of Peterborough.

700. *Egbert, Albert,* and *Eaubald,* Archbishops of York, superintended and completed the erection of York Cathedral during the eighth century.

FROM THE TIME OF CHARLEMAGNE, FROM THE
NINTH TO THE FOURTEENTH CENTURY.

Perhaps no sovereign ever gave more employment to architects than Charlemagne ; throughout
the whole of his vast dominions he erected extensive buildings of various descriptions, but unfortunately, no written memorials inform us who were
the architects.

840. *Romualdus* built the first Cathedral of Rheims,
supposed to be the earliest example of Gothic
Architecture.

900. *Tietland* erected the Monastery of Einseidela,
called the Hermitage of the Virgin, in Switzerland.—*Tioda*, a Spanish architect, employed by
King Alphonso.

1016. *Buschetto* of Dulichio, of Greek extraction, built
the Cathedral or Duomo of Pisa, one of the most
sumptuous edifices of that period, and the earliest
example of the Lombard ecclesiastical style.—
Aldhun, Bishop of Durham. First Cathedral of
Durham.

1020. *Pietro di Ustamber*, a Spanish architect, by
order of Ferdinand of Castile, built a magnificent
church, in which is now the sepulchre of Ustamber,
with an inscription importing that he was famous

for supernatural abstinence, and for working miracles. His greatest miracle, probably, was the Cathedral of Chartres.

1046. *Alfred*, Bishop of Worcester.

1070. *Alvaro Garzia*, of Estella, in Navarre.

1089. *Lanfranc*, Archbishop of Canterbury.

1092. *Remiquis*, Bishop of Lincoln.

1095. *Karilepho*, Bishop of Durham, began the Cathedral of Durham.

1100. *Gundulph*, Bishop of Rochester, built Rochester Castle, White Tower in the Tower of London; rebuilt Rochester Cathedral.—*Odo*, Prior of Crayland.

1115. *Ernulph*, Bishop of Rochester, completed Gundulph's works.

1123. *Alexander*, Bishop of Lincoln, rebuilt Lincoln Cathedral.

1139. *Raimond* of Montfort, rebuilt the Cathedral of Lugo, for which the bishop, canons, and nobles, stipulated to give the architect an annual salary of two hundred soldi, and in case of their happening any change in the value of the specie, thirty-six changes of linen, seventeen loads of wood, shoes and boots as many as he might require; every month, two soldi for meat, a quart of salt, and a pound of wax!

St. Giovanni, a nobleman of Ortego, and *St. Domingo* of Calzada, practised architecture from a desire of doing good. They repaired roads, cleared forests infested by banditti, built bridges, hospitals, and churches.

1150. *Dioti Salvi*, built the Baptistry of Pisa.

Buono, a Venetian, built the celebrated Tower of St. Mark at Venice.

Sugger, of St. Denis, was distinguished for his skill in Gothic architecture; he built the Abbey and Church of St. Denis, near Paris.

1170. *Pietro di Cozza*, of Limena, built the celebrated Great Hall of Padua.

1174. *Gulielmo*, or *Wilhelm*, a German architect; with the assistance of Bonnano of Pisa, he built the famous bell tower of Pisa, called the Leaning Tower. The inclination of this tower from the perpendicular is fifteen feet. It has been a question whether this inclination was occasioned by accident or design. It has stood for ages just as it now appears; the probability is, that the foundation on one side gave way when the tower was partly completed, and being repaired with promptitude, it remained firm, but slanting in such a way that it was impossible to give it an upright position.

1175. *William of Sens;* Canterbury Cathedral.

1201. *Isembert* of Kaintes.

Peter of Colechurch built London Bridge.

1209. *Berham*, overseer of the works of Salisbury Cathedral.

Fitz Odo, master of the works at Westminster, under Henry III.

1220. *Robert de Lusarche* gave the design for, and commenced the Cathedral of Amiens, which was completed by Tomaso de Charmont and his son Rinaldo, in 1269.

Etienne de Bonneveil constructed the church of the Trinity at Upsal in Sweden, after the model of Notre Dame at Paris.

Poore, Bishop of Salisbury, began Salisbury Cathedral.

1237. *Melsonby*, Bishop of Durham, built Durham Cathedral.

1250. *Jean d'Echelles*, built the portico of the Cathedral of Notre Dame, at Paris.

Pierre de Montereau built the Chapel of Vincennes, the Chapel of Notre Dame, in the convent of St. Germain, near Paris, &c.

Eudo de Montreuil, a French architect, whose style was dark and heavy.

St. Gonsalvo, *St. Pietro*, and *St. Lorenzo*, were Dominican friars, who were architects in Portugal, about this period.

Lapo, a German, who practised his art in Italy.

Nicola da Pisa mixed the Gothic with the Lombard style, and erected many churches and convents in various parts of Italy.

1270. *Fuccio*, a Florentine sculptor and architect, built

the church of Santa Maria, on the Arno, at Florence.

Ferrante Maglione, a disciple of Nicola da Pisa, built the Cathedral of San Lorenzo, at 'Naples, and many other splendid edifices.

Marsuccio, a Neapolitan sculptor and architect.

1280. *Arnolfo,* the son of the German Lapo, learned the art of his father, which he successfully practised at Florence. His works were much admired.

Pietro Perez, of Spain, built the Cathedral of Toledo.

Robert de Coucy rebuilt the Cathedral of Rheims.

Erwin von Steinbach, a German: the celebrated Cathedral of Strasburgh was under his superintendence as architect, for twenty-eight years. Among the specimens of Gothic Architecture, in Europe, this is the most stupendous. In the interior, near one of the large piers of the transept, is the statue of Erwin, which appears leaning over the balustrade of the upper corridor, looking at the opposite piers. The ornaments in the frieze of this church show the taste of the times in which they were conceived. A pig carrying the holy water, followed by pigs and asses clothed in sacerdotal habits; a procession of asses, a fox enshrined, and other similar extravagances were chosen to satirize the times; it is doubtful if the satire, thus perpetuated, had a salutary effect.

Giovanni of Pisa, son and disciple of Nicola of

Pisa, was a sculptor and architect, who acquired early in life, a great reputation. He erected the Campo Santo of Pisa, a public cemetery, where he was afterwards buried. Giovanni was called to Naples by Charles I. of Anjou, where he built the Castel Nuova, and many other admirable works. His churches and other buildings are grand and cheerful.

1300. *Agostino* and *Angelo of Sienna*, were brothers, and the most illustrious disciples of the school of Giovanni of Pisa.

Andrea of Pisa was an excellent sculptor and architect; he made the design for the Castle of Scorperia, at the foot of the Appenines; and though he built some churches, was more distinguished for military, than civil architecture.

Giotto, a famous painter, was also an architect. He was born near Florence. At the age of ten years, he amused himself by drawing figures of men, animals, buildings, &c., upon stones, and in the sand, while occupied as a shepherd-boy.

Taddeo Gaddi excelled his master Giotto, in architecture and painting.

1308. *William Boyden*, an English architect, built Caernarvon Castle.

1310. *A. de Bek*, Bishop of Durham, England.

1319. *Henry Latomus*, Abbot of Eisham, England.

J. Helpstone, an English architect.

1326. *Hugh de Eversden*, Abbot of St. Albans, England.

1330. *Walter Weston* and *Thomas of Canterbury*, built St. Stephen's Chapel, Westminster.

Andrea di Cione Orgagna, a poet, painter, sculptor, and architect, was born at Florence, where he was admired for his universal genius.

Giacomo Lanfrani of Italy, built the Churches of St. Francis at Imola, and of St. Antonio at Venice.

1340. *Jean Rauy*, a French architect, finished the Cathedral of Notre Dame, at Paris.

1350. *J. de Lincoln*, master of the works in the King's Chapel, Westminster.

William of Wykeham, Bishop of Winchester; built New College, Oxford, part of Winchester Cathedral, and planned a part of Windsor Castle.

1354. *Calendario*, a Venetian, built the porticoes around the Place of St. Mark's, Venice.

Walsingham, Prior of Ely; *Rede*, Bishop of Chichester.

1395. *J. Boterell, Nicholas Walton, Stephen Lote*, and *Gainsborough*, English architects of the fourteenth century.

Chichele, Archbishop of Canterbury, founded All Soul's College, built a monument for himself in Canterbury Cathedral, made additions to that Cathedral, Lambeth Palace, &c.

ARCHITECTS OF THE FIFTEENTH CENTURY.

Filipo Brunelleschi was a Florentine, born in
1377.   He studied diligently at Rome the ancient
works of art, to qualify himself for his profession.
When he was about thirty years of age, he attended an assembly of architects and engineers,
convoked at Florence to deliberate on the comple-
tion of the Cathedral.   Brunelleschi gave his
opinion, that a double dome could be raised to a
sufficient height, and sustained, without a mass
of timber-work.   So preposterous was this considered, that he was turned out of the assembly,
for having presumed to insult the good sense and
judgment of so many celebrated artists.   By
drawings and models, Brunelleschi demonstrated
the practicability of his scheme, but the prejudice
against him was such that he returned to Rome.
After his departure, a more careful and dispas-
sionate examination of his drawings and models,
induced the deputies entrusted with the comple-
tion of the Cathedral, to send for the daring
architect.   He undertook it with ardour, and completed it as far as the lantern.   Michael Angelo
afterwards said it would be almost impossible to
surpass this dome.   Brunelleschi was the first in
this century who attempted to revive the ancient

Grecian and Roman Architecture. He built several splendid edifices, and left some of them incomplete for want of encouragement. He was a friend to young artists and a father to the poor. His merit as an architect was more generally acknowledged after his death than in his lifetime, which proves that his genius and taste were in advance of the age in which he lived.

1400. *Michellozzo Michellozi*, a Florentine, constructed many splendid edifices in various parts of Italy.

Giuliano da Majano, a Florentine, built the magnificent palace of Poggio, which is a perfect square; triumphal arches, fountains, &c.

1422. *Roger Keyes*, architect of All Soul's College, Oxford.

1450. *Christobolo*, an Italian, was employed by Mahomet II., to build a Mosque at Constantinople, on the ruins of the Church of the Holy Apostles.

Baccio Pintelli, a Florentine, built at Rome the Convent and Church of Santa Maria del Popolo, and many other edifices in various parts of Italy.

Bartolomeo Bramantini, a Milanese, built the Church of San Satiro at Milan, and other fine works.

Giovanni del Pozzo, a Spaniard.

Andrea Ciccione, a Neapolitan.

Ridolfo Fiorivanti, a Bolognese. His reputation procured him the patronage of the Czar of

Muscovy, for whom he erected several churches, &c.

1458. *W. Orchyarde,* architect of Magdalen College, Oxford.

Francesco de Georgio of Sienna.

Leon Baptista Alberti, one of the greatest Italian architects, was born at Florence, and educated for a priest, but finally devoted himself to the fine arts. He was a sculptor, a painter, a poet, and a mathematician, but he is better known for his treatise on architecture, which is an admirable commentary on Vitruvius, and the many superb edifices with which he adorned the Italian cities. He was canon of the Cathedral of Florence; a true nobleman, liberal and courteous. Even the rival artists of the time have celebrated his amiable and generous character, and acknowledged his superior genius.

1472. *Farleigh,* Abbot of Gloucester, England.

Beauchamp, Bishop of Sarum.

Wayneflete, Bishop of Winchester. Founder of Magdalen College, Oxford.

Bramante d'Urbino, a celebrated Italian, first applied himself to painting, but at length devoted his fine genius entirely to architecture. He studied the ancient works, and became the first architect of that period. Michael Angelo said of him, "It cannot be denied that Bramante is superior in architecture to all others since the time of the ancients." He carried Raphael the painter to Rome, where he instructed him in architecture. His name has been immortalized by his grandest work—the design of St. Peter's at Rome. Bramante was also a poet and musician. He has been accused of being so anxious to see the effect which his buildings would produce, that he caused them to be executed with too much celerity, so that they soon needed repairs. His ardent, enthusiastic temperament led him, doubtless, into errors, which a man of less genius might not have committed. He died in 1514, at the age of seventy, universally lamented.

Francesco Giamberti, a Florentine.

1479. *Ventura Vitoni*, a pupil of Bramante.

J. Alcock, Bishop of Ely.

J. Morton, of Cambridge, England.

1500. *Gabriello d'Agnola*, a Neapolitan.

Gian Francesco Normando, a Florentine.

Pietro Lombardo, a Venetian.

Martino Lombardo, a Venetian.

John Cole, an Englishman.

Sir Reginald Bray, designed the Chapel of Henry VII. at Westminster; and other works at St. George's Chapel, Windsor.

George Hylmer, St. George's Chapel, Windsor.

1507. *Giuliano di Sangallo*, a Florentine, built many churches and palaces in Italy, which have been admired for their magnificence.

Simone Cronaco, a Florentine.

SIXTEENTH CENTURY.

1506. *Leonardo da Vinci*, born near Florence, was a celebrated painter, but he gave much attention to architecture, planned an aqueduct at Milan, and wrote various works on the art.

Fra Giocando of Verona, built many bridges, especially that of Notre Dame, at Paris. He was engaged with Raphael and Sangallo in carrying on St. Peter's at Rome.

Novello da San Lucano, a Neapolitan.

Rafaelle D'Urbino, one of the most celebrated painters in the world, continued the erection of St. Peter's after the death of his master, Bramante, and was employed upon many other buildings in Italy.

W. Bolton, supposed to have designed Henry VII.'s Chapel.

John of Padua, an Italian, employed by Henry VIII. in England.

W. Gibbes, last Prior of Bath.

Andrea Contucci, an Italian, built many fine edifices in Italy and Portugal.

Bartolomeo and *Guglielmo* of Bergamo, in Italy.

Maestro Filippo, a Spaniard, restored the Cathedral of Seville.

1520. *Giovanni di Ololzago*, of Spain, blended the

modern Greek style with Gothic, in the manner called *Arabatedescho*.

Giovanni Alonzo, of Spain.

Antonio San Gallo, an Italian, was employed upon many magnificent works by Leo X.

Baldasare Peruzzi was an Italian, who early exhibited genius for painting, and was patronised by Pope Alexander VI. He studied architecture, and wrote a commentary on Vitruvius. He died by poison, in 1536, and was buried by the side of Rafaelle in the Pantheon at Rome. His architectural style was in fine taste.

1530. *Marco di Pino*, of Sienna.

Andrio Brioso, of Padua.

Ferdinando Manlio, of Naples.

Giovanni Merliano da Nola, an Italian.

Giovanni Gil di Houtanon, planned the Cathedral of Salamanca.

Giovanni Maria Falconetto, of Verona.

1540. *Pietro de Uria*, a Spaniard, built a splendid bridge over the Tagus.

Alonzo de Cobarrubias, a Spaniard.

Diego Siloe, of Toledo, built the Cathedral at Granada.

Girolamo Gengu, of Urbino, and his son Bartolomeo, constructed many palaces and churches in Italy.

Michelo San Micheli, of Verona, built some fine

cathedrals in Italy, but was chiefly distinguished for his skill in fortification.

Philibert de Lorme, of France, commenced the Tuileries at Paris.

G. Allesi, an Italian, built the Escurial in Spain, and many palaces at Genoa "the Superb."

Sante Lombardo, a Venetian.

Giacomo Barozzi da Vignola, called *Vignola*, from the place of his birth, was educated at Bologna, from whence he went to Rome, where he completed his architectural studies in the Academy of Design. He was employed in France and Italy upon many churches and palaces, and was appointed architect to Julius III. On the death of Michael Angelo, he continued St. Peter's. His treatise on architecture has been much read, and his work on perspective considered quite ingenious.

Giulio Pippi, or *Romano*, from his birthplace, Rome, was a distinguished architect, whose style was cheerful and pleasing.

Michael Angelo Buonarotti, of Florence, the celebrated sculptor, painter, and architect, was employed in continuing St. Peter's, and constructing the great dome of that cathedral. When he was made chief architect of St. Peter's, he was advanced in years, and from a religious feeling, stipulated that he should receive no pecuniary remuneration for that work. He was of noble birth, and his father in vain attempted to divert his wonderful genius from the fine arts. In the course of his long life he left many specimens of his bold and original plans in architecture.

Eustace Marshall, of England, clerk of the works to Cardinal Wolsey, and chief architect of Henry VIII.

1550. *Damiano Forment*, of Spain.

Sebastiano Doya of Flanders was employed by Charles V. and Philip II. It is said, that falling ill, he employed as the only remedy abstinence, of which he died.

Martino de Gainza, Alonzo Berruquete, Pietro de Valdevira, Pietro Ezquerra, Ferdinando Ruiz, and *Machuca,* Spanish architects of the sixteenth century.

Antonio Fiorentino, a Florentine.

Jacopo Talli, a Florentine, employed at Florence, Venice, and Naples, in building magnificent edifices.

Theodore Havens, built Caius College, Cambridge, in the eccentric and affected style that prevailed at that time in England.

Domenico Testocopoli, a Greek; built several churches and convents at Madrid, in a massive, gloomy style.

Garzia d'Emere;
Bartolomeo di Bustamente;
Giovan Battista di Toledo; Spanish architects.

24

1567. *John Thynne*, built Somerset House.

1570. *Giovanni d' Herrera*, continued the Escurial, and built the bridge of Segovia at Madrid, and the Palace of Aranjuez.

Pierre de Lescott, of France.

Sebastiano Serlio, of Bologna, employed by Francis I., at Fontainbleau; and at Venice on the Palace of Grimani.

Bartolomeo Ammanati, built the Palace Pitti, at Florence, and the beautiful bridge of St. Trinita, which is much admired for its stability and lightness. He built the celebrated Rucellai Palace at Rome, and the Jesuit's College.

Nicholas Abate, of Modena, a celebrated painter, was also an architect; employed by Francis I.

Andrea Palladio, of Vicenza, from his earliest years devoted himself to architecture, and having acquired a knowledge of classic literature, he applied to the study of Vitruvius, and the remains of Roman art. There are many works by this famous architect in Italy. He was the familiar friend of the learned and great, yet so kind and considerate towards his workmen, that he gained their affection and veneration. His treatise on architecture, published at Venice, in 1570, has passed through many editions. His style was majestic and simple, his outlines are bold and easy, and none of his buildings want character.

Giorgeo Vasari d'Arezzo, was a great painter

and architect, and an intimate friend of Michael Angelo. Vasari built a number of edifices in various places, but that for which he is justly renowned, is his " Lives of the Artists."

Pierre de Wit, a Fleming, was called " Il Candido." In a church which he erected, in the centre of the white marble pavement, the print of a human foot is represented; standing at this point, not a window is visible, although there are a great many as high as the naves. This century was fruitful in such architectural whims.

Pirro Ligorio, a Neapolitan nobleman, was employed under Paul IV., on St. Peter's, but disagreeing with Michael Angelo, the Pope deprived him of the charge. He was also a painter and engineer.

John Shute, an Englishman, who was distinguished as a painter and architect, during the reign of Elizabeth.

1600. *Robert Adams*, superintendent of royal buildings to Queen Elizabeth.

Louis de Foix, of France.

Jaques Androuet du Cerceau, was architect to Henry III., of France.

Vincenco Scamozzi, of Vicenza, the supposed inventor of the angular Ionic capital. He wrote a book on " Universal Architecture," and built two or three theatres.

Carlo Maderno, a sculptor and eminent architect. During his public career, he witnessed a succession of ten popes, by all of whom he was regarded with favour.

1608. *John Warren*, architect of St. Mary Church Tower, Cambridge.

Sir H. Wotton, author of "The Elements of Architecture," 1624.

Inigo Jones, was an admired English architect, in the reigns of Charles I. and II. Walpole says, "Vitruvius drew up his grammar, and Palladio showed him the practice," of his art. He built Surgeon's Hall, the Chapel of Lincoln's Inn, and many other buildings in England; improving in that way the taste of his countrymen.

Giovanni Batista Alioti, of Ferrara, was employed by the Italian nobles in building splendid palaces and other edifices.

Pierre le Muet, of France.

Francesco Borromini, an Italian, repaired to Rome at the age of seventeen, for the study of sculpture and architecture. There he was employed upon several edifices, the reputation of which induced the King of Spain to send for him and to patronise him. He was extravagant, and singular in his architectural designs, departing far from established rules; in consequence, his buildings were many of them left unfinished. He was severely censured by the critics, and rival artists supplanted him; his misfortunes produced occasional alienation of mind; in one of his paroxysms, he seized a sword and gave himself a wound of which he died; aged sixty-eight.

Alessandro Algardi, an Italian, employed at Rome.

Lorenzo Bernini, an Italian sculptor and architect, at the early age of ten years attracted notice by his uncommon genius for sculpture. His skill as an architect was shown in the piazza, colonnade, and staircase of St. Peter's at Rome. He was sent for by Louis XIV., to complete the Louvre, but when he saw the design by Perrault, he nobly said that his coming to France was useless, where there were architects of the first class. He died in 1680, in the eighty-second year of his age.

François Mausart, was born at Paris, where he received his education as an architect. He was so anxious for perfection in his works, that he sometimes demolished them when nearly completed, if he discovered even a trifling fault that might be remedied. In consequence of this extreme fastidiousness, he completed but few important works.

Alonzo Cano, a Spaniard, so distinguished for his skill in architecture, sculpture, and painting, that he was called "the Michael Angelo of Spain." He was a passionate, violent man, whose whole life was tumultuous, and filled with adventure.

Claude Perrault, of Paris, was educated for the

medical profession, but was led by his genius to the study and practice of architecture. His master-piece was the front of the Louvre, executed by the command of Louis XIV.

François Blondel, was first a mathematician and military engineer, but afterwards devoted himself to architecture, and was appointed by Louis XIV. to superintend all the public works in Paris. He was also Director and Professor in the Academy of Architecture, established in France in 1671.

Antoine le Pautre, a French architect, published a work entitled "Les Œuvres d'Architecture d'Antoine le Pautre," in 1652.

Jaques le Mercier, a French architect.

FROM 1610 TO 1710.

Chrismas Gerard, an English architect and sculptor.

John Evelyn, an Englishman.

Sir Christopher Wren, was the son of an English clergyman, who was chaplain to Charles I. He was educated at the University of Oxford, where he was appointed Professor of Astronomy. In 1665, he went over to France, to study architecture at Paris. On his return from that city, he was appointed architect for the reparation of St. Paul's Cathedral. After the great fire of London,

1666, he drew a magnificent plan for a new city, which was perfectly practicable, but in consequence of disputes about private property, was never carried into execution. His genius was employed, however, in rebuilding many of the public edifices and palaces which had been destroyed. More than fifty churches were built by him in London; besides, Chelsea and Greenwich Hospitals, the Monument, Custom House, &c. &c. The church of St. Stephen's, Walbrook, has been much admired, but St. Paul's is his master-piece and monument; for there, after his long and active life was he buried, at the age of ninety-one. He was knighted, twice sat in Parliament, and was President of the Royal Society.

Robert Hooke, the associate of Wren in building many edifices in London.

FROM 1710 TO 1774.

John Benson, the successor to Wren.

Carlo Fontana, an Italian.

Julis Hordouin Mausart, a Frenchman; built the Dome des Invalides, la Galerie du Palais Royal, &c., &c.

Francesco Fontana, an Italian.

H. Aldrich, an English clergyman.

Sir John Vanbrugh, in the reign of Queen

Anne, was the leading architect in England. Walpole said of him, "He wanted all ideas of proportion, convenience, propriety. He undertook vast designs, and composed heaps of littleness. He seems to have hollowed quarries rather than built houses. The laughers, his contemporaries, said, that having been confined in the Bastile, he had drawn his notions of buildings from that fortified dungeon." Blenheim, which he built for the Duke of Marlborough, was an expensive pile, much ridiculed by the wits of Queen Anne's court; although it has since been considered the finest modern house in England.

Robert de la Cotte, a Frenchman; he finished the Dome des Invalides and the Chapel of Versailles.

Nicholas Hawksmoor, a pupil of Wren, and assistant to Vanbrugh.

Alexander Jean Baptiste le Blond, a Frenchman, who was employed in Russia by Peter the Great.

Germain Boffrand, a French architect, whose style of building was formed after the model of Palladio. He was employed upon a great number of edifices at Paris, and drew designs for several German princes. He had a taste for literature, and wrote comedies. His "Book of Architecture" was printed at Paris, in 1745. He lived to the advanced age of eighty-seven years.

James Gibbs, was born at Aberdeen in Scotland.

He studied architecture in Italy, and on his return, practised the art in England. His style, though mechanically correct, has not been greatly admired.

William Kent, was born in Yorkshire, England, and studied in Italy. His taste has been much admired.

Edmund Bouchardon, of France.

FROM 1774 TO 1837.

Francois Cuviller, a Frenchman, employed by the Elector of Munich.

Francis Blondel, was born at Rouen, was a practical architect, and wrote several valuable works on the art. He was royal professor at the Louvre, and architect to the King.

Earl of Burlington, England.

George Dance, England.

John Brettingham, England.

John Rodolphus Perronet, a French architect, skilled in the construction of roads and bridges.

Jacques Germain Soufflot, a French artist, who built a part of the church of St. Genevieve.

Nicholas Antoine Boulanger, an accomplished scholar, an engineer and architect, was born in Paris, and employed in various works in France.

Sir William Chambers, was of an ancient

Scottish family. He was first employed in mercantile pursuits, and made a voyage to China. On his return to his native country, he introduced the Chinese style into gardens and ornamental buildings. He was patronised by Lord Bute, and afterwards by George III. His works have a chaste correctness of detail, though as a whole, they are not imposing. He showed a want of taste in despising the ancient Grecian Architecture. His treatise on Civil Architecture is considered a valuable work.

Joel Johnson, an Englishman.

James Stuart, an English architect of much celebrity.

Robert Adam, was born at Edinburgh, in 1728, and was educated in the University of that city. He was at first devoted to painting, but on going to Italy, he became a student of architecture, and an enthusiastic lover of the art. After he returned home, he was patronised by the Earl of Bute, and subsequently by George III. His style, founded as it was upon a careful study of Roman buildings, has been justly admired.

James Adam, brother of Robert, was his colleague and assistant.

James Wyatt, was born in Staffordshire, England, about 1743. He studied architecture in Italy, and such was his enthusiasm and perseverance, that he " had measured with his own hand every part of the dome of St. Peter's, at the imminent danger of his life, as he was obliged to lie on his back on a ladder slung horizontally, without cradle or side rail, over a void of three hundred feet." At the age of twenty, he returned to London with his taste highly cultivated. Wyatt was President of the Royal Academy. Among his principal works, are the Palace at Kew, Fonthill Abbey, Huntworth Church, Doddington Hall, &c. He was invited by the Empress of Russia to settle at St. Petersburg, but declined the offer. He died at the age of seventy, in 1813.

Sir John Soane: this eminent architect was a native of Reading, in Berkshire, England. He was born, September 10th, 1752, and died, January 20th, 1837, in his eighty-fourth year. Soane was the son of a bricklayer. He early discovered genius for architecture, and was placed at the age of fifteen as a pupil with Mr. Dance to learn the art. In 1772, he was a student of the Royal Academy, and received a silver medal for a drawing. Four years afterwards, he obtained the gold medal for the best design for a triumphal bridge. He was introduced to George III., by Sir William Chambers, and soon after was sent to Rome to pursue his studies for three years. After his return, he was appointed clerk of the works of St. James's Palace, and subsequently architect to the Royal Woods and Forests, Professor of Architecture to the Royal Academy, &c., &c. In 1831, he received the honour of knighthood. He bequeathed his large collection of works of ancient and modern art, (The Soane Museum,) to the British nation, said to have been worth 60,000 pounds sterling. In 1835, the architects presented him with a splendid medal, in token of their respect for his talents and munificence. His love for his art was extraordinary, and almost to the last moment, he was engaged in the study of it. The illness that terminated his long and useful life, was of short duration, and he died apparently without the slightest pain.

John Linnell Bond, of England, died November, 1837. As an architect, he was in knowledge, judgment, and taste, inferior to none of his contemporaries.

Note.—It would be very desirable to add here, a list of eminent American architects, but so many of the most distinguished are still living, that we must deny ourselves the pleasure.

A GLOSSARY OF ARCHITECTURE.*

Abacus. The upper member of the capital of a column.

Abutment. The extremity of a bridge.

Acanthus. The leaf which forms one of the ornaments of the Corinthian capital.

Acanthus.

Acropolis. A citadel, a Greek stronghold or fortress.

Acroterium. A pedestal or base placed on the angle, or on the apex of a pediment.

Adit. The approach or entrance to a building.

Admeasurement. Adjustment of proportions.

Adytum. A retired or sacred place in ancient temples, which no one but the priest was permitted to enter.

Affectation. In architectural composition, an unnatural or over-strained imitation or artifice.

Aisle. When a church is divided in its breadth into three parts, the two extreme outward divisions are called *aisles*, and the central division, the *nave* or *middle aisle*. A passage left open for walking through.

* Principally abridged from Stuart's "Dictionary of Architecture."

Alcove.   A recess.

Altar.   A place on which offerings or sacrifices were made to the gods.

Alto-relievo.   High relief.   Sculpture projecting nearly as much as if the objects were isolated and complete.

Ambo.   A raised platform; a marble pulpit.

Amphiprostylos.   A temple which has a portico in both fronts.

Amphitheatre.   An edifice formed of two semicircles united, with seats arranged all around it, and an area in the centre called the *arena.*

Anchor.   An ornament shaped like an anchor or arrow-head, used with the *egg* ornament to decorate mouldings.   The anchor or arrow and egg ornament is peculiar to the Ionic and Corinthian orders.

Angels.   Brackets or corbels with the figures or heads of angels.

Annulets.   The fillets or bands that ornament the Doric capital.

Antæ.   Pilasters attached to a wall.

Aperture.   A small or large opening.

Aqueduct.   An artificial channel made for conveying water from one place to another.

Arabesque.   A building after the manner of the Arabs.   Sentences from the Koran, interwoven with foliage and geometrical figures for ornament.

Arcade.   A series of arched openings, with a roof or ceiling.

Arch.   A mechanical arrangement of separate inelastic bodies in the line of a curve, which preserves a given form when resisting pressure.   *Circular arches* are called *arches* by old writers by way of eminence.

Circular Arch.

A Rampant or Stilted Arch, rises from imposts.

Rampant Arch.

A Saracenic Arch. Commonly called a *horseshoe* arch.

Horseshoe.

Pointed or *Gothic Arches*, are mostly formed by the intersection of two arcs of a circle ; among these are the

Lancet Arch. Formed on an acute-angled triangle,

Lancet.

and the arch formed upon an equilateral triangle.

Equilateral
Triangle.

The *Tudor Arch.* Used during the reigns of Henry VIII., James I,, and Elizabeth.

Tudor

The *Ogee Arch.* Used frequently in the Decorated and Perpendicular Gothic.

Ogee.

The *Cinquefoiled Arch.* Met with occasionally in the Early English.

Cinquefoiled.

The Romanesque Arch. Sometimes called the Saxon and the Norman Arch; it is semicircular, and generally has double or triple arches, ornamented with mouldings.

Romanesque Arch.

Archway. An aperture in a building covered with a vault.

Archeion. The treasury of a temple.

Architect. One who designs and superintends the erection of buildings.

Architectonical. Skilled in architecture.

Architectural. Concerning, or relating to, architecture as a decorative art.

Architecture. The art of building; naval, military, and civil. It is *essential*, and *ornamental*.

Architrave. That part of the entablature which rests immediately upon the columns.

Area. A small court or place sunk below the general surface of the ground, before and level with the floor of the basement story of a building.

Arena. The middle or body of a temple; the plain space in the middle of an amphitheatre.

Arris. In general language an *edge*.

Artificers. Persons who work with their hands, and manufacture any article in iron, brass, wood, &c.

Artisan. Artificer or mechanic, not an artist.

Astragal. A small moulding, having a semicircular profile.

Athenæum. A public place, wherein the professors of the liberal arts held their assemblies.

Atlases. Statues of men which supported entablatures; called by the Greeks, "Persians."

Atrium. A court supported by porticoes in the interior division of ancient Roman houses.

Attic. A low story erected over an order of architecture to finish the upper part of the building. The upper story of a house.

Balcony. A kind of open gallery projecting from the walls of buildings, usually of iron fashioned into fanciful figures.

Baluster. A small column or pillar belonging to a balustrade.

Balustrade. A railing or enclosure, for use as in staircases, or for ornament, as a finish for the top of a building.

Band. A flat member or moulding.

Baptistry. An apartment, or edifice, where baptism is administered.

Bas-relief. } The representation of figures, projecting from a
Basso-relievo. } background, without being detached from it.

Battlement. A parapet, or wall, with indentations; first used in fortifications; afterwards for ornament on churches and other buildings.

Bay-Window.

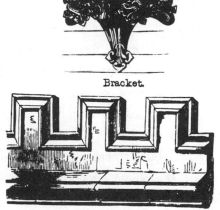

Bracket.

The Battlement.

Bay-Window.   A   projecting   window, sometimes called an oriel window.

Bead.   A moulding, of a circular section.

Belfry.   That part of a steeple in which the bells are hung.

Belvidere.   A turret raised above the roof of an observatory.

Bracket.   An   ornamented   projection,   to support a lamp, a statue, &c.

Break.   A projecting part of the front of grand buildings.

Bronze.   A compound metal used for statues, &c.

Buttress.   A mass of masonry, serving to support the side of a wall.   Gothic buttresses are placed on the exterior sides of the building, between the windows and at the angles.

Canopy.   A covering for an altar, throne, or pulpit.

Capital.   From the Latin *caput*, head; the head of a column.

Carrara Marble.   White marble, much used by the ancients for statuary.

Caryatides.   Female   figures,   clothed   in long garments, supporting an entablature, in place of columns.

Castle.   A fortified building, with towers, battlements, &c.

Catacombs.   Subterraneous places for burying the dead.

Catharine-Wheel.   A circular ornamented window.

Cathedral.   The head church of a diocese.

Caulicoles, or *Cauliculi.*   Slender stems under the leaves of the Corinthian capital.

Canopy.

Capital.

Ceiling. The inner roof of a building.

Cella. The sanctuary of a temple.

Cemeteries. Places where the bodies of the dead are deposited.

Cenotaph. An honorary tomb or monument.

Centering. The name used for the turning of an arch of stone, or brick.

Chancel. That part of a church in which the communion table is placed; usually enclosed with lattice-work.

Chapiter. See Capital.

Chevron. An ornament in Gothic Architecture, sometimes called *zigzag*, used for mouldings.

Choir. The part of a church where the singers are placed.

Choragic Monuments. Were erected by the Greeks, in honour of the leader of a chorus who gained a prize.

Chord. The right line which joins the two ends of an arc.

Cinquefoil. An arch having five interarches or foils.

Circumference. The boundary line of circular bodies.

Circus. A large ovate building for the exhibition of popular games and shows.

Citadel. A castle or fortress, generally occupying the highest part of a city.

Clerestory. The higher story, with small windows, in Gothic buildings.

Cloacæ. The common sewers of ancient Rome.

Cloister. The principal part of a regular monastery.

Clustered Column. Several slender pillars, attached to each other, in the Gothic style.

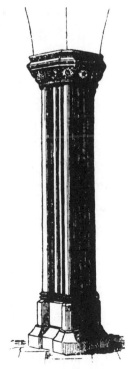

Clustered Column.

Clustered Capital. The capital of a clustered column.

Colonnade. A row of columns ; when in
front of a building, they are termed
porticoes, when surrounding it, *peris-
tyle.*

Clustered Capital.

Column. A round pillar, the parts of which
are, the *base*, *shaft*, and *capital.*

Composite Order. An order formed by the Romans from the
Corinthian and Ionic.

Concave. Arching into the plane
of the surface ; a common or
vulgar expression for concave,
scooped out.

Concentric. Having a common
centre.

Cone. A solid which is bounded
by two surfaces, of which,
one called the *base*, is a circle,

Composite Order.

and the other, ending in a point, called the *vertex*, a convexity.

Conservatory. A building for the protection of plants.

Construction. The art of building from the architect's designs.

Contour. The outline of a body.

Convex. Swelling externally out from the plane, in a circular form.

Coping. The upper tier of masonry which covers a wall.

Corbeils. Sculptured baskets of flowers or fruit ; sometimes placed
on the heads of Caryatides.

Corbels. Carved stones projecting from the wall to support a parapet,
serving in the place of brackets or modillions, and under weather
mouldings of doors and windows.

Corbel Table. A series of semicircular arches which cut one another in a wall supported by timbers, with their ends projecting out, and carved into heads, faces, &c.

Corinthian Order. The order with a capital of Acanthus leaves, said to be invented by Callima-chus.

Corona. The projecting brow of a cornice.

Corridor. A long gallery, or passage, in a mansion, connecting various apartments.

Cottage. A small house or habitation.

Cottage Ornée. An ornamented cottage.

Corinthian Order.

Cottage Ornee.

Coupled Columns. Columns arranged in pairs.

Course. A continued layer of bricks or stones in a building.

Court. An open area before or behind a house, or in the centre.

Cramp. A piece of iron, bronze, or other metal, used to hold together stones in buildings.

Crest Tile. The tile on the ridge of a house.

Crockets. The small buds or bunches of foliage, used in Gothic

Architecture, to ornament spires, cano-
pies, pinnacles, &c., the larger branches
at the top being termed *finials*.

Cross-Beam. A large beam going from
wall to wall.

Crown. The upper part of a cornice, including the corona.

Crypt. A subterranean vault, generally
beneath ecclesiastical edifices. They
probably were first used by the early
Christians as secret places of worship.

Finial.

Cube. A solid of six equal square sides.

Cubit. An ancient measure, equal to about a foot and a half.

Cupola. A dome.

Cusps. The parts of the foils and quatrefoils.

Cylinder. A figure whose base is a circle, and whose curved superficies is everywhere at an equal distance from the axis or line
supposed to pass through the middle.

Cylindric Ceiling. Vulgarly termed a *wagon-headed ceiling;* a
ceiling vaulted in the shape of the segment of a cylinder.

Cyma, or *Cima.* An undulating moulding, which is generally the upper
one of a cornice, when it is called
cymatium. The *cyma recta*, is
composed of a concave and convex
moulding, the former being uppermost.

Decoration. Anything that enriches or
gives beauty to a building.

Decorated Style. The middle style in
Gothic Architecture.

Days, or *Bays.* In Gothic Architecture,

Decorated.

the compartments formed in tall windows, by the introduction of mullions.

Decagon. A plane figure having ten sides and ten angles.

Dentils. Ornaments in a cornice, in the form of teeth.

Design. A drawing or plan of an intended building, projected by the architect, according to the rules of art.

Diameter of a Column. A line passing through it at the base.

Diastyle. A term applied to a building with columns at the distance of three diameters from each other.

Diminishing of a Column, is the difference in the top and bottom diameters, found in all regular orders.

Diminished Arches. Arches less than a circle.

Dome. An arched or vaulted roof.

Domestic Architecture. That branch of the art, which relates to private dwellings, including cottages, farmhouses, &c.

Domicile. A small house.

Donjon. The massive tower in the interior of ancient castles, to which the garrison might retreat in case of necessity.

Doric Order. Of the three orders of Grecian Architecture, this is the oldest and most original.

Dormant, or *Dormer Windows.* The attic stories of houses were commonly used as sleeping apartments, or *dormitories ;* the windows opening from these rooms, on the inclined plane of the roof, were hence called Dormant or Dormer windows.

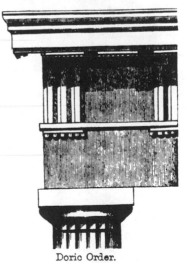

Doric Order.

Dove-tailing. A mode of fixing two boards together by indentures in one, and projections in the other, the shape of a dove's tail.

Drawbridge. A bridge made to draw up or let down at pleasure.

Eaves. The overhanging edges of a roof.

5.9

Egyptian Capital.

5.9

Egyptian Capital.

Echinus.

Egyptian Column.

Early English.

Early English. The earliest Gothic style, with lancet windows.

Echinus. A convex moulding ornamented with eggs and darts.

Edifice. Building, fabric, erection.

Egyptian Architecture. The style used by the Egyptians.

Elizabethan or *Tudor style.* The style which prevailed when the earlier and purer Gothic had degenerated; during the reigns of Henry VIII., Elizabeth, and James I.

Entablature. That member of a building which includes the architrave, frieze, and cornice.

Fabric. A term generally applied to a large building.

Façade or *Face.* The exterior front of a building.

Facettes. Flat projections between the flutings of columns.

Fascia or *Facia.* A band, a flat member in an entablature or other part of a building.

Fauxbourg. That part of a city which is without the gates, and the fortifications.

Fillet. See Annulet and Band.

Flamboyant. A term applied to the *flowing* tracery of a Gothic window.

Floor. The bottom of a room.

Florid Style. The elaborately ornamented Gothic.

Fluting. Longitudinal cavities cut on the shaft of a column or pilaster.

Flying Buttresses. An arched buttress formed of a flat arch, or part of an arch, abutting against the sides of another arch or vault, to prevent their giving way in that direction.

Foliage. An ornamental distribution of leaves.

Font. A vessel in Christian churches of marble or stone, to contain the water of baptism.

Flamboyant

Foot. A measure of twelve inches.

Forum. A public place used for assemblies, markets, &c.

Foundation. That part of a building or wall which is below the surface of the ground.

Fountain. A building out of which water is made to flow for the supply of towns and cities.

Fresco. The most ancient method of ornamenting houses, by painting on stucco while it was soft and damp.

Frieze. That part of the entablature between the architrave and cornice.

Gable. The upright triangular end of a building, in classical architecture called a *pediment.*

Gallery. An apartment of much greater length than breadth.

Gaol. A prison or place of confinement.

Garret. The apartment in the roof.

Gothic Architecture. The pointed architecture of the middle ages.

Granite. A primitive rock composed of quartz, feldspar, and mica.

Grecian Architecture. The architecture practised in Greece, including the three orders, Doric, Ionic, and Corinthian.

Greek Cross. A cross having the transverse part equal to the other part.

Green-house. See Conservatory.

Groined Ceiling. A surface formed by three or more curved surfaces, so that every two may form a groin, all the groins terminating at one extremity in a common point.

Groove or *Mortice.* The channel made to receive the tenon.

Grotesque. A fantastic style of ornament, found in ancient buildings.

Grotto. An artificial cave.

Ground Floor. The lowest story of a building.

Ground Plan. An outline or drawing of the foundation of a building.

Guttæ. Ornaments of a conic form on the cornice of the Doric order, supposed to represent drops of water.

Gymnasium. The public edifices of the Greeks for education.

Hall. The first large apartment in a house; a court of justice; a manor house.

columns, measured

of which are orna-

six

, or

ts to

rivate

alids.

Hindoo Co-
lumn, &c.

ing-house or other

of giving ladies an

ic Capital.

erving ice.

ding.

door-post or pier, and

Ionic capitals.

brick.

e.

tube, and falling

p of an arch or

ding of an arch.

passages.

us turnings and

tersecting Arches.

style.

. The space between tw
afts at the base.

The space between dentils.

er. The space between pilasters.

Order. The Grecian order, the capitals
mented with volutes.

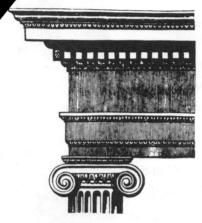

Io

Ionic Order.

Ionic Capital. The most highly ornamented of th

Jack Arch. An arch of only the thickness of one

Jambs. Door-posts; the upright sides of a fire-pla

Jet d'eau. Water thrown into the air from a pipe o
into a basin below.

Joining. The smaller wood-work of a building.

Keep. The strongest part of the old English castles

Keystone. The stone placed in the centre of the t
vault.

Label. In Gothic Architecture, the drip or hood-moul

Labyrinth. A building full of numerous and intricat

Labyrinth Frett. An ancient ornament, with numerou
evolutions.

Lacunaria. The sunk panels or coffers in ceilings.

Lancet Arch. The sharp-pointed arch, in the Gothic

Lantern. A turret placed above a building and pierced with windows.

Lattice. A reticulated window.

Lazaretto. A hospital for persons sick with contagious disorders.

Lean-to. A small building whose side walls and roof project from the wall of a larger building.

Level. A surface which inclines to neither side.

Library. A building or apartment to contain books.

Line. The figure which has only length.

Light-house. A high building with a light to guide ships at sea.

Lintel. The horizontal piece which covers the opening of a door or window.

Loop. A small slit, or narrow window.

Losange or *Lozenge.* A figure of four sides, with two acute, and two obtuse angles.

Lunette. A cylindric or spherical aperture in ceilings.

Machicolations. Small projections or apertures in old castles, through which melted lead and stones were thrown upon assailants.

Mansion. A large house.

Mantel-piece, or *Mantel tree.* The name formerly given to the beam of wood supporting the breastwork of a chimney.

Marble. A stone of compact texture and fine grain, found in almost every country of Europe, and in Asia, Africa, and America. Its varieties are almost innumerable. Among the most valuable marbles of antiquity, were the *Pentelican, Parian,* the marble of Mount *Hymettus,* of *Thasos,* of *Lesbos,* of *Luna* in Etruria, of *Philleus,* of *Phrygia,* all pure *white.* The *black* marble of *Phrygia.* A marble resembling ivory, called *Chernites.* The *Numidian* marble, or *rouge antique.* The black marble of Tænarus. The celebrated *black translucent* marble from the Isle of *Chio.* The *black obsidian* from *Ethiopia.* The *green* marble of Mount Taygetes, known by the name of *verde antique.*

The *black-veined Cyzican* marble. The marble of *Carytus* is a *mingled green;* of *Mount Atrax* in *Thessaly*, of *mingled white, green, blue*, and *black;* the marble of *Memphis*, resembling the *skin of a serpent*, called in Italy, *Il serpentino antico.* The *black* and *red Mygdonian* marble. The Corinthian marble was *yellow;* that of Cappadocia, called *Marmor Phengites*, was *white* with *yellow spots.* The *Rhodian* marble was marked with spots resembling *gold.* The marble of Melos, *yellow,—jaune antique.*

Masonry. The art of joining stones, for the formation of walls, &c.

Moresque. The style of building peculiar to the Moors and Arabs.

Mausoleum. A sepulchral monument.

Medallion. A circular tablet with raised figures.

Members. The different parts of a building.

Menagerie. A building for rare and foreign animals.

Mensuration. The science that treats of the magnitude of bodies, superficies, and lines.

Meros. The centre of a triglyph, in the Doric order.

Metope. The space between the triglyphs in the Doric frieze.

Milliare. The Roman mile-stone.

Minaret. A high slender turret, rising by different stages, each of which has a balcony; attached to Turkish mosques.

Modillion or *Modillon.* An ornament used under the projection and in other parts of buildings; most frequently in the Corinthian order.

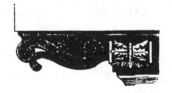

Modillion.

Mole. A pier of stone to shelter ships from the violence of the waves.

Monastery. The habitation of monks.

Monolithol. Works constructed of one stone.

Monopteral. A kind of temple which had only a cupola sustained by columns, without walls or cell

Mortar. The calcareous cement used in building, composed of burnt limestone and sand.

Mouldings. The small projecting orna- ments of columns, &c.

Mullions. The framework of a Gothic window.

Mural. Belonging to a wall.

Museum. A repository of scientific and literary curiosities.

Mutule. A projecting ornament of the Doric cornice.

Nave. The middle part of a church.

Niche. A cavity or hollow in a wall for the reception of a statue.

Obelisk. A monolithic pillar of a rec- tangular form, diminishing from the base to the top.

Niche.

Observatory. A building for astronomical purposes.

Odeum. A kind of theatre among the Greeks for poetical and musi- cal exhibitions.

Oriel. A projecting window.

Ornaments. The smaller or more detailed parts of a work that serve to beautify and enrich a building.

Ovolo. The principal member of the Doric capital.

Palace. The dwelling-house of a king, prince, bishop, &c.

Palisades. Pales or stakes set up for an enclosure.

Panel. A thin board, having its edges in- serted into a surrounding frame.

Pedestal. The square support of a column, statue, &c.

Oriel.

Pediment. The triangular member of a building, which surmounts a portico; an ornament of a triangular form finishing the front of a building, the top of windows, doors, &c. In a pediment, an entablature, conformed to the order of the building, encloses a space called the *tympanum.*

Pendant. A hanging ornament in Gothic groined roofs.

Penetrale. The most sacred part of a temple.

Penitentiaries. Formerly, small houses where the monks retired for penance; at present, houses of imprisonment.

Pentagon. A figure of five sides and five angles.

Pentastyle. Having five columns in front.

Peperino. A stone much used by the Romans in building; that found near Tivoli is called *travertino.*

Pendant.

Peribolos. A walled court, sometimes surrounding a temple.

Peridome. That part of the periptere, which was left between the columns and the walls.

Periptere. A range of insulated columns, distant from the walls, surrounding the exterior of a temple.

Peripteral. Surrounded with a periptere.

Perpendicular. When a straight line stands upon a horizontal straight line, so that the angles on each side are equal, or right angles.

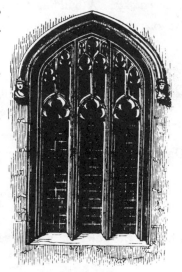

Perpendicular Style.

Perpendicular Style. In Gothic Architecture, the last period, or Florid Gothic.

Persians. Figures of men supporting entablatures.

Persian Architecture. The style used by the Persians.

Persian Capital.

Perspective, linear. Shows how the lines which define figure appear to the eye of the spectator, according to the point on which the eye is fixed, and the distance of the objects.

Pharos. A lighthouse.

Piazza. A continued archway or vaulting, supported by pillars.

Pier. A mass of stone supporting a vault; the arches of a bridge.

Pilaster. A square column, generally engaged in the wall, having its proportions and ornaments of the order of the building on which it is placed. The Greeks used them to strengthen the walls of the cella of temples, and called them *antæ*.

Persian Capital.

Pilaster.

Pinnacle.

Pile. Timber driven firmly into the ground for foundations.

Pillar. Sometimes used as synonymous with column; more pro-

26

perly, a supporter to arches having no fixed proportions, in Saxon, Norman, and Gothic Architecture.

Pinnacle. The roof of a house, terminating in a point, and in some instances with an ornamental finishing.

Pitch. The vertical angle of a roof.

Plan. The draught of a building, taken on the ground-floor, showing the form, size, distribution of the rooms, &c.; a *perspective plan,* is exhibited with diminution, according to the rules of that science. The *raised plan* of a building is the *elevation.*

Plane. A surface which coincides everywhere with a right line; a surface which is everywhere perfectly true and level.

Plank. A name given to timber which is less than four inches thick, and thicker than a board which is an inch and a half.

Plinth. The lower member of a base, or the support for the base of a column.

Pointed Style of Architecture, called the Gothic.

Polygon. A many-sided figure.

Porphyry. A hard stone susceptible of a fine polish, much used by the ancients.

Portal. The arch over a door or gate; a gate.

Portcullis. A strong grating of timber and iron, made to slide up and down in a groove within the portal of a castle.

Portico. A long covered space, usually supported by columns, the sides being open.

Postern. A small door or gate for private ingress to a castle.

Profile. The perpendicular section of a building.

Projection. A branch of perspective.

Pronaos. The front porch of an ancient temple.

Propylæ. Buildings of great magnificence, before the entrance of ancient temples.

Propylon. A vestibule or avant-porte.

Proscenium. The front part of the stage of the ancient theatres.

Prostyle. Temples with columns only in front.

Pseudodipteros. A mode of arranging the columns of a temple, in which the two fronts had eighteen columns, and the sides fifteen or sixteen.

Pulpit. The place in a church whence the sermon is pronounced.

Pylône. Lofty pyramidal masses of masonry, placed at the entrance of temples and palaces by the ancient Egyptians.

Pyramid. A solid having one of its sides, called the *base*, a plane figure, and the other sides triangles, their points joining in one point at the top, called the vertex.

Pulpit.

Quadrangle. Any figure with four angles and four sides.

Quarry. A place out of which stones are taken.

Quatrefoil. Supposed to be derived from quatre-feuille, four leaves; an ornament with four cusps.

Quoins. Stone or other materials put in the corner of buildings to strengthen them.

Rafters. The secondary timbers of a house, which are let into the great beam.

Rampart. A bank of earth, to protect from the cannonading of an enemy.

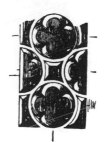

Quatrefoil.

Recess. A depth of some inches, (or feet,) in the thickness of a wall.

Rectangle.   A figure whose angles are all right angles.

Refectory.   An eating-room.

Relievo.   The projecture of an architectural ornament.

Reservoir.   An artificial pond or basin to collect water.

Reticulatum.   A kind of masonry among the Romans, in which the stones were laid diagonally.

Ridge.   The top of a roof, which rises to an angle.

Right Angle.   An angle of ninety degrees.

Right-line.   A line perfectly straight.

Roman Architecture.   The manner of building among the Romans.

Roman Ionic.   The alteration made by the Romans in the Grecian Ionic order.

Roman Ionic.

Romanesque.

Romanesque.   The architectural style which resulted from the decline of the art at Rome, *e. g.*, Saxon, Norman, Lombard, &c.; an imitation of Roman Architecture.

Rose Window.   A circular Gothic window; a Catherine wheel.

Rotunda.   A building which is round, within and without.

Rough-casting.   A coarse mode of covering cottages with mortar.

Round Churches.   Round ancient structures in England, supposed by some to have been built by the Jews.

Rural Architecture. That part of architecture which relates to the construction of picturesque and rustic dwelling-houses in the country.

Rustic. A mode of building in imitation of nature; the stones left rough on the outer surface.

Salient. Projecting.

Saloon. A lofty hall, usually vaulted at the top.

Saracenic Architecture. The architecture of the Arabs, Moors, Saracens, &c.

Sarcophagus. A tomb or coffin made of one stone.

Sash. The frame which holds the glass in windows.

Saxon Architecture. The architecture of the Anglo-Saxons; a barbarous imitation of the architecture of Rome.

Scaffold. A frame of wood for masons and builders to stand upon, while working on the higher parts of an edifice.

Sepulchral Monument. Tombs for the interment of the dead.

Seraglio. The palace of an Eastern prince; more particularly the apartments of the women.

Shaft. The cylindrical part of a column, between the base and the capital.

Shingles. Small pine or other boards used for the covering of roofs.

Shrine. The tomb of a saint; place of deposit for a sacred relic.

Skylights. Windows placed in roofs to give light to staircases and attic apartments.

Slating. Covering roofs with slates.

Sleepers. Timbers laid upon walls for supporting the ground-joists of floors.

Soffit. The under part of a cornice.

Sounding-board. A board placed over a pulpit to increase sound.

Spire. A steeple which diminishes to a point.

Stadium. The open space where the athletæ exercised in running.

Stairs. Steps to ascend from the lower part of buildings to the upper.

Stanchion. A prop or support.

Steeple. An appendage to a church, to contain the bells, rising either in the form of a tower or spire.

Stone. The substance which is employed in all buildings intended to possess durability. Granite, marble, freestone, &c.

Story. A floor or flight of rooms.

Stucco. Cement of various descriptions.

Stylobate. The uninterrupted basis below the columns of a temple or other edifice.

Surbase. The mouldings immediately above the base of a room.

Syenite, or *Sienite.* A stone found in the neighbourhood of Syene, in Egypt, resembling granite, of which obelisks were frequently constructed.

Tabernacle. The temporary edifice used by the Israelites in the wilderness. A large tent.

Temple. An edifice destined for religious worship.

Terra-cotta. Baked earth.

Theatre. A building appropriated to the representation of dramatic spectacles.

Timber. Wood used for building. *Ash* is tough. *Elm* liable to warp and shrink. *Beech* hard and close. *Poplar* not durable. *Birch* tough but not durable. *Walnut* seldom used. *Oak* durable. Chestnut, for inside work, stains. Pine, brittle.

Tomb. A monument raised over the dead.

Torus. A large semicircular moulding used in the bases of columns.

Tout-ensemble. The general or whole expression.

Tower. A lofty building of several stories.

Transept. An open passage across the body of a church, at right angles with the nave and choir.

Tracery. The ornamenting of Gothic windows.

Trefoil. An ornament in Gothic Architecture, consisting of three cusps in a circle.

Triclinium. The room in a Roman house where company was received, and seats placed for their accommodation.

Triforium. The space between the aisles of a church and the clerestory.

Triforia. Three galleries, or ranges of seats, above each other, in churches or cathedrals.

Triglyph. An ornament of the Doric frieze, consisting of three parallel nicks, and supposed by some to represent the end of beams.

Triumphal Arch. A monument to commemorate a victory.

Truncated. Cut short.

Turkish Architecture. See Saracenic Architecture.

Turret. A small tower.

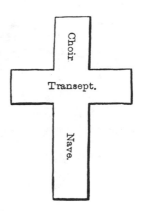

Turret.

Tuscan Order. Not properly an order, but a Roman style, having the frieze ornamented with triglyphs and metopes.

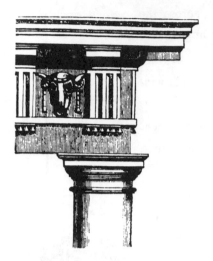

Tuscan Order.

Vane.

Tympanum.   The plane triangle of a pediment.

Type.   The canopy over a pulpit.

Unity.   A harmonious agreement of all the parts of a building.

University.   A collection of buildings for the most liberal education.

Urn.   A vase, designed to preserve the ashes of the dead.

Vane.   A plate of metal, fixed on the summit of a steeple or other
convenient place, to show the direction of the wind.

Vase. A beautiful vessel, used for various purposes among the Greeks,
Etrurians, and other ancient people.

Vault.   An arched roof, so contrived that the stones which form it,
support each other.

Veneer.   A thin piece of valuable wood, for covering wood of a more
common kind.

Venetian Window.   A window with three separate apertures.

Ventilation.   Free admission of air.

Vertical.   Opposite.

Vestibule.   The entrance or waiting room, to ancient buildings.

Vestry.   A room adjoining a church where the ministerial vestments
are kept.

Villa. A country mansion for the wealthy.

Volute. A spiral scroll, in the Ionic and Composite capitals.

Vomitoria. Gates or doors in the ancient amphitheatres, by which the spectators entered.

Wagon-headed Ceiling. See Cylindric Ceiling.

Wainscot. The wooden lining of walls, generally in panels.

Walls. A body of masonry, of a certain thickness, formed of stone or bricks.

Water-table. A projection placed to carry off water.

Weather-boarding. Boards lapped over each other, to prevent rain from passing through.

Window. An opening in a building to admit light to the interior.

Wood. (Ornamental.) Ebony, Rosewood, Mahogany, Curled Maple, Bird's-eye Maple, Black Walnut, &c.

Wreathed Columns. Columns twisted in the form of a screw.

Xenodochium. A hospital or inn among the Greeks for the reception of strangers.

Xystus. A spacious portico where the Grecian athletæ exercised during winter.

Zeta.   A small withdrawing chamber.

Zocle.   A low square member used instead of a pedestal to support a column.

Zotheca.   A small room or alcove in Grecian villas, which might be separated from the room to which it adjoined, by curtains or windows.

INDEX.

A.

B.

C.

D.

E.

N.

THE END.